The Muses, the Masses, and the Massey Commission

The Massey Commission is widely celebrated as the watershed event in Canadian cultural history. Formally called the Royal Commission on National Development in the Arts, Letters and Sciences, the commission was created in 1949. Two years later it made its recommendations, from which came much of Canada's current government support system for culture, including the Canada Council. Paul Litt explores the origins, activities, and impact of the Massey Commission, and the contexts – political, social, and cultural – that shaped it.

The proceedings of the commission saw a range of various interests coalesce into an effective national lobby group for the cause of Canadian culture. Influential figures in universities, national voluntary associations, and the government all took part, alongside enthusiastic members of local cultural groups across the country.

During the commission's work it became clear that cultural nationalism had become a force to be reckoned with, a natural expression of the pride Canadians felt in their wartime accomplishments and their new international status in the postwar world. And cultural issues provided a focus for all the anxieties Canadians felt about life in the modern world: the challenge of communism, the fears of technology epitomized by The Bomb, and the rapid growth of mass culture through the media.

In response to these concerns, the Massey Commission looked to traditional high culture as a source of humanistic values upon which Canada could build a unique and independent liberal democratic postwar society. Its legacy continues to shape Canadian cultural policy.

PAUL LITT is a Toronto historian interested in Canadian cultural and intellectual history.

THE MUSES,
THE MASSES,
AND
THE MASSEY
COMMISSION

Paul Litt

University of Toronto Press

Toronto Buffalo London

© University of Toronto Press 1992
Toronto Buffalo London
Printed in Canada

ISBN 0-8020-5003-4 (cloth)
ISBN 0-8020-6932-0 (paper)

Printed on acid-free paper

To Michelle Seville

Canadian Cataloguing in Publication Data

Litt, Paul
The muses, the masses and the Massey Commission

Includes bibliographical references and index.
ISBN 0-8020-5003-4 (bound) ISBN 0-8020-6932-0 (pbk.)

1. Canada. Royal Commission on National Development
in the Arts, Letters and Sciences.   2. Arts –
Canada.   3. Canada – Cultural policy.   I. Title.

FC95.4.L5 1992   354.710085   C92-093217-7
F1021.2.L5 1992

This book has been published
with the help of a grant from the
Canadian Federation for the Humanities,
using funds provided by the
Social Sciences and Humanities Research Council
of Canada.

Contents

ACKNOWLEDGMENTS vii

Introduction 3

Part One

1 The Origins of the Commission 11
2 The Cultural Elite and the Culture Lobby 38
3 The Promotional Tour 56

Part Two

4 Liberal Humanism 83
5 Liberal Humanist Nationalism 104

Part Three

6 The Battle for the Air Waves 123
7 From Scholarships to University Funding 146
8 Hand-Outs for Longhairs 167
9 Cultivating the Hinterland 186

Part Four

10 The Report 207
11 Response and Implementation 223

Conclusion 245

vi / Contents

APPENDIX A: Submissions to the Commission 255
APPENDIX B: Public and Private Meetings of the Commission 269
APPENDIX C: Parody of a Commission Meeting 273
PICTURE CREDITS 276
NOTES 277
PRIMARY SOURCES 311
SELECT BIBLIOGRAPHY 315
INDEX 319

Acknowledgments

My interest in the Massey Commission began with a suggestion made by Brad Adams that led further than either of us then expected, and a decade later I am not sure whether I should thank him or not. At the very least I can say that his contribution made a difference. An earlier version of this study was prepared as a doctoral dissertation at the University of Toronto, and I am grateful to my PHD supervisor, Dr Robert Bothwell, for providing valuable criticism and judicious enthusiasm during the writing process. He allowed me the freedom necessary to work things out on my own, but could be counted on for help in clearing the numerous obstacles in the graduate school steeplechase. I am also indebted for advice and resourceful scholarship administration to Susan Macdonald, then graduate secretary at the Department of History, and one of the few people I met there who seemed to know how the system worked. Professor Paul Rutherford and Professor John English also deserve my thanks for reading the manuscript and contributing insights which I have incorporated during subsequent revisions.

In researching this subject I was fortunate to be able to interview a number of people who had first-hand experience with the Massey Commission or the government of the day. The Rev. Georges-Henri Lévesque, the Hon. J.W. Pickersgill, Mr Guy Roberge, Dr Claude Bissell, Mr Douglas LePan, and Mr Vincent Tovell were all very generous in sharing their time and knowledge of the commission with an interested but uninformed neophyte. It was gratifying to see that they were still enthusiastic about the subject; without their help this study would not have been possible. I am similarly indebted to Mrs Kate Nichols, who was kind enough to write to me about her sister, Hilda Neatby, and her work on the commission.

The Saskatchewan Archives Board and the Government Publications Section of the John P. Robarts Research Library at the University of Toronto gave me access to valuable private papers in their collections. Mr James Whalen of the National Archives of Canada and Mrs Laurenda Daniells of the Special Collections Division of the University of British Columbia Library were particularly helpful in directing me to relevant records in their depositories. I would also like to thank the editorial staff at the University of Toronto Press: Gerry Hallowell for his staunch support, Laura Macleod for her enthusiastic guidance, and Ken Lewis for his scrupulous copy-editing.

The most important contributor to the writing of this book was my wife, Michelle, whose companionship made life a pleasure no matter how the writing was going. My parents also deserve acknowledgment for providing moral support and an overdraft service at critical moments. Finally, Joey was a constant companion, although he tended to sleep through the good parts. Any errors that remain in this work are more my fault than his.

The Royal Commission on National Development in the Arts, Letters and Sciences. Left to right, Arthur Surveyer, Georges-Henri Lévesque, Vincent Massey (chairman), Hilda Neatby, and N.A.M. MacKenzie

The commission in session in Saskatchewan

Prime Minister Louis St Laurent receiving a copy of the Massey
Report from Vincent Massey, 1 June 1951

National Liberal Convention, 5–7 August 1948, Ottawa.
Mackenzie King, the prime minister, congratulates
Louis St Laurent on his election as leader of the Liberal party.
Brooke Claxton (extreme left) and C.D. Howe (extreme right)
look on.

National Film Board offices in Ottawa, 1947

The Victoria Building in Ottawa, home of the National Museum,
the Geological Survey, and the National Gallery in the 1940s

A string quartet under the direction of Eugene Karsh of the NFB in recital during a retrospective of Canadian painting at the National Gallery, Ottawa, June 1945

OPPOSITE

A group of Canadian artists from the Kingston Conference visit the National Gallery in June 1941.

Patrons crowd the foyer of the Odeon Theatre for the opening performance of Canada's first festival of ballet, Winnipeg, May 1948.

Public Archives, Sussex Drive, Ottawa, 1953

The Public Archives of Canada and the National Library,
395 Wellington Street, Ottawa, 1967

A contemporary radio production, 'Nazaire et Barnabé,' with
Ouila Légaré and Georges Bouvier, on CKAC Montreal, 1950

Lloyd Saunders, Regina sports announcer for CKCK, interviews the
Montreal Canadiens' Maurice Richard (left) and Elmer Lack in the
late 1940s.

One of the NFB's rural circuit film audiences, 25 November 1942

A weekly evening art class at the Public School, Yellowknife,
NWT, 1953

A demonstration of television at the CBC building on Dorchester Street, Montreal, 30 November 1951. Front row, left to right, Davidson Dunton, chairman of the CBC Board of Governors, W.A. Robinson, chairman, House of Commons Committee on Radio, and D.A. Fleming, MP for Eglinton

The Rev. Georges-Henri Lévesque, the Rt Hon. Vincent Massey, and the Hon. Brooke Claxton arriving for the inaugural meeting of the Canada Council, Ottawa, 30 April 1957

The Muses, the Masses, and
the Massey Commission

Consider your birthright; think who you are.
You were not made to live like brutes,
but to pursue virtue and knowledge.

Dante, *The Divine Comedy: Inferno*, 26.118–20

Introduction

A royal commission on government cultural activities might well be expected to be a tedious affair, absorbed in the minutiae of policy revisions for an endless array of bureaucratic programs and agencies. The ponderous title of the Royal Commission on National Development in the Arts, Letters and Sciences seemed to promise as much when it was appointed in 1949. But the Massey Commission, as it became known after its chairman, Vincent Massey, became a celebrated chapter in Canadian cultural history through a broad and imaginative interpretation of its mandate. Although it was specifically directed only to investigate broadcasting, federal cultural institutions, government relations with voluntary cultural associations, and federal university scholarships, it parlayed these instructions into a crusade for Canadian cultural nationalism. The result, in the spring of 1951, was a report that offered a keen diagnosis of Canada's cultural predicament and a number of bracing remedies.

The Massey Commission has long been associated with the dawn of a new era in Canadian cultural affairs. It issued the first clear warning about the dangers of dependence upon American culture in the postwar world and proposed a deliberate and coordinated strategy for state-sponsored Canadian cultural development. This strategy included endowing federal cultural institutions with the resources they needed to play leading roles in national cultural life and asserting the federal government's right to fund university education. The com-

CBC

creation
of Can
Council

mission also affirmed the Canadian Broadcasting Corporation's control over unruly private radio station owners within the public broadcasting system and endorsed a similar model for television development. The centrepiece of its recommendations, however, was the creation of the Canada Council, an arts funding body that would provide transfusions of cash for Canadian artists and scholars. Given the commission's broad conception of federal cultural responsibilities, it is not surprising that the Canadian public came to think of it as nothing less than a general investigation of culture in Canada and began calling it 'The Culture Commission.'

The commissioners justified transforming their enterprise into a 'general survey of the arts, letters, and sciences in Canada' on the grounds that the government's cultural responsibilities could only be appreciated in the context of Canada's wider cultural life.[1] Nevertheless, the expansion of their mandate was based in politics as much as logic. Leading figures in universities, national voluntary associations, and government were behind the founding of the Massey Commission. This cultural elite created the commission to protect its interests in public broadcasting and federal cultural institutions, then prodded the commissioners, who were drawn from its ranks, towards recommending funding for the universities, cultural organizations, and research of its members. It won wide support for the commission through general publicity and by exploiting its direct connections with voluntary associations across the country. Most of these organizations, whether directly involved in cultural activities or not, stood to benefit from an expanded government presence in the field. They coalesced into a vocal national lobby that emboldened the commission and persuaded the government of the political importance of its work. The Massey Commission was a formative exercise in interest group politics for a cultural community adapting to the possibilities of a peaceful and prosperous postwar society.

The commission was interested not just in culture in Canada, but in Canadian culture. As the commissioners themselves put it, their work was 'concerned with nothing less than the spiritual foundations of our national life.'[2] They operated on the premise that their enterprise deserved the support of all patriotic citizens because culture was what bound Canadians together and distinguished them from other nationalities. It followed that the Canadian state had an obligation to support the cultural activities which legitimized its very existence. In short, the Massey Commission was driven by cultural nationalist ideology as well as interest-group politics. Although these motive forces run throughout Canadian cultural history, the unique conditions of postwar Canada affected them profoundly. The Massey Commission was a critical passage in the history of these themes; like a prism, it was coloured by them but also refracted them into the future with altered hue and intensity.

The Massey Report is widely credited with ushering in a new era of significant government support for culture in Canada. As a result it has come to serve as something of a creationist myth for Canadian cultural nationalists in recent years. The essentials of the parable are simple: before Massey, barbarism; after Massey, civilization and arts subsidies for all.[3] Idolizing the Massey Commission in this way is nothing new. Over the years it has been cited in different ways to serve all manner of nationalist teachings.

The Massey Report was hailed as a symbolic step forward in national development from the moment it hit the bookstores. Drawing on the popular saga of Canada's 'progress' from colony to nation, nationalists noted that just as political, military, and diplomatic autonomy had been earlier stages on the road to national independence, now the young nation, confident and optimistic following its wartime feats, was discovering its cultural identity. The Massey Commission reflected a new stage of national development that would see a coarse, adolescent Canada mature into a civilized adult.[4]

Nationalists have also hailed the Massey Commission as one of many examples of Canada's distinctiveness from the United States. According to this interpretation, the Massey Report's misgivings about mass culture reflected a conservative temperament that makes Canada a distinctive community in North America and justifies an independent Canadian nationality. Accordingly, the commission's general strategy of state intervention to foster Canadian culture has been described as a typically Canadian form of public policy based in a concern for the national community over untrammelled liberal individualism. As such it is seen as a continuation of the nation-building policies of the nineteenth century – the National Policy adapted to the information age.[5]

The instructiveness of the Massey Commission is seemingly endless.

It has also been used to illustrate the venerable theme of national unity through French-English accommodation. In this instance it is pointed out that its commissioners, both French Canadian and English Canadian, articulated a vision of a national culture based on bicultural toleration and cross-pollination. The tradition of English-French collaboration epitomized by leadership duos such as Baldwin and LaFontaine and Macdonald and Cartier is extended in the recent practice of calling the commission the 'Massey-Lévesque Commission,' a well-intentioned gesture that nonetheless abuses history by elevating commissioner Georges-Henri Lévesque to a status as co-chair that he never actually enjoyed.[6]

Indeed, the Massey Commission has been revered sufficiently to earn the most flattering confirmation of historical importance: dismissive revisionism. Over the years Canadian cultural discourse has become less obsessed with the themes of national independence and unity and increasingly concerned with issues of gender, class, ethnicity, regionalism, and social justice. As a result, many commentators have taken a dimmer view of the commission. They agree with the cultural nationalists' assertion that the Massey Commission had a conservative bias, but for them this is cause for criticism rather than celebration. In their portrayals the Massey commissioners become a bunch of stuffy college dons trying to force a good dollop of 'culchah' down the throat of a gagging Johnny Canuck. They criticize the commission for patronizing the common man, failing to appreciate the virtues of modern mass democracy, and promoting an aristocratic high culture. In this view the Massey Commission represented a reactionary elitism geared towards preserving the establishment culture and values of a bygone day in a new era of cultural pluralism.[7]

There is some truth to all of these characterizations, but none of them rests upon a close historical analysis of the Massey Commission and its times. By presenting the commission in its historical context, this study offers an opportunity to judge how much it can bear of the symbolic freight that has been heaped upon it over the years. At the same time it may serve both as a case study in Canadian cultural nationalism and as a window on some overlooked features of Canadian society at the mid-point of the twentieth century. For those who prefer their history unencumbered by pedantry, there may also be some intrinsic interest in this account of ideologies clashing and interest groups battling over the spoils of government influence, media control, and cultural power in postwar Canada.

PART ONE

1

The Origins of the Commission

= fr. min of nat def.

It may seem odd that the initiative within the Canadian government that resulted in a royal commission on culture came from a minister of national defence. It brings to mind the 1960s image of daisies in gun barrels. But cabinet ministers get their portfolios because they are politicians, not because they are specialists, and the Hon. Brooke Claxton was certainly no blinkered militarist. In fact, most of his early political experience had come from his involvement in cultural politics. With his background in national voluntary associations, his political connections, and his nationalism, Claxton embodied three factors that were critical to the creation of the Massey Commission.

When Claxton joined the Liberal cabinet in 1945, he became the cultural community's unofficial representative inside the government and often proposed new policies in cultural affairs. In April 1946, for example, he urged Prime Minister Mackenzie King to consolidate the administration of the government's cultural institutions and to put Vincent Massey in charge of them upon his return from his post as high commissioner in London. The only problem with this proposal was that King did not particularly want Massey involved in his government or his government involved in culture. The days of 'Babbitt Rex' as prime minister were numbered, however, and Claxton decided to bide his time until the advent of a new regime.[1]

His chance came two years later as the Liberal party readied itself for leadership succession and policy review at the National Liberal

Clax asked King to get Massey involved in his gov't but King did not want to.

Convention of August 1948. Claxton was on the committee appointed by the National Liberal Federation to refine resolutions that were to be put before the convention. The committee had received proposals urging greater support for 'such activities as the National Gallery, a National Library, Dominion Scholarships, and the like.'[2] Claxton eagerly embraced the opportunity to draft a resolution that would incorporate these suggestions into a single declaration on cultural affairs.

Claxton's proposal languished near the bottom of the committee's list of resolutions, but the various headings he gave it – 'The Spirit of Canada,' 'A Distinctive Canadian Way of Life,' and 'A Richer National Life – a Canadian Culture' – defied its lowly ranking. So too did the eloquent language he employed to introduce it:

> The Liberal Party of Canada believes that the future of the nation depends upon things of the spirit as well as material progress. It believes in the existence and development of a Canadian spirit, uniting the various traditions and creative abilities of our people, enriching the lives of all Canadians and widening our contribution to the community of nations.[3]

Such inspiring nationalistic rhetoric was required because cultural initiatives had to overcome both indifference and hostility within the party. Although the government was developing a more interventionist disposition in managing the economy and planning the foundations of the welfare state, it was a long step from these material responsibilities to involvement in cultural affairs. Traditionalists in the party regarded the idea as a scheme cooked up by highbrows to serve their marginal interests at the expense of the average taxpayer.

Claxton's invocation of a 'Canadian spirit' was also necessary to lend thematic unity to the seemingly diverse collection of endorsements and initiatives that composed his resolution. He shrewdly began his list on a down-to-earth level with two relatively practical proposals: the beautification of the national capital and the improvement of national parks. The resolution then progressed from the mundane to the esoteric. Next came a declaration of the party's support for the Canadian Broadcasting Corporation (CBC) and the National Film Board (NFB). The CBC's role in developing 'Canadian artistic abilities' was applauded; the contribution of private radio in the same sphere questioned. Immediate action on the long-promised but perpetually de-layed National Library was urged in a section that also demanded increased resources for existing federal cultural institutions. Higher education was included with the proposal that existing federal aca-demic scholarships be developed into a comprehensive scholarships scheme, and Claxton also proposed national scholarships and com-petitive awards for the arts. To bring things back down to earth after this novel idea, an uncontroversial endorsement of the Historic Sites and Monuments Board concluded the resolution.

Although Claxton's proposal encompassed diverse elements, most fit into four basic areas of activity: public broadcasting, federal cul-tural institutions, scholarship, and the arts.[4] The last implied an en-tirely new area of government activity, and there is no evidence that any such proposal had been put before the resolutions committee. As Claxton later noted, however, such demands had been made 'to the Advisory Committee on Reconstruction and in other connections.'[5] He was referring to the fact that for the previous half-decade Ca-nadian artists had been lobbying unsuccessfully for some form of government support.

Claxton was trying to help the artists by slipping aid for the arts into a resolution which otherwise addressed only existing government cultural responsibilities. But his blending of scholarships and awards for the arts with the expansion of federal academic scholarships did not escape notice. Mackenzie King and his cabinet vetted all the con-vention resolutions. Then Claxton's proposal was reviewed by the resolutions committee, amended with the views of the cabinet in mind, and passed 'in a preliminary way.'[6] In the process all references to government aid to the arts were purged. Claxton's extravagant preamble linking the future of the nation to spiritual as well as ma-terial progress was entirely excised. Gone too were such faint com-mitments as the allusion to the 'artistic abilities' developed by the CBC. Evidently a sense of responsibility for the arts was too much to expect from a government that only half-heartedly fulfilled its existing cul-tural obligations.

Even this radical surgery was not enough to placate all of the op-ponents of Claxton's initiative. On the eve of the convention, the resolutions committee met in Claxton's absence and decided to kill his entire proposal. As the convention began, organizations which had submitted declarations in favour of cultural initiatives to the National Liberal Federation were outraged to discover that there was no reflection of their concerns on the convention agenda. As Claxton recalled a few months later, this 'led to a number of enquiries being made.'[7]

One group in particular, the Canadian University Liberal Federation (CULF), was determined to make trouble over the issue. It decided to put the missing proposal before the resolutions committee as an independent resolution of the university Liberal clubs. But the resolutions committee, claiming that it had been overwhelmed with business, adjourned without dealing with the issue. The CULF took this as a further affront and resolved to make its grievance public that very afternoon by putting its proposal forward as a motion from the floor, even though officially the last resolution had already been considered by the convention.

Claxton was not happy to hear of the CULF's plan. On the one hand, he felt responsible for its disillusionment, having encouraged the clubs earlier in the year to submit resolutions to the convention. Still, he wanted to avoid any public display of acrimony that would hurt the party's image, and he also feared that forcing the issue would cement opposition and harm the long-term prospects of the culture lobby. In the end he managed to placate the dissidents by promising that he would bring their concerns to the attention of the cabinet.

A battle had been lost, but it was still possible to win the war. Although the opportunity for a party endorsement of cultural initiatives had passed, there were other ways of obtaining the same objective. The cultural community had been asking for government action on the arts since before the end of the war, and at the same time private radio interests had been calling for a royal commission on broadcasting.[8] It soon became apparent that a royal commission was Claxton's ultimate aim. That fall he talked to his friend Jack Pickersgill, head of the prime minister's office. They agreed that it would be futile to push such a proposal as long as Mackenzie King remained in office. The changing of the guard would come that November, however, and King's successor, Louis St Laurent, might regard the idea more favourably.[9] Pickersgill discussed the matter with Lester Pearson, secretary of state for external affairs. Pearson was sympathetic. An experienced diplomat, he hoped that a commission on cultural matters would put the improvement of Canada's image abroad on the public agenda. Canada was assuming a new prominence in the postwar international scene, and Pearson felt that the country's cultural life, or lack of it, would be an important part of its growing international reputation.[10]

It was natural that Claxton would suggest that the ideal chairman for such a commission would be his friend Vincent Massey. Massey had been at loose ends since returning from his posting as high commissioner in London in 1946, and government insiders were trying to find something new for him to do. Pearson met Massey in Europe in early November 1948 and afterwards wrote to Pickersgill from Paris, confiding that Massey was restless in his largely ceremonial post as chancellor of the University of Toronto and wanted more important work. He was not without alternatives, having been offered the position of master of Balliol College at Oxford that fall. Massey was reluctant to leave Canada, however, if there was some way he could make a contribution to his native country. Pearson had a useful suggestion for Pickersgill:

Recalling our talk in Ottawa when you put forward a very interesting suggestion indeed, I expressed the hope to Mr. Massey that he would not make any final decision on the Balliol matter until he had returned to Canada, which will be in about ten days.

What I have in mind is that you, on behalf of Mr. St Laurent, might give him a call in a fortnight and ask him to come to Ottawa for a chat. Even if nothing concrete resulted I think it would be a very good thing if Mr. St Laurent could have a few words with him. The Royal Commission idea which you mentioned seemed to me to be an imaginative and excellent one and Massey would, of course, be admirable for that work ... Will you mention the matter to the Acting Prime Minister and see if his reaction to this suggestion is the same as mine?[11]

Claxton now had his friends in the prime minister's office and in the cabinet working with him, and together they began to exert their considerable influence upon Louis St Laurent.

Later that month Claxton presented St Laurent with a memorandum which detailed his proposal for a royal commission to deal with cultural affairs. This time he did not try to include an overt commitment to arts subsidies but prudently restricted the proposal to a review of public broadcasting, government cultural institutions, and federal academic scholarships. He introduced its terms of reference with another nationalistic preamble but was careful to give good political reasons for it as well. Claxton stressed that a royal commission would meet the demands of a number of active and articulate political constituencies. There were many influential Canadians who were deeply concerned about cultural matters:

> Included among such people is a very considerable proportion of the 50,000 or more teachers in Canada, a very large number – sometimes estimated at half a million – of people, particularly in small towns and rural communities, who regularly attend the showing of films arranged through the various outlets established in connection with the National Film Board, university staff and students and a good proportion of the people who read books, and so on.[12]

Here was a portentous moment in the history of the nation: 'people who read books' had been singled out as a significant political constituency. Ordinarily these people would be Liberals, Claxton contended, but in these parlous times they probably were leaning towards the CCF. Something should be done to reclaim their affections. Moreover, a commission on culture would also capitalize on the postwar nationalism of the Canadian public: 'This also has a very definite appeal to the very large number of Canadians who have a distinct national conscience and who feel that everything should be adopted to encourage national culture and strengthen national feeling.'[13] By presenting his proposal as a matter of political expediency, Claxton wooed the pragmatist opposition he faced within the government with the kind of practical political argument they responded to best. He was warning them that if they clung to their old principles they risked being bypassed by a more progressive electorate and would suffer the consequences at the polls in the upcoming election.

Claxton was also doing his best to justify a course of action that he personally favoured. But there were solid grounds for him to stress that there was political advantage to be gained. His proposal did indeed suit the temper of the times and answer the demands of a variety of special interest groups across the country. A confident and ambitious Canadian nationalism had grown out of the great accomplishments of the nation during World War II and the new international prominence Canada enjoyed in the postwar world. National confidence was expressed and reinforced by developments ranging from the admission of Newfoundland to Confederation to legislation making the Supreme Court of Canada the court of final appeal in the land. For a generation weaned on the 'colony to nation' theme of progressive national independence, it seemed that Canada had come of age constitutionally, diplomatically, and militarily. A cultural nationalism that cultivated a unique culture identity was an appropriate capstone for the nation-building process. In internationalist circles there was also general agreement with Pearson's feeling that now that Canada was rubbing shoulders on the world stage with older nations with venerable cultural traditions it should do something to match their refinement. Postwar nationalism gave government cultural initiatives a broader base of popular support and a new political relevance.

This nationalism was bolstered by a strain of utopianism. Expectations of a brave new world had been raised by wartime rhetoric and the ecstacy of victory. It was a feeling that found bureaucratic expression in the Marsh Report, with its blueprint for the welfare state, and in the House of Commons Special Committee on Reconstruction and Re-establishment, where Canadian artists had demanded state patronage for the arts. In fact, the word *reconstruction*, taken literally and liberally, aptly captured the contemporary hope that out of the wartime trial by fire had come the opportunity to forge a better world. The idealism inherent in this postwar mood buoyed expectations that the government should concern itself with esoteric matters like culture and extend its nation-building efforts by becoming an active agent of cultural nationalism.

Historian Donald Creighton could still feel the spirit of the times as he described the postwar mood less than a decade later: 'Unquestionably the nation was more conscious than ever before of its corporate identity, its separate interests, its distinctive point-of-view. It was making a far more vigorous and serious effort than it had ever done to free itself and find itself.'[14] It was this spirit that had inspired Vincent Massey to write his 1948 book on Canadian culture and nationalism, *On Being Canadian*. Significantly, he had prefaced one chapter with a telling quotation from Matthew Arnold:

> Again and again I have insisted how those are the happy moments of humanity, how those are the marking epochs of a people's life, how those are the flowering times for literature and art and all the creative power of genius, when there is a *national* glow of life and thought, when the whole of society is in the fullest measure permeated by thought, sensible to beauty, intelligent and alive.[15]

Massey's inference was clear. Canada was enjoying such a happy moment, and the time was ripe for a flowering of Canadian culture. For those familiar with British history, Arnold's comment brought to mind the Elizabethan period, when English power and culture had burgeoned in a symbiotic alliance. With the coronation of Queen Elizabeth II the parallel became even more exact. As Creighton recalled, 'a new Queen had ascended the throne of Canada and the second Elizabethan age had begun.'[16] In this atmosphere it was not unnatural that small-town Ontario businessmen set up a Shakespearian festival in a tent by the Avon River in Stratford, Ontario, in the summer of 1953.

The Canadian cultural community was bursting with anticipation of a new postwar order in which the arts would gain a deserved prestige in the life of the nation. Arthur Phelps, an English professor at United College, University of Manitoba, who followed the Canadian cultural scene closely, had expressed the rise of such expectations even as the war wound down:

> Some of us are tempted to believe that there is possible now a vital polarization of national interest in the Arts, stimulated not only by the widespread national awakening which is political and economic, but also by the modern conditions of easier communication suited to draw together an erstwhile too much dispersed country. It seems to me that the Artists' Brief presented to the Parliamentary Committee was but the expression of a conviction

already matured in the consciousness of the Canadian people: the conviction that the artistic interests of Canadian life need recognition and encouragement now, and that recognition and encouragement can be practical on a large scale now ... Canada is ready for something which might one day become a Ministry of Fine Arts as well established and as necessary for the nourishment of natural resources as a Ministry of Mines and Fisheries. That something as an intermediary step, might be a Commission set up and empowered under wide terms of reference.[17]

Phelps's recognition of the impact of 'easier communication suited to draw together an erstwhile too much dispersed country' was significant as well. Although he was referring to the recent organization of artists on a nationwide basis, the phenomenon had become evident years before in the formation of a variety of other national organizations with interests in cultural affairs.

The roots of post–World War II cultural nationalism can be traced back to World War I. Pride in Canada's wartime accomplishments and the increased autonomy Canada assumed as the British Empire devolved into the Commonwealth inspired a variety of national voluntary associations that rose into prominence in the 1920s. Claxton, then a lawyer and a lecturer in constitutional law, had participated enthusiastically in four of the most active of these organizations: the Association of Canadian Clubs, the Canadian Institute of International Affairs (CIIA), the Canadian League (eventually absorbed into the CIIA in its various branches), and the League of Nations Society. In his memoirs he recalled that 'the objectives of these four organizations coincided and their memberships overlapped. For quite a long time the key people in each organization came from much the same group of people in Ottawa, Winnipeg, Montreal, Toronto, and other Canadian cities. They had "interlocking directorates." While the leaders in these movements may have kept changing their hats, they kept playing the same tune and that was "O Canada, our home, our native land." '[18] Though these organizations did differ somewhat in composition and emphasis, they shared general patriotic and educational goals. By disseminating information and fostering discussion about national issues, they hoped to foster democratic responsibility and a Canadian consciousness. They also shared a general conviction that the state, moved by enlightened public opinion and guided by expert judgment, should be the prime agent of social progress.

The leaders of this movement were based in the East, where they had solid political connections, and they used their nationwide contacts to mobilize local elites across the country.[19] They found an ideal cause and demonstrated the effectiveness of their network when Graham Spry and Alan Plaunt founded the Radio League in 1929 to promote implementation of the Aird Commission's recommendation for a publicly owned national broadcasting system. It was a goal perfectly suited to the educational, nationalistic, and interventionist inclinations of the national voluntary associations.[20] Claxton knew Spry from his work with the Canadian Clubs and had attended Oxford with Plaunt. Claxton and Spry used their connections from the Association of Canadian Clubs and other groups to get national and local voluntary associations to pass motions in favour of public broadcasting. The resulting deluge of telegrams, resolutions, and letters of support from across the country helped convince the parliamentary committee investigating the issue to endorse the Aird Report.

The members of the Massey Commission would all come from the national voluntary associations of the interwar years. The CIIA, for instance, included among its active members Vincent Massey, Hilda Neatby, Norman MacKenzie, and Arthur Surveyer – all of whom were destined to become commissioners.[21] MacKenzie and Massey were as deeply involved in this and related voluntary associations as Claxton. Massey had been a staunch supporter of the Radio League, and MacKenzie was associated with Claxton in the League of Nations Society and the Association of Canadian Clubs as well as the CIIA.

Although this elite was predominantly English Canadian, there was an equivalent network in French Canada. Another commissioner-to-be, Georges-Henri Lévesque, was co-founder of the Société d'éducation des adultes du Québec, the Quebec equivalent of the Canadian Association for Adult Education (CAAE), and a member of the Société des écrivains canadiens – the French-Canadian counterpart to the Canadian Authors Association. He was also active in the French-Canadian cooperative movement as the founder and first president of the Quebec Co-operative Council from 1939 to 1944, and as an adviser to the Corporation des agronomes de la province de Québec. As the war effort increased awareness of the need for bicultural amity, the connections between the two elites strengthened. Lévesque worked closely with the CAAE and became a member of the Canadian Youth Commission, an association which included Claxton and MacKenzie among its active members. In 1948 he received his first honorary doctorate – from the University of British Columbia, where Mac-Kenzie was president. In 1949 Lévesque was inducted into the Royal Society of Canada, and in 1951 he would become president of the Canadian Political Science Association.

Members of this cultural elite were generally well educated, white, middle-class, and male, and their interaction led to friendships which reinforced their shared interests. Claxton, for example, first met Jack Pickersgill at a CIIA study conference in Montreal in May 1934. At the same conference he was befriended by Vincent Massey and his wife, and received an invitation to Batterwood, the Massey estate, the following year. The way in which similar connections were made and cultivated by countless other insiders has prompted one observer to comment that 'Canada in the first half of the twentieth century appears to have operated in the fashion of a country club.'[22] One of the members of the club called its outlook 'the hotel room interpretation of Canadian enterprise' because when a meritorious cause emerged 'a small group of interested people in a hotel room somewhere in Canada' would meet and plan a crusade.[23]

Future commissioner Hilda Neatby was an obvious exception to the rule. Being younger and female, she could hardly qualify as a member of an old boys' network. But like Lévesque and MacKenzie, she was an academic. And although Claxton, Pearson, Pickersgill, Massey, and Surveyer were not pursuing university careers, they too had graduate degrees or had held university appointments in the past. The cultural elite was an intellectual elite, but activism in voluntary associations and an involvement in government were also defining characteristics of its members.

The growth of professional organizations of academics in the interwar years had also provided a focus for this group's activities. In commenting on the activities of national voluntary associations in his memoirs, Claxton noted that 'parallel developments were taking place in the learned societies which were revived or established in the first postwar years.'[24] He was referring to the development of groups such as the Royal Society of Canada, the Canadian Historical Association, the Canadian Political Science Association, the Canadian Psychological Association, and the Royal Canadian Geographical Society. Academics were trying to increase their impact upon society by using a network of organizations and journals to spread their ideas and influence the political process. They were simultaneously attracted to national voluntary associations because they saw them as vehicles through which they could publicize their ideas and develop important connections.[25] In addition, the academic emphasis on fact gathering and public enlightenment meshed nicely with the educational goals of the national voluntary associations. MacKenzie, Neatby, and Lévesque were representative of the extensive overlapping of membership between the two types of bodies that provided an organizational framework for the cultural elite.

These organizations provided valuable experience in national affairs for a generation waiting for power. As they rose to higher levels of political responsibility in the 1940s, Claxton and his cohorts brought with them the values they had pursued all along: nationalism, a belief in cultivating democracy through education, and a faith in government intervention under expert guidance. Claxton, Pickersgill, and Pearson were all members of a rising clique of politicians for whom issues such as public broadcasting and university education were of great importance.

The arts community was one of the last cultural constituencies to emerge as an effective lobby group on the national scene. Its organization began in June 1941 with a conference in Kingston, Ontario, arranged by artist André Biéler, head of the Department of Fine Arts at Queen's University, with the support of Queen's, the National Gallery, and the Carnegie Corporation. The artists were concerned about their marginal status in Canadian society and impressed with how Roosevelt's New Deal in the United States had provided government support for artists through its Works Progress Administration. The conference featured discussions on weighty subjects such as 'the function of art in a democracy,' but it was also intended simply for artists to get to know one another and cultivate a vocational consciousness.[26]

The Kingston Conference of Artists was the first national conference of artists in Canadian history, and it sowed the seeds of further organization. Over the next year the Federation of Canadian Artists was formed with Biéler as chairman 'to unite all Canadian artists, related art workers and interested laymen for mutual support in promoting common aids: the chief of these is to make the arts a creative factor in the national life of Canada and the artists an integral part of society.'[27] In other words, Canadian artists were tired of being the have-nots among the educated elites and were determined to elbow their way up to the government trough alongside other privileged interest groups. With the establishment of the Special House of Commons Committee on Reconstruction and Re-establishment (the Turgeon Committee), the artists saw a perfect opportunity to lobby the government for support.

On 21 June 1944, a coalition of artists' groups, represented by a committee that included such luminaries as conductor Sir Ernest MacMillan and painters Lawren Harris and A.Y. Jackson, presented a brief to the Turgeon Committee. Their trip to the capital would later be immortalized by artists as a historic 'March on Ottawa' to win recognition of their importance in the life of the nation. Canada, they claimed, had an uncultured populace and underemployed artists; aid to the arts would solve both problems. The government should help build community centres in towns across the country and establish a funding body for the arts. The Turgeon committee was impressed with the artists' arguments and passed on their proposals to the government of Mackenzie King, suggesting that it consider establishing either an agency to administer aid to artists or a ministry for cultural affairs. The artists, for their part, established the Canadian Arts Council (CAC) in December 1945 as a lobbying group that could continue to press their cause.

In April 1946 Herman Voaden, president of the Arts Council, wrote to Mackenzie King to reiterate the demands made before the Turgeon committee. King ducked the issue, claiming that he was too busy to meet with the CAC. It is interesting to note that this was the same month in which Claxton approached the prime minister with his proposal for consolidating the administration of federal cultural institutions. There was, if not conspiracy, at least mutual awareness and common purpose between Claxton and the artists' lobby. However, the artists do not deserve the position they often occupy at the front and centre of accounts of the Massey Commission's origins. Claxton had failed to get arts subsidies past the early drafts of his convention resolution, and he was reluctant to risk his entire package of cultural initiatives in pursuit of this one goal.

The artists were still outsiders in the lobbying game, while the cultural elite, interconnected through national voluntary associations, academia, and government, was an influential group with an established stake in existing government institutions. Claxton was on firm ground when he emphasized in his memorandum to the prime minister the political gains to be made from catering to an educated leadership class that operated within a network of national and local organizations across the country. He was also right to note that the postwar temper of the nation made the general public particularly amenable to cultural nationalism. But satisfying these conditions did not necessarily require a radical new initiative such as subsidies for artists. Prime Minister St Laurent made this distinction himself when he responded positively to Claxton's proposal for a royal commission with the proviso that he did not think that the government should be 'subsidizing "ballet dancing." '[28]

The prime minister was more interested in politically sensitive issues affecting existing government responsibilities. There were pressing problems facing some of the prominent federal institutions in which the cultural elite and the government shared a common interest. The most troubling was the inadequate funding of the Canadian Broadcasting Corporation. The CBC's ability to make long-term plans was undermined because it was never assured of enough money to implement them. Even its existing operations were suffering as its income decreased in real value year by year. By 1948 the CBC's financial difficulties had reached crisis proportions. Most of its money came from an unpopular and widely evaded licence fee of $2.50 that was levied on radio sets by the Department of Transport. Claxton, Pickersgill, and St Laurent were strong supporters of public broadcasting who wanted the CBC to get secure funding, insulated from political influence, so that it could adequately fulfil its mandate. But faced with the prospect of increasing the unpopular licence fee, they were eager to find alternative sources of revenue or to shift responsibility for an unpopular decision elsewhere.

This was not the only broadcasting problem facing the government. The Canadian radio broadcasting system included a large number of private stations in a public system supervised by the CBC. Private broadcasters were unhappy with the CBC, which was committed to providing national coverage and quality programming. They could attract more listeners, sell more advertising, and lower costs by offering American-produced commercial programming. They demanded an independent regulatory body for radio in the hope that they could win more freedom under a different regulatory system.

The Canadian Association of Broadcasters (CAB), the private station owners' lobby group, relentlessly publicized its cause throughout the late 1940s, and in time Conservative MPs took its side and began to attack the CBC in the House of Commons. The Liberal party supported the existing system of regulation by the CBC, but the fact that the public broadcasting system had become a partisan issue was itself a matter of concern for those who contemplated its long-term prospects. Meanwhile the CAB's constant carping was creating the impression that there was a crisis in radio. Two Montreal newspapers and the two most prominent national magazines, *Maclean's* and *Saturday Night*, called for a royal commission to investigate broadcasting. For the CBC's friends in government, a royal commission offered a way of providing an 'objective' and authoritative ruling on the issue that could vindicate the status quo without dragging the CBC into the mud of party politics.[29]

The broadcasting mess was compounded by the impending advent of television. All the questions that plagued radio broadcasting applied to television as well but were exacerbated by uncertainty about the nature of the new medium. The government wanted to develop a television system under the authority of the CBC that would be modelled after the radio system. Since television promised to be incredibly expensive to develop in Canada, the CBC wanted to proceed cautiously. Yet the availability of television south of the border made some action imperative. The Canadian public was clamouring for the new technology, and to delay too long risked institutionalizing dependence upon American broadcasters. Meanwhile, private broadcasters, eager for an entré into a potentially lucrative new field, boasted that they could provide television service for Canadians if only they were granted licences and freed from the shackles of CBC regulation. The Conservatives took up the cause of the private interests on this issue as well, creating another thorny problem that might best be dumped into the lap of a royal commission.

NFB became a gov't headache

cutbacks

On top of all of this, the National Film Board had become a government headache. During the war, commercial film producers had worked in harmony with the NFB to produce propaganda and instructional films for the war effort. When the NFB budget was reduced after the war, much of the contract work given to private producers was reduced by cutbacks. Private film-makers were disgruntled and claimed that they should be given most of the film work done by the NFB. It should function only as a contracting and distribution agency, they argued; instead it was a state monopoly that hogged film production. Similar complaints came from photographers who felt that the NFB undercut their prices for prints because it was subsidized by the government.

Both these lobbies found a voice in Parliament through opposition members who began to pick away at vulnerable aspects of the NFB, both real and imagined. One real weakness was that the NFB's accounting system, an unorthodox product of the Board's anomalous administrative position in the civil service, was complex and chaotic. Accusations of mismanagement and extravagance rang out from the private sector. There were also rumours being spread that the NFB was inundated with communist sympathizers. A secretary who had worked briefly at the Board was implicated in the Gouzenko scandal, and this was enough to provide enemies of the NFB with evidence that the entire organization was a Red propaganda machine.[30]

The royal commission proposed by Claxton was politically attractive because it could be assigned a number of issues that held more risks than rewards for the government. It could confirm the government's policies, or warn if they were unpopular and offer alternatives, without exposing the government itself to any political flak. The overt political motives for a commission on the CBC and the NFB could be camouflaged by adding some less controversial government responsibilities to its mandate and making it seem to be a general commission on cultural affairs. Anyone interested in the plight of institutions such as the National Gallery, the Public Archives, or the National Museum was aware that they suffered from the lack of any coordinated or determined government cultural policy. The Public Archives were run by the Department of Agriculture, for example, while the National Gallery was stuck behind the dinosaur collection in the National Museum building. Many considered it a national embarrassment that

Canada had no National Library. Institutions that were supposedly 'national' in character in fact played a limited role beyond their headquarters in Ottawa. Claxton's memorandum pointed out that 'these various agencies have been developed to meet particular needs without having on the one hand a single concept or on the other hand regard for the needs of the different provinces or localities.'[31] Moreover, as the 1948 Liberal convention had demonstrated, various voluntary associations were lobbying for the improvement of government services in their areas of interest. Alone their demands had made a negligible impact, but once the government decided that something had to be done about the CBC and the NFB, a review of its other cultural responsibilities filled out the mandate for a royal commission quite nicely. If such a commission aroused cultural nationalism across the land that could help counteract some of the private sector opposition to government policies in broadcasting and film, so much the better.

There was another cultural problem that lurked in the wings as Claxton framed his proposal. Canadian universities were experiencing a grave financial crisis which the federal government was powerless to alleviate. Like the CBC, the universities were seeing their revenues decline at a time when greater demands were being made upon their services. There was an increasing desire for university education as postwar optimism and prosperity raised Canadians' expectations of life. But the provinces claimed that they lacked the resources to boost their contributions to universities (which made up about a third of the average university's budget). Student fees had been raised higher than most university officials considered wise and still provided only about half of the universities' costs. Meanwhile, endowment revenue was declining in relation to total expenses. The universities had been getting about 10 per cent of their funding from federal grants which paid for the education of veterans through the Direct Veterans Assistance (DVA) program. This revenue was already declining, however, and the entire program was scheduled to end in 1951. The universities were cutting corners to reduce costs but had reached the point where they felt that their educational standards were jeopardized. The short-term picture was bleak enough, but as they observed the climbing birth rate, the universities grew even more apprehensive about their ability to cope with long-term demand.

The academic associations of the cultural elite ensured that the universities would be among the cultural concerns brought to the government's attention. There were serious political obstacles to a federal bailout, however. The British North America Act specified that education was a provincial responsibility. A federal initiative in the field was likely to provoke constitutional controversy, particularly with Quebec, where Premier Duplessis jealously guarded his province's constitutional prerogatives as the front line of defence for French-Canadian culture. Duplessis's influence in his province always worried St Laurent, for Quebec was critical to his political fortunes and those of his party. The postwar period saw bitter wrangling between the provinces and the federal government over taxing powers and jurisdictions, and Duplessis was the most vociferous defender of provincial rights in every phase of this acrimonious dispute. St Laurent was genuinely concerned about the universities, but he was reluctant to hand Duplessis another issue by which he could portray the Liberals as centralizers threatening French-Canadian cultural survival.

Claxton and Pickersgill were disappointed by St Laurent's timidity in this area, but they surreptitiously hoped that a royal commission could find some indirect way for the federal government to help the universities. The commission could be asked to review the federal system of university scholarships, which would give it an opening to survey the university scene in general. It might heighten public awareness, gauge public opinion, or perhaps even raise public support for some kind of federal action. And once it was launched, who could tell what an 'independent' inquiry might choose to recommend?

Even if the commission steered clear of education, it was likely that its cultural interests alone would provoke protests about a federal invasion of provincial jurisdiction. Claxton anticipated constitutional objections of this sort, pointing out in his memo to St Laurent that the national governments of other federal states such as the United States and Australia had national libraries, scholarship schemes, and other large cultural projects.[32] But remembering his experience on the convention resolutions committee, and well aware of St Laurent's fear of controversy in Quebec, Claxton steered clear of any specific mention of funding for the arts or universities in his formal proposals for the commission.[33] He was determined to avoid controversy, at least until the commission was safely launched.

Besides, there was no need to make controversial directives public when the commission would be staffed by like-minded members of the cultural elite. Vincent Massey, Claxton's nominee to chair the commission, could be counted on to steer the commission along a suitable course. Massey was the obvious choice for the appointment: he was knowledgeable about cultural affairs, he was a Liberal, and he was available. Few other Canadians had his combination of experience in the arts and politics. As his biographer noted, 'his career had made him either a patron or an informal critic of every institution and activity that would come under scrutiny. In some areas of the arts – in Canadian painting and modern drama – he was by way of being an expert.'[34] Massey, then sixty-one, had been an amateur actor in his youth and was an active patron of painters and musicians throughout his life. Through the Massey Foundation, the legacy of his family's farm implement manufacturing fortune, he had endowed and then supervised the construction of Hart House at the University of Toronto as a model cultural centre for the formation of young men. Moreover, he had served on the boards of a variety of cultural institutions, including the Royal Ontario Museum and National Gallery of Canada. During his tenure as high commissioner in London, he became the only Canadian ever to be appointed to the National Gallery and the Tate Gallery in Britain. In this capacity he had helped prepare a report that recommended reforms of the Victoria and Albert, Tate, and National Galleries. Finally, as Canadian minister to the United States from 1926 to 1930, and high commissioner to London from 1935 to 1946, Massey had ample first-hand exposure to the two nations that most influenced Canadian cultural life.

Certain aspects of Massey's personality have won him notoriety as a snobbish prig. Some of his colleagues thought him an actor willing to transform himself to suit his audience, while others defended him as a shy and misunderstood figure. He loved things British, in particular pomp and circumstance, and would have liked more such traditional pageantry in Canadian life. As a young man he had been something of an aesthete, with ethereal concerns both high-minded and prissy. His later diplomatic career served as a corrective, perhaps at the cost of a studied stuffiness. Throughout his tenure as high commissioner in London, Mackenzie King had worried about these characteristics, fearing that Massey's anglophilia and susceptibility to aristocrats' blandishments put Canada's real interests at risk.

Part of the reason that Pearson and Pickersgill were looking for something for Massey to do was that they had him in mind as the ideal figure to become the first Canadian governor general, and they wanted to keep him on the back-burner until the time was right for such an appointment.[35] The fact that in some ways Massey was more British than the British themselves made him the perfect bridge candidate for the Canadianization of the vice-regal office. ('Fine chap, Vincent,' Lord Cranborne, Lord Privy Seal in Churchill's government was once reported to have remarked, 'but he does make one feel a bit of a savage.')[36] St Laurent, however, had a drawer full of letters opposing the appointment on the grounds that Massey was too elitist.[37] He wanted to give Massey a test run across Canada to see how he would do as governor general, and the chairmanship of a royal commission was the ideal vehicle. Massey was summoned to see the prime minister in Ottawa on 6 January 1949. There St Laurent proposed that he chair a commission that would review 'the relation of Government to the cultural field, co-ordination of existing institutions, radio, television, UNESCO.'[38] St Laurent probably told Massey that a successful commission would put him high up on the short list for the governor general's office.[39]

The speech from the throne which opened Parliament on 26 January 1949 formally announced the government's intention to appoint a royal commission to study the government's cultural institutions, Canada's international cultural relations, and related matters. The Co-operative Commonwealth Federation supported the idea of the commission from the start. But Conservative leader George Drew attacked the proposal in the ensuing debate for being too vague, for having a built-in bias in favour of public broadcasting, and for infringing on provincial rights inasmuch as it implicitly concerned education.[40] Drew's criticisms hit at many of the vulnerable aspects of the commission proposal. But St Laurent replied that the commission was 'restricted to the activities of federal agencies – activities which are the concern of the Canadian nation.'[41] Warming to his subject, he began to defend the idea of such a commission against the very criticisms which he had first expressed in his aversion to underwriting ballerinas: 'There is another side to human life that is quite as important as the dollars and cents resulting from trade. Upon that side of the normal activities of civilized, Christian human beings, sufficient attention has not been focused nationwide.'[42] Searching for illustrations of such endeavours, the best examples that the prime minister could think of were Barbara Ann Scott and the Royal Canadian Air Force hockey team, Canada's Olympic representatives. It was broadcasting problems, however, that weighed heaviest on his mind. In a lengthy speech he quoted R.B. Bennett's reasons for establishing a public broadcasting system in 1932 to remind the opposition of the Conservative origins of the CBC.

Massey, meanwhile, put off accepting the chairman's post. He talked things over with members of his wife's family and with friends whose advice he valued. There was little chance that he would ultimately refuse the position – it was too well suited to his talents and interests. He thought with pleasure of the long association between cultural patronage and the vice-regal post in Canada. By delaying his acceptance, however, he maintained bargaining power that he could use to eradicate some of his lingering concerns about the project. At first he worried about the feisty criticisms of the leader of the opposition, but he was on good terms with Drew and probably reached a private understanding with him that the Conservatives would lay off the commission until they saw what it recommended. That left his worries about the support that the commission would get from the government itself. Massey thought that the announcement of the commission in the throne speech had been underplayed, and fretted about the depth of St Laurent's commitment to the project. His doubts were finally dispelled by reassurances from Pearson and others that there was strong backing for the project in the cabinet. He was promised that the government would not ignore the commission's recommendations. However, there was still resistance within certain areas of the government to funding the arts directly, an idea that Massey was determined to pursue. In his final discussions with St Laurent, Massey probably secured his private approval to pursue this line of investigation. Fellow commissioner Georges-Henri Lévesque later concluded that Massey had the establishment of an arts council in mind (he had pushed the concept in his recent book, *On Being Canadian*) and that St Laurent agreed to the possibility of such a recommendation as a condition of Massey's participation.[43] Finally, Massey accepted the position in mid-February.

Massey discussed the appointment of other commissioners with the prime minister and members of the cabinet. Although Massey's assent was secured in each case, the cabinet made the final decision. According to some accounts, it was not always a rational process. A story went around Ottawa that painter Lawren Harris was rejected out of fear that the enterprise would become known as the Massey-Harris commission, thereby confusing national culture with agriculture.[44] In general, however, there was a concern for achieving a geographical and sectional balance that reflected the way in which federal cabinets were chosen. The chairman, Massey, came from Ontario, there was a representative of the Prairies, and care was taken that one French Canadian came from Quebec City and the other from Montreal. Norman MacKenzie, then president of the University of British Columbia and engaged in directing its postwar expansion, represented both Coasts because he was a native of Nova Scotia and had been president of the University of New Brunswick from 1940 to 1944.

MacKenzie was not chosen for the commission on the basis of his reputation as a lover of culture. He was no stranger to high culture, but he tended to be more of a populist both in his cultural preferences and his political instincts. He was, however, a former president of the National Conference of Canadian Universities (1946–8), a member of an advisory committee to the federal government on veterans' education, and a noted advocate of federal funding for universities. 'Larry,' as friends called the gregarious fifty-five-year old, was also chummy with numerous Liberal party insiders, including Claxton, Pearson, and Pickersgill. No doubt he was recommended as a commissioner by this group to ensure that, whatever the commission's terms of reference, federal funding for universities would receive serious consideration. Pearson phoned MacKenzie to ask him to serve on the commission, and Massey probably did the same. Massey followed up with a letter on 22 February 1949 imploring MacKenzie to say yes.[45]

MacKenzie had just turned down a chance to serve on the Royal Commission on Transportation. But this new commission was different. In consulting one of the university's governors he wrote that 'my own feeling is that I should accept because it does deal with matters of great importance to the University and to education.'[46] The board of governors of UBC saw the direct relevance of the Massey Commission to the interests of the university and readily agreed.[47] On 3 March 1949 MacKenzie let Pearson know that he wanted the appointment.

By the time MacKenzie replied, only one another commissioner, Arthur Surveyer, had been chosen. St Laurent took a special interest in the selection of representatives from Quebec, and Surveyer was his choice. A founding partner in the leading civil engineering firm in eastern Canada, Surveyer, Nenniger and Chenevert, he was a capable and sophisticated man of affairs, well known and respected in Canada at the time. Surveyer's business credentials were impeccable. His firm was heavily involved in hydro-electric developments in Quebec and elsewhere and had an impressive stable of blue-chip clients. At seventy-one he was an elder statesman of the business community with a clutch of prestigious company directorships.

Surveyer's appointment filled multiple criteria in the cabinet-making process. He was a francophone from Montreal with connections to the English commercial community of that city. He represented not just business, but modern technology, and it was expected that he could provide the commission with expertise on the technical side of broadcasting. Although he represented constituencies that were traditionally hostile to government cultural initiatives, he had a record of involvement in voluntary associations and government affairs which suggested a public spiritedness that transcended the narrowness of his professional background. Since he had served on the National Research Council from 1942 to 1948, he could also be expected to provide some insight into its scholarship schemes. This background, combined with the fact that he was no stranger to university circles, being a PHD and a member of the Cercle universitaire in Montreal, made him a multi-purpose commissioner.

Hilda Neatby, assistant professor and acting head of the Department of History at the University of Saskatchewan, was chosen as the commission's representative from the Prairies. Historian George Brown of the University of Toronto (and probably his colleague Frank Underhill, one of Neatby's intellectual mentors) recommended her to Massey. Massey had never met her, but he was favourably impressed by articles she had published on education. Still, Neatby's appointment was something of a surprise. She was not well known outside of Saskatchewan, and she was a woman – and, at forty-four, a relatively young one at that. The commission needed a historian, however, and she was bilingual. Indeed, French-Canadian history was one of her main interests. Neatby thought that her work with women's associations in the West was another reason she was chosen. She may well have been right, for although the appointment of a woman was by no means a necessary token in 1949, Claxton had considered it appropriate for such a commission from the very beginning. This was a reflection of the common perception of the arts as 'feminine' pastimes, foreign to the rough-and-tumble masculine world where the business of making a living allowed little time for such frills. But it was also an inarguable fact that women dominated local cultural associations across the country. A female commissioner would help the commission relate to a significant portion of its clientele. If the government was seeking a token woman for the commission, however, it certainly got more than it bargained for: Neatby had an imperious will and strong intellectual convictions that would make her a force to be reckoned with on the commission.

This left only the choice of a second francophone representative for the commission. Since Surveyer's representativeness as a French Canadian was qualified by his multiple roles and anglo-business associations, this appointment would be especially important. St Laurent and Massey each composed a short list, and at the top of both was the name of Georges-Henri Lévesque, the forty-six-year-old Dominican priest who was founder and dean of the faculty of social sciences at the Université Laval. Lévesque was a good friend of the prime minister, who had also taught at Laval; St Laurent personally phoned Lévesque and asked him to join the commission. Lévesque was surprised, and demurred, fearing that he knew too little English to take on the job. St Laurent reassured him on this point and also quelled his misgivings about leaving his duties at Laval by arguing that his appointment would lend his faculty prestige.[48] Eventually the prime minister talked him into accepting. Since Lévesque was an outspoken opponent of the Duplessis regime whose selection was bound to annoy the Quebec premier, it seems that St Laurent had resigned himself to a confrontation with Duplessis about jurisdictional authority over culture. By selecting Lévesque he was equipping the commission with a French-Canadian spokesman who had enough prestige and credibility to offset some of the premier's influence.

As a group these commissioners were unlikely to deviate far from the government's way of thinking. Massey, MacKenzie, and Lévesque were all known sympathizers of the federal Liberals who would probably endorse government policy on the CBC and the NFB. All the commissioners held postgraduate degrees, and only Surveyer had not held a university teaching post; they were therefore all likely to favour an extended national scholarship scheme, if not direct federal aid to universities. Moreover, most of the commissioners had been directly involved with one or another of the federal cultural institutions (Surveyer with the National Research Council, Neatby with the Public Archives, Massey with the National Gallery, and MacKenzie with the NFB). These relationships made their sympathies in this area somewhat predictable as well.

The choice of commissioners has often been criticized for not including any artists (although Massey had been an actor, Lévesque was known to play the fiddle, and Surveyer claimed to be an amateur painter). But this was understandable since the commission was not officially intended to concern itself directly with the arts. Most of the commissioners were friends-of-government insiders who belonged to the same quasi-academic cultural elite and were more concerned about national culture than the arts per se. Since the commission was founded to protect and advance the favourite causes of this elite, it is not surprising that its composition reflected its origins and purposes.

The commission of appointment that established the commission on 8 April 1949 included instructions for it to make recommendations upon the principles behind Canadian radio and television broadcasting, federal cultural institutions, Canada's relation with UNESCO, national scholarships, and the federal government's relations with national voluntary bodies involved in cultural affairs. The biggest change between these terms and the ones Claxton originally outlined for St Laurent was the addition of government relations with voluntary bodies. This conjured up a legion of possibilities. It implied that the government did have some responsibility for maintaining a direct relationship with voluntary associations in addition to the indirect relations that derived from their mutual involvement in existing federal cultural institutions. Since the term 'voluntary associations' was broad enough to include many cultural organizations which sponsored arts activities, there was an opening for the commission to investigate the possibility of government funding for the arts. Although the inclusion of national scholarships suggested that the related issue of university aid might come under scrutiny as well, it was preceded by the disclaimer that such federal activities should be examined 'with full respect for the constitutional jurisdiction of the provinces.'[49] Officially, at least, Claxton's and Pickersgill's ambitions for action on university funding were still restricted by St Laurent's continuing concern about stirring up constitutional controversy.

Nevertheless, with the establishment of the Massey Commission, the federal government assumed a new degree of responsibility for the cultural life of the nation. The Aird Commission had already brought involvement in the field by prompting the government to create a public broadcasting system, and the government had haphazardly acquired a number of other cultural responsibilities over the years. But merely by establishing the Massey Commission the government implied that it had a more general responsibility in cultural affairs and that it intended to approach this responsibility in a more conscious and coordinated fashion. It was also likely that this sphere of responsibility would be expanded substantially by the new commission. A few problems in cultural affairs had been lashed together with enough loopholes to allow for nothing less than a full-scale investigation of the nation's cultural life. Massey would take advantage of this open mandate to conduct a comprehensive survey of the Canadian cultural scene and to assert broader federal initiatives in the cultural sphere.

The Massey Commission was the product of both long-term trends and immediate circumstances. A nationalistic cultural elite that had been growing in influence since the 1920s found that specific political problems and a sympathetic national mood in postwar Canada created an opportunity to force its interests onto the public agenda. Still, the commission was launched as something of a Trojan Horse. Not only did its creators hope that it would serve as a disguised vehicle for finding some answer to the problem of university funding, they were careful to veil the likelihood that it would recommend arts subsidies as well. It would be wrong, however, to see this as a deception foisted upon the Canadian public. Claxton's guile was aimed first at getting the commission established by the Liberal government. Once it was launched, public reaction would largely determine just how far the Massey Commission could go. Claxton and his allies were betting that this would be farther than certain members of the government were willing to venture at the time. From its beginnings, then, the Massey Commission was intended to be not just an investigation, but a combined publicity venture and public opinion survey. It was designed as a catalyst to activate and concentrate the otherwise disparate political pressure of special interest groups in the cultural field. As such it reflected Claxton's experience in cultural affairs, indeed, the *modus operandi* of the cultural elite as a whole. The Massey Commission was born of the same belief in public education that had distinguished national voluntary associations since the 1920s and from a faith in the same lobbying methods which won the Radio League its historic victory in the 1930s. This was no surprise, since the commission itself was a product of the cultural nationalism of that same generation as it came into power and found the opportunity to pursue its ideals through public policy.

Comm prod of the cult nationalism
+ pursue its ideals thru public policy

2

The Cultural Elite and
the Culture Lobby

The word *elite* can conjure up images of aristocratic cliques embroiled in conspiracy and intrigue. There was nothing quite so melodramatic about the cultural elite of which the Massey Commission was a part. Its role in the founding of the commission demonstrated that it was not an exclusive clique, but a loose network of friendships and professional associations among leaders in academia, voluntary associations, and government. It was an elite, however, in the sense that it was a definable, privileged group that wielded significant influence in Canadian society. Through their leadership positions, its members were able to exert their influence informally from the national to the local level. The one constant during the hectic early months of the commission's existence was the sustained effort of the cultural elite to create broad and effective culture lobby to support the commission's work.

The cultural elite was part of a broader, public-minded intelligentsia whose influence in Canadian politics grew noticeably towards the mid-point of the twentieth century. Many within this group had abandoned traditional humanistic and religious approaches to social and political problems in favour of the empirical methods of the social sciences. The Massey Commission's cultural mission ran counter to this trend, but as one historian has noted, intellectuals in public life were not a dogmatic band, but 'a pool of available talent ... there were continual formings and reformings of elements into structured bodies to promote their concerns.'[1] Some support for the Massey Commission came from social scientists who had little interest in culture *per se* but did want government aid for their professions. The nationalistic goals of the commission also won it general approval. But the cause of culture was most appealing to those who clung to humanistic values in an age of science.

The humanist point of view maintained some potency despite the dominant scientific ethos of the era because Canadian intellectuals still bore with them the imprint of their Christian upbringings and educations.[2] Among the commissioners this paradox was personified in Lévesque, who as a social scientist and a priest represented both empirical and metaphysical values. Lévesque was conscious of this seeming contradiction. In 1952 he would give an address entitled 'Humanisme et sciences sociales' – no doubt a product of his reflections upon this subject during his work for the commission – which argued that the social sciences were simply the necessary means for the fulfilment of humanist goals in the modern world.[3] He made it clear that his commitment to the social sciences was motivated by and subordinated to humanism. The cultural elite consisted of those members of the Canadian intellectual elite who felt the same way and responded to the Massey Commission as an opportunity to promote such values in Canadian society.

One less ambiguous effect of the rise of the social sciences was that the intelligentsia placed a much greater emphasis on state intervention as a means of resolving social problems. Although in general public opinion was moving in this direction as well, laissez-faire principles were still deeply ingrained in Canadian society. Perhaps in the ideal democracy the average citizen would be educated to the need for state action, but the reality of Canadian politics was that public advocacy was required to make new state initiatives politically acceptable. When Massey was asked by executives of the Canadian Library Association in 1947 how they should go about winning support for a national library, he described how knowledgeable insiders went about effecting change:

The plan of action which he outlined ... emphasized the value of collaboration with other Canadian organizations having a direct interest in the establishment of a national library ... he stated that the 'important thing at the moment would seem to be the mobilization of public opinion and the maximum amount of publicity,' reasoning that 'if the public is made aware of the problem, there will undoubtably be some favourable reaction to it in the Canadian press daily and weekly.' This would convince the authorities in Ottawa that there was a real demand for a national library. Once the government was committed to the project and definite steps had been taken, then the movement would acquire its own momentum.[4]

If not the ideal form of education in a liberal democracy, public advocacy of this sort was at least the acknowledged method of building a democratic consensus and forcing action within the political system.

Many members of the elite had gained experience in managing public opinion through involvement with the work of the Wartime Information Board (WIB). The board's purpose had been to make Canadians happy and cooperative with the government's war effort, and after the war its techniques were used by Claxton to win support for government policies and, by extension, for the Liberal party. The humanist cause of the Massey Commission would be informed by the WIB's social-scientific methods of 'public opinion sampling combined with an integrated media blitz.'[5] Although the commissioners would not apply any such formal social-science techniques, their approach to managing public opinion would be roughly the same.

When the five commissioners gathered for their first official meeting on the morning of Monday, 2 May 1949, their discussions were dominated by concerns about how to ingratiate themselves with the Canadian public. Commissioner and former WIB chairman Norman MacKenzie was worried: they were already being referred to as the 'Commission on Culture,' a title that suggested an elitist enterprise irrelevant to the common man.[6] At least the damage this caused would be limited to English Canada. Lévesque noted that francophones had given the commission a similar nickname, but that culture did not have the same 'unhappy associations' in French Canada.[7] There was no way to shed the unwanted label, but the commissioners were equal to the larger issue it raised. Their basic strategy for promoting their cause was to organize their friends, confound their enemies, and seduce the uncommitted majority of the general public. This last goal was underlined by Lévesque's advice that they keep in mind 'the educational value to be expected from hearings of the Commission throughout Canada and ... the valuable publicity which could thus be given to its work.[8]

At a press conference the next day, reporters picked up on Massey's deliberately populist tone. 'Massey Arts Inquiry not "Highbrow" Affair; He Shuns Word "Culture,"' pronounced the headline in the Toronto *Globe and Mail*.[9] Other newspapers generally echoed this message. 'Commission Won't War on Juke Boxes: No Attempt in Arts Probe to Dictate Tastes, Says Massey' was the banner in the Vancouver *Sun*.[10] Like many of its competitors, the Winnipeg *Free Press* quoted Massey at length on this point:

'I am always a bit shy about the word "culture." It has a sort of highbrow ring about it. And highbrow is the last thing in the world we want this inquiry to be.'

The chairman was asked if there was any idea of a crusade against juke boxes, soap operas, disc jockeys and grade B movies.

'Heavens, no!' Mr Massey exclaimed laughing. 'We can't impose our taste on anybody.'[11]

Massey's jocularity rings hollow to those who suspect that he was, at heart, a juke-box basher. But the least hint of elitism could alienate public opinion. Massey promised that a popular summary of the commission's report would be published for the general public. He was also careful to plant the commission's standard on the solid common ground of Canadian nationalism, proclaiming that its work would be a 'step forward in the development of Canadian feeling and national unity.'[12]

Only after popular suspicions of the commission's cultural mission were addressed did the reporters move on to other issues. Massey soothed the fears of provincial autonomists by promising that the commissioners would 'toe [the] constitutional line' and not enter the field of 'formal education.'[13] He also hinted at the creation of a UNESCO commission and an arts funding body. Although this was the first public sign that the commission would consider funding for the arts, it provoked surprisingly little comment from the reporters. Many had no doubt heard the idea bandied about for years but were unaware of the controversy it had generated within the government.

Massey was pleased by the response to his appearance. Over two dozen reporters had shown up, and he was 'surprised to find that there was considerable interest in the Commission amongst the newspaper men.'[14] In fact, the Ottawa press corps was probably predisposed to give the commission favourable publicity. Its centralist perspective made it sympathetic to the commission's nationalist goals. Parliamentary correspondents, more literate and better educated than most Canadians, were less likely to denigrate culture. Indeed, prominent journalists like B.K. Sandwell, Wilfrid Eggleston, and George Ferguson were closely associated with the cultural elite and could be counted on to be unofficial publicists for the commission.[15]

There were some limits to the good press that the commission could expect. The average reporter would not push cultural elitism too far beyond his readers' tolerance. Many ended up straddling the issue, catering to popular suspicions of high culture in one sentence and emphasizing the commission's patriotic mission in the next. Sometimes, too, their biases were decided for them by the business interests of media proprietors. These factors, however, would emerge most strongly at a later date; for the time being, the commission enjoyed a honeymoon with reporters.

While the commission's image was being orchestrated in public, important administrative matters were being resolved behind the scenes. The search for staff members was conducted within the same academic, voluntary, and governmental circles from which the commissioners were drawn. Well before the first meeting of the commissioners, Massey was in search of a suitable secretary for the commission. He considered this position to be extremely important; he had always used secretaries to great advantage, delegating responsibility to them and expecting in return a critical contribution.[16] This time it was particularly vital to find someone who could write with style to help produce an impressive and convincing final report. An efficient secretary would also ensure that the commission's day-to-day operations ran smoothly, so that it would maintain the best possible public image.

Massey's first choice was Douglas LePan, who had worked under him in the high commission in London. LePan, however, was working on a book of poetry, *The Net and the Shield*, and turned down the offer. Massey wrote to MacKenzie for advice:

> I am rather troubled about the problem of a Secretary for the Commission. Several men have been suggested but most of them seem inadequately qualified. It is, as I think you will agree, absolutely vital that we should get the right man. I should like your opinion on one suggestion, – that of J.E. Robbins of the Education Branch of the Bureau of Statistics. Do you know him and what would you think of his qualifications? I think the secretary must be a person with sound judgement, a strong personality, good address, and an interest in and grasp of the problem we have to deal with. I hope I have not been describing a nonexistent superman.[17]

MacKenzie in turn asked his assistant, Geoffrey Andrew, for suggestions. Andrew thought that Robbins did not have the panache that Massey desired and suggested other names that MacKenzie forwarded to Massey.[18]

MacKenzie's dependence upon Andrew in this matter showed that the commission had already acquired an important if unofficial staff member. Like his boss, Andrew came from northern Nova Scotia and had attended Dalhousie University. He had gone on to Oxford and later taught at Upper Canada College (UCC), where he met and married Margaret Grant, daughter of UCC principal W.L. Grant and a niece of Massey's wife, Alice. Andrew had been secretary at the Wartime Information Board, where MacKenzie was chairman.[19] MacKenzie later brought Andrew to UBC as his executive assistant. While MacKenzie was primarily concerned with what the commission could do for the universities, Andrew was interested in its broader cultural mission and freely offered advice in this area. They were a formidable team. MacKenzie knew everyone and how to get things done, while Andrew supplied administrative support, critical acumen, and a familiarity with cultural issues.

In this case, however, the advice from UBC would not carry the day. Massey's eventual choice for the commission's secretary was Archibald (Archie) Day, an External Affairs officer. Day was recommended to Massey by Gilbert Norwood, a classics professor at the

University of Toronto, by Lester Pearson, and by T.W. MacDermott. MacDermott, then under-secretary of state, wrote that Day was a cultured man with many of the attributes Massey sought: 'He writes well; has a great gift for conversation; a very civilized sense of humour and considerable drive and organization power.'[20] Day, a classicist who had attended the University of Toronto as an undergraduate and the University of London for a PHD, had taught at Toronto, McMaster, and Queen's. During the war he had served at Canadian military headquarters in London, joining External Affairs upon his return. An impish sense of humour leavened Day's erudition; he would prove capable of running the day-to-day affairs of the commission and parodying them at the same time. It was rumoured that sometimes his high spirits were topped up from a handy bottle.

Other important administrative posts were filled with less urgency. René Garneau was chosen as the francophone associate secretary on the recommendation of Lévesque. Garneau had been educated at the universities of Montreal, Laval, and Paris. Like Andrew, he had served on the Wartime Information Board with MacKenzie; he had also held the post of assistant librarian of the parliamentary library of the Province of Quebec. Along the way he had written speeches for Mackenzie King and St Laurent. His emerging reputation as a man of letters was an important factor in his appointment to a position in which he would be responsible for the French version of the report.

Massey had a significant public relations role in mind for the commission's lawyers as well. They would be mercenaries deployed at public hearings to combat hostile witnesses. By having its lawyers ask the tough questions on controversial issues such as radio, television, and the NFB, the commission could retain an aura of impartiality while ensuring a vigorous representation of its views. The position of counsel was first offered to Brigadier Sherwood Lett, a prominent West Coast lawyer, but he turned it down because of previous commitments. By August the post had been filled by Peter Wright, a friend of Brooke Claxton from McMillan, Binch in Toronto. Wright had been a colonel during World War II and was a nephew of the late Chief Justice N.W. Rowell, who had also been his father's law partner. Later that year Guy Roberge, a lawyer from Quebec City, was appointed as associate counsel. Roberge was suggested to St Laurent by his secretary, Jules Léger, because of his experience with copyright law and his connections in the arts community. He would take over from Wright in public hearings in French Canada and the Maritimes. His recruitment brought to the commission yet another member of the Quebec City elite already represented by Lévesque and Garneau – a circle in which the prime minister could be included as well.

In a fashion typical of the cultural elite, friends were sounded out and strings pulled as a network of connections was employed to staff the commission. The smugness of the insiders was palpable to Hilda Neatby when she arrived in Ottawa for the commission's first meeting. She 'found the bland self-satisfaction of the eastern establishment ... a little disconcerting at first. [She had] the feeling that everyone who saw her inspected her covertly to be sure nothing was crawling on her.'[21] But one of the elite's strengths was its ability to recognize and absorb new talent, and it was not long before Neatby began to feel like an insider. Soon she was preparing memoranda on a possible 'Canadian Arts Council,' the Public Archives, and the National Library. The other commissioners were assigned special tasks as well. As expected, Surveyer took on the technical side of broadcasting, and MacKenzie was made responsible for the study of federal activities in the field of scholarship and research. This left the chairman and Lévesque to support Neatby in considering arts funding and the state of major cultural institutions. The chairman was also busy with administrative duties, and it was clear that Lévesque would bear an extra burden as the commission's French-Canadian spokesman.

The manner in which the commission pursued its inquiries also reflected the coziness of relations among leading figures in cultural circles. The commissioners were on friendly terms with the administrators of many of the government agencies they were supposed to be investigating. Massey, of course, was linked to the National Gallery as a director and patron. He would surrender the chair during the Gallery's public hearing in a token display of conscientiousness about conflict of interest, but this gesture only underlined the fact that the Gallery had friends in high places. Close connections also existed with other federal cultural institutions. Kaye Lamb, the Dominion archivist, appeared regularly on commission sub-committees and at public hearings. The commission also stayed in intimate contact with Davidson Dunton, the young chairman of the board of governors of the CBC. At an early commission meeting Massey was pleased to report that 'Mr. Dunton was very happy about the general approach to problems of broadcasting which the Royal Commission was making.'[22] This was the start of a beautiful friendship. Dunton assured Massey, if he needed any assurance, that the CBC would be happy to provide any information that the commission needed. Of course, the commissioners had a legitimate need for information and opinions which only officials like Dunton could provide. Nevertheless, as fellow members of the cultural fraternity they interacted more like partners than as investigators and subject.

The commissioners also planned private sessions so that specialists in various fields could present their views in a setting where the lack of time and secrecy at public hearings would not restrict their comments. They soon concluded that private appearances by such authorities would not be enough, but that special studies of certain subjects should be commissioned. Surveyer and Lévesque were assigned to decide whose services should be solicited and what subjects they should address. Typically, authors were selected from names suggested by the commissioners or their contacts. The list of contributors would read like a 'Who's Who' of the Canadian cultural elite, including figures from national voluntary organizations like E.A. (Ned) Corbett of the CAAE, academics like Massey's nephew George Grant, journalists like B.K. Sandwell, and prominent artists like Sir Ernest MacMillan.

At the same time attempts were made to muzzle rival elites. It was agreed that the Canadian Association of Broadcasters should be approached, possibly by Walter Gordon, to see if one of its representatives could present the case of the private broadcasters to the commission in camera. Perhaps some discussion among reasonable men behind closed doors could save the CBC from some of the unfavorable publicity that would result from more public complaints by the CAB. Surveyer carried the idea of business representation too far, however, when he suggested that the heads of U.S. broadcasting networks be brought in to give their thoughts on Canadian broadcasting. The other commissioners were not receptive to the idea; they had no interest in soliciting hostile opinion unless it could save them from having such views aired in public. They discouraged briefs from other undesirable sources as well. When the British Columbia CCF inquired whether it could appear before the commission, the commissioners contemplated the danger of opening their hearings to partisan political representations and decided to refuse the request. Later M.J. Coldwell, leader of the federal CCF, wrote to protest this decision, but the commissioners held firm.

The provinces were another potential source of trouble. Both Massey and Lévesque met with the prime minister at different times to plot the commission's course through the minefields of federal-provincial relations. It was argued that provincial government buildings should not be used when holding meetings outside Ottawa – there was no sense in giving fears of federal incursions into the provincial sphere a visible manifestation. As it turned out, relations with the provinces would be surprisingly amicable, with one notable exception. When a letter explaining the commission's plans was sent to the premiers, Quebec's Premier Duplessis replied: 'Nous respectons l'opinion contraire et les membres de votre commission, mais nous sommes d'avis que le mandat conferé à votre commission par les autorités fédérales se rapporte à des problèmes qui découlent de la jurisdiction exclusive des provinces, c'est-à-dire, à des problèmes éducationales. En conséquence le gouvernement du Québec est d'opinion qu'il ne doit pas acquiescer à votre mandat ni participer à son exécution.'[23] Behind this firm but polite rejection lay a deep-seated antagonism between Lévesque and Duplessis. The priest was an outspoken critic of the Duplessis government and in the summer of 1949 irritated the premier still more by taking the workers' side in the bitter Asbestos strike. The commissioners were painfully aware that Duplessis could make trouble for them down the road.

Their Quebec hearings, however, were still months away; the opening of public sessions in Ottawa was a more pressing concern. The commissioners recognized that their hearings provided an ideal forum in which to generate the publicity and political pressure necessary to win government acceptance of their recommendations. Massey had secured St Laurent's permission to use the Supreme Court building in Ottawa in order to lend the proceedings a prestige and solemnity befitting their national importance.[24] The commissioners agreed that they should read all briefs beforehand to avoid the boring ritual of having them read aloud at hearings. Instead, witnesses would be asked to summarize their arguments, emphasizing their conclusions, and then answer questions from the commissioners.

They also decided to delay the opening of public hearings until after the federal election on 27 June to avoid any entanglement in electoral politics. There was also the possibility that the Liberals could lose, which would change the political climate severely enough to warrant a serious reconsideration of existing plans. They decided to open their hearings in Ottawa in late July. To the commissioners' relief, the electorate subsequently returned a Liberal majority, ensuring that they would continue under the government that had appointed them to pursue their mutual goals. But their hearings were postponed again when they decided that Lévesque, who was travelling to Europe for a UNESCO conference that summer, should make a side trip to study the British broadcasting system while he was overseas. It was thought that at the same time he could confer with the directors of the British Council and the Arts Council of Great Britain to gather some information about arts funding. Lévesque also took it upon himself to check on television developments in Switzerland, Holland, and Denmark, where his travels took him in the early summer. It was mid-July before he made it to London, and his extended visit set back the opening of the commission's hearings until early August. In the interim Neatby conducted an informal study of television in the United States during a visit to New York.[25]

The opening series of public hearings, which ran from 3 to 8 September in Ottawa, were dominated by the government cultural institutions, national voluntary associations, and professional organizations of the cultural elite. The first week of hearings focused on federal cultural institutions like the National Museum, the National Gallery, the National War Museum, and the Public Archives, with the Library of Parliament following the next week. Afternoons were often set aside for tours of these institutions. Special sessions on issues such as scholarships and broadcasting were interspersed over the following weeks with appearances by leading national cultural associations like the Dominion Drama Festival, the Canadian Writers' Foundation, and the Royal Society of Canada.

The presence of government cultural institutions at the commission's first sessions was natural enough: they were based in Ottawa and the official subjects of the commission's investigation. It was revealing, however, that the only other organizations with a prominent presence in the opening sessions were the national organizations of the cultural elite. With one or two exceptions, they were the only non-governmental bodies to appear before the commission in its first Ottawa hearings. They were there by special invitation because the commissioners wanted to hear what they had to say. Moreover, they had nationwide influence, knew how to promote their interests before the public and in the government, and would serve as the vanguard of the developing culture lobby.

Their presence also demonstrated that the cultural activities of the federal government had become a focus of attention for a number of organized interest groups across the country. The Canadian Historical Association made an appearance to support the Public Archives, and the National Film Society of Canada came to endorse the NFB. The Canadian Federation of Agriculture (CFA) and the Canadian Association for Adult Education, which together had helped the CBC adapt BBC experiments with organized listening groups to the Canadian scene, appeared before the commission as solid allies of their public partner. There were even strong representations for government cultural institutions that did not yet exist. The Canadian Library Association pushed for the continued pursuit of plans for a national library, while a number of educational associations demanded a federal commission for UNESCO. The CAAE's brief noted that the connections between national voluntary associations and the government had tightened during the war and hoped that the Massey Commission might be a step towards making such closer relations permanent in peacetime.[26]

As the commission toured the country, it would be able to rely on the backing of these same cultural interests at the local level. But Canada also boasted hundreds of other voluntary associations, national and local, that had at least a peripheral interest in the commission's work. The presence of the Canadian Federation of Agriculture in support of the CBC was just one such example. For a variety of reasons, labour unions, churches, and women's groups also had a stake in cultural issues. Farmers' groups and labour unions wanted to obtain for their memberships the same cultural advantages enjoyed by the urban middle class. Rural Canadians in particular regarded the CBC and the NFB as their cultural lifelines. For Canadian churches, culture was related to education and invoked their traditional concern with enjoining social values. Women's groups, on the other hand, were often deeply involved in local cultural pursuits and in related professions such as teaching. It would not take much to persuade these groups that their interests were at stake in the commission's work, and their support would create an extensive and powerful culture lobby from coast to coast. The real organizational challenge for the cultural elite was to reach beyond its own pet organizations to rally these related constituencies to its cause.

Some of these groups were spurred to action by the general publicity accorded the commission, but others needed more direct encouragement. The Canadian Association for Adult Education played a critical role in motivating these marginal sympathizers. It provided a link between the cultural elite and important non-profit organizations across the country. Ned Corbett, the director of the CAAE, was a friend of Massey and MacKenzie, both of whom had been involved with the CAAE on a variety of projects over the years. During the interwar years Corbett had been active in many other leading national voluntary associations, including the Radio League. His extensive connections in cultural circles were underlined by the CAAE journal, *Food for Thought*, when it noted after the summer hearings of 1949 that 'most of the submissions came from organizations and governmental agencies with which the CAAE maintains close working relationships.'[27]

Cultural development was a natural cause for adult educators to embrace, and Corbett used his contracts with grassroots organizations across the country to rally support for the commission. The Joint Planning Commission (JPC), a body created by the CAAE to coordinate goals and share information among various organizations in the field of adult education, was at the centre of this effort. It included representatives from the Canadian Library Association, the Canadian Council of Churches, the Ontario Federation of Labour, the Canadian Federation of Agriculture, the University of Toronto, the National Farm Radio Forum, and the Citizen's Forum.[28] The CAAE used the JPC to encourage other voluntary associations to present briefs to the Massey Commission and to provide them with information and opinions that would help them to do so. Without explicitly directing their efforts, the CAAE managed to mobilize support for the commission's work and coordinate opinion around a few central issues.

The CAAE's efforts were paralleled in the arts by the promotional enterprise of the Federation of Canadian Artists (FCA). The FCA distributed five hundred or more copies of its brief and the commission's terms of reference to its own branches, various other arts and cultural organizations, and members of the press. Its covering letter urged recipients to make presentations to the commission and to seek local newspaper coverage and other forms of publicity for their hearings.[29] The commissioners themselves also played an active role in trying to mobilize support for their cause. As their cross-country itinerary was being organized, they noted a dearth of submissions from Saskatchewan. At her colleagues' behest, Neatby wrote letters to influential figures in her native province to stir up more interest. MacKenzie later contacted key people in the East to see if they too could generate greater support for the commission in appropriate quarters.[30] Without such behind-the-scenes organization and promotion, the Massey Commission's schedule would not have been as impressively crowded from one city to the next.

These efforts were successful in creating a broad culture lobby which extended beyond organizations with a direct interest in government cultural activities. Voluntary associations with primary interests outside of the culture sector would become the second most important presence in the commission's hearings. The 473 representations to the Massey Commission can be divided into eight basic categories. Ranked in descending order by the number of submissions received from each category, these groups were:

1. Voluntary Associations/Institutions in the Arts, Letters, and Sciences
2. Other Voluntary Associations/Institutions
3. Professional Organizations in the Arts, Letters, and Sciences
4. Individuals
5. Private Broadcasters
6. Government Institutions/Departments
7. Business Organizations
8. Universities

Most of these groups can be further subdivided into national, regional/provincial, and local categories. A breakdown of the origins of the briefs produces the following table:

Type of Organization	Total number of briefs	National	Provincial /regional	Local
1. VAI–ALS	149 [31.5%]	31 [6.6%]	33 [7.0%]	85 [18.0%]
2. Other VAI	94 [19.9%]	51 [10.8%]	22 [4.7%]	21 [4.4%]
3. PO–ALS	63 [13.3%]	25 [5.3%]	25 [5.3%]	13 [2.7%]
4. Individuals	41 [8.7%]	–	–	41 [8.7%]
5. Pvt. bctrs	41 [8.7%]	3 [.6%]	4 [.8%]	34 [7.2%]
6. Government	36 [7.6%]	17 [3.6%]	18 [3.8%]	1 [.2%]
7. Business	27 [5.7%]	16 [3.4%]	5 [1.1%]	6 [1.3%]
8. Universities	22 [4.7%]	2 [.4%]	–	20 [4.2%]
Total	473 [100%]	145 [30.7%]	107 [22.6%]	221 [46.7%]

The one distortion in these figures is that most of the individuals listed were in fact representing some organized cultural interest. Nevertheless, it is clear that the commission succeeded in attracting almost every interest group that could conceivably benefit from government-sponsored cultural development. The business interests and private broadcasters, who were generally hostile to government cultural enterprise, ended up being outnumbered seven to one in its hearings. 'From the very beginning of our work,' Massey would later boast, 'we were amazed at the extent of public interest, goodwill, and co-operation ... The enthusiasm was invoked by the nature of the work itself.'[31] Whether enthusiasm for culture or good organization was the cause, a wide array of Canadian voluntary organizations had acted on the belief that their interests were at stake in the work of the commission. The creation of this culture lobby from coast to coast was evidence that the cultural elite's connections branched across the country.

But these extensive branches were not always balanced by deep roots in Canadian society. It was clear that many local voluntary associations did not necessarily represent the interests of their communities as a whole. As a friend of Neatby's warned:

Voluntary societies are not always good. They often have very narrow goals, are machinery for the expression of personal advancement, persist long after their usefulness because the officers need them to maintain their status in the community, have difficulty developing and changing as the needs of their members change. It is customary to describe government workers as bureaucrats, but nothing is more bureaucratic than a society that hasn't changed its officers in ten or twenty years.[32]

Professor J.D. Mawdsley of the University of Saskatchewan later elaborated: 'This is the history of most of these societies. At some time or other there is an enthusiast who is a key man. He often leaves and then there is a down drop.'[33] In short, many local voluntary associations resembled forlorn outposts of special causes rather than vigorous grassroots enterprises. Massey's claim that there was an overwhelming public response to the commission must be considered with this in mind.

Even with many large national voluntary organizations it was debatable whether briefs submitted to the commission reflected the feelings of their rank and file. Two farmers from the Niagara peninsula, Howard Prentice and John Pollock, appeared before the commission to complain about the Canadian Federation of Agriculture brief. They supported the private radio side of the broadcasting controversy and protested that they had 'had no opportunity of examining, let alone approving, that brief before it was presented to you nor have we had a chance to examine it yet.'[34] Many members of constituent organizations of the CFA, the farmers claimed, did not even realize they were affiliated with the national body. Similar questions arose regarding the representativeness of pro-culture briefs from Canadian labour unions. The leaders of these organizations nevertheless presented their views as representative of their membership on the basis that they reflected resolutions that had been passed at conventions or executive meetings.

This was a sensitive issue because it touched directly upon the commission's Achilles' heel: the popular suspicion of high culture. The cultural elite liked to think that it spoke for the interests of all Canadians. In their report the commissioners would brazenly claim that 'we have had before us a complete cross section of the Canadian population' and that 'a large proportion of the public of Canada has been directly represented.' This was hogwash. They later conceded that 'most of the briefs and most of the interviews came to us from organized societies. We heard little from the citizen who represented no one but himself.' Nevertheless, they were satisfied that through these voluntary associations they had 'heard the voice of Canada.'[35]

Neatby would later argue that the commissioners had proceeded in as democratic a fashion as practicality allowed. Pure representations of public opinion were a fanciful ideal in any working democracy: 'The whole question of the use of the briefs was discussed with much care and was considered as a serious and difficult problem ... An effort was made to offer a fair analysis of opinions expressed ... The summaries of the briefs were offered as the views of those Canadians who were sufficiently interested ... to care to express any views at all.'[36] The commission's hearings, then, did not provide as accurate a sampling of public opinion as a poll or a plebiscite, yet they did offer a forum in which those who were concerned and motivated could make their opinions count. 'It may have been a mistake to describe these as most representative of Canadian listeners,' Neatby concluded in a discussion of opinion on broadcasting, 'but if this was a mistake, then the whole system of representative government is a mistake.'[37]

To endow this pragmatic conception of how things worked with some of the populist appeal it so obviously lacked, the commissioners went out of their way to portray voluntary associations as more than just special interest groups. Instead, they were bulwarks of democracy, agencies through which ordinary citizens made the type of unselfish contributions that democracy depended upon. It was only natural and just that such disinterested effort should be influential in Canadian society. 'To develop an informed public opinion and to guide it into effective channels is [an] important function of the voluntary society,' the commissioners would write; such societies could be 'counted on, when occasion arises, to express sane and intelligent views on public matters.'[38] In essence this was yet another defence of representative democracy, but in its eagerness to maintain public approval the commission tried to present itself in as populist a light as possible.

In any event, it was clear that within a few months of its formation the Massey Commission had won the support of a significant assortment of interest groups. At the core of the culture lobby was an elite of well-educated, principled, and like-minded leaders who wielded influence across the nation. This cultural elite roused support from all manner of voluntary associations, professional organizations, and cultural institutions that were attracted to the cause, in part at least, by a desire to promote their own interests. It was an articulate sector of Canadian society, and the Massey Commission gave it a cause to fight for and a national forum in which to voice its concerns. The commission had mobilized a constituency that would generate interest in its report and maintain political pressure for government action in cultural affairs. In the process the commission itself was transformed from a stolid official investigation into something of a national crusade. The highbrows were on the march.

3

The Promotional Tour

The cultural elite's success in attracting support across the country meant that by mid-summer of 1949 the Massey Commission was well on its way to fulfilling the first part of its three-pronged plan to rally its supporters, confound its enemies, and seduce the uncommitted public. The last two goals were equally important and would preoccupy the commissioners throughout the rest of their work. Even before the end of its first Ottawa hearings it was clear that the commission faced two major sources of opposition. The first came from Quebec nationalists, who were already portraying the commission as a threat to French-Canadian culture. There was also open resistance from businessmen, particularly broadcasters, who had pecuniary interests that were endangered by federal cultural activities. The commission would have to parry these challenges in its public hearings and in the press. Winning over general public opinion was a more subtle and complex business. The commissioners' supposition that most Canadians harboured egalitarian suspicions of high culture was reinforced by what they heard as their hearings progressed. They responded by continuing to distance themselves from the word *culture* and emphasizing instead the national and popular purposes of their mission.

The commission set about its work in a country that was still adjusting to the changed environment of the postwar world. Canadians were savouring the fruits of victory and beginning to believe that prosperity had come to stay. It was the start of an era which would

the era of [handwritten annotation in margin]

come to be associated with the baby boom, suburbia, bigger cars, expressways, naïve futurism, and a happy-go-lucky ethos epitomized in radio shows like 'The Happy Gang.' According to stereotypes of the 1950s, Canada was entering the decade in which the American Dream, upholstered in vinyl and gilded in chrome, materialized for many North Americans. Life in postwar Canada was not, of course, as puerile as 1950s nostalgia would have it. Just flipping through the pages of contemporary periodicals reveals a more sober, serious society struggling with a wide variety of issues and interests.

Can entering the decade of the Amer. Dream [handwritten annotation in margin]

An avid anticipation of television service was evident in the coverage given the subject by national magazines. In the 15 January 1949 issue of *Maclean's*, Blair Fraser had an article entitled 'Why They Won't Let You Have Television,' and two months later the CBC's plans for the new medium were explained in *Saturday Night*. The March issue of the *National Home Monthly* was more sensationalistic; in 'Television: The New Monster,' novelist The Callaghan breathlessly announced that 'a cultural time bomb is being thrown into Canadian homes, and panic is hitting the entertainment industry.'

Canadian magazines also gave a good deal of attention to more traditional cultural issues. Articles on Canadian achievements in the arts appeared frequently in *Maclean's*, while the highbrow *Saturday Night* kept on top of university affairs and regularly celebrated Canadian composers, musicians, playwrights, poets, novelists, painters, and dancers. Even the more populistic *National Home Monthly* had the odd piece on the arts. Its October 1949 issue featured an article on Robertson Davies and the summer theatre movement which lauded the development of such Canadian cultural activity. But Morley Callaghan may have been more in tune with the magazine's audience when he took pains to distance himself from the uppity literati in one of his columns. He facetiously told his readers 'how to talk to highbrows' with their 'mumbo-jumbo of sex and economics' and concluded with an endorsement of the wisdom of the common man. Perhaps it was the Canadian rather than the Thespian accomplishments of Davies and his crew that won endorsement; articles like 'In Search of a Canadian' in September 1950 showed that the *National Home Monthly* embraced a cultural nationalism similar to that of its competitors.

Can mags more attant to more trad cult issues. [handwritten annotation in margin]

But learning to live with the Bomb and the Cold War were more pressing contemporary concerns. In a 15 January *Maclean's* article, Matthew Halton drew some disturbing conclusions about the meaning of the recent NATO Pact: 'It's plainly a spectacular distance that the democratic world has come since it reluctantly realized a year or so ago that there was no peace on earth, that its nations must live in a state of continuous crisis, and that it had no hope of bargaining with Russia or stopping the Communist technique of aggression in country after country unless it was economically rejuvenated and militarily strong.'[1] 'Russia Won't Attack,' *Maclean's* assured its readers in one article and then went on to confide in another that 'The Death Ray Is Here' and 'there is no real defense against the death rays locked in the atom bomb.' *Saturday Night*, in contrast, emphasized four days later that 'Peaceful Atomic Energy Is Man's Best Friend.' The postwar world order presented Canadians with issues that were both ambiguous and profound.

At least the merits of capitalist democracy were generally agreed upon. 'Let's Fight Communism with Democratic Weapons,' *Maclean's* suggested. The *National Home Monthly* offered a popular primer on the merits of capitalism. 'Hello Mr. Average Canadian, I'm Pete (Average) Profit,' declared a clean-cut, hard-working cartoon character. Pete went on to demonstrate that he was not as big as people thought he was, and that his existence was assured only by thrift and perseverance. 'Boy, do I lead a risky life!' he exclaimed. Poor Pete was hounded by the spectre of socialism on the one hand and the constant risk of bankruptcy on the other.

The virtues of a free enterprise society were clearer still in the advertising that dominated Canadian magazines. 'Dollar for Dollar – you can't beat a Pontiac!' ran a typical car ad, 'So *Big!* So *Good!* So *Beautiful!*' This was advertising at its best: quantitative, moral, and aesthetic virtues were extolled simultaneously to mythologize a midsize sedan. The pitch for a rival model appealed to Canadians' faith in technological progress. 'Here They Come – The New Futuramics,' it proclaimed, 'They're Here! They're New! They're Futuramic! With Hydramatic Drive!' The North American love affair with the car may have been particularly intense, but similar appeals were used to sell a wide array of consumer goods. '"Craven A" will not affect the throat,' consumers were assured on one page and then enticed on the next with the '*extra* leisure hours' to be gained by using the 'Time and Labor-saving features' of a new brand of stove. This ceaseless barrage of advertisements probably had more of an impact on most readers than occasional articles on Canadian culture, especially since the latter did not even exist in the pages of the American magazines that Canadians read most.[2]

This impression was borne out by what the commission heard in its public sessions. The average Canadian's appreciation of high culture was portrayed as either limited or non-existent. H.L. Keenleyside, appearing before the commission on behalf of the Association of Canadian Clubs, argued that press, movies, and radio were the greatest cultural influences in the country.[3] A Vancouver *Sun* columnist was inspired by the commission's visit to expand on this very point:

> We in B.C. are proud of our modern artists. True, we cannot understand them. But this is not necessarily a disadvantage. In fact, if we COULD understand our artists, we might not be so proud of them ... You will find that B.C. people yield to none in their love of music ... Our favourite B.C. musical instruments are the Radio, the gramaphone [*sic*] and the juke box. We have some of the finest young jukebox players in the country ... Our symphony orchestra is really something. Only a few years ago we used to think that symphony concerts were pretty high-brow. Now we know better ... You will find you can get coffee and soft drinks and everything right in the concert! It is almost as good as a hockey game.[4]

The Canadian Youth Commission (CYC) had recently concluded a study showing how young Canadians aged fifteen to twenty-four filled their leisure hours. It revealed that they spent most of their spare time talking, listening to the radio, reading, dating, and dancing. About 27 per cent went to at least one movie a week; 17 per cent to two or more a week. But only about a third played on a sports team, and half did not belong to a group or club of their peers. 'Very few,' the survey concluded regretfully, 'have any interest in cultural activities.' The same thing was probably true of their parents, the CYC surmised.[5]

In short, the commissioners were aware that their enterprise was being launched into a society that was not wildly enthusiastic about its mission. The public's opinion of high culture seemed to range from indifference to suspicion. This prejudice presented a formidable obstacle to the fulfilment of the commission's aims, yet there were ways of offsetting it. For the duration of its public hearings the Massey Commission would be in the public eye. It could expect extensive media coverage as it criss-crossed the country holding public hearings, coverage that could be orchestrated to neutralize opposition, overcome indifference, and forward its aims.

The commission had already made a splash in the papers during its opening Ottawa sessions. Its most newsworthy hearings were on universities and broadcasting, issues on which opposition was already organized and vociferous. The National Conference of Canadian Universities dropped a bombshell on the afternoon of 23 August. Disregarding scruples about provincial rights and the warnings of French-Canadian nationalists, it made a bold demand for direct federal aid for university education. The proposal grabbed headlines. Massey had probably wanted to be circumspect about this treacherous issue, but it was now out in the open once and for all.

The battle of the broadcasters came in the first week of September when the commission heard first from the CBC and then from the private broadcasters' umbrella organization, the Canadian Association of Broadcasters (CAB). Anticipation had been heightened by the leaking of the CBC brief to a Montreal newspaper. Mindful of the controversy and public interest surrounding broadcasting policy, the commissioners took great care in preparing their questions for these sessions. Wright was assigned the tricky task of questioning both combatants in a way that would bring out the main points the commissioners wanted emphasized without overtly betraying their sympathy for public broadcasting. Despite all the assurances of good intentions and mutual respect, however, the tensions between the two sides were palpable. The Ottawa hearings ended in an ominous atmosphere of unresolved acrimony.

The general public's attitudes about government cultural activities were never expressed very strongly in the commission's hearings. For ordinary Canadians the prospect of appearing before a royal commission, with its elevated official status and its eminent commissioners, was very intimidating. A Western witness would comment that 'I feel somewhat like a prisoner at the bar.'[6] To relieve anxiety about up-coming appearances, Day would often brief those about to appear on the type of questions they would be asked. Nevertheless, it was still a nerve-wracking experience. Even Eric Arthur, a professor of architecture who was used to public speaking, joked to Neatby about 'the strain of "examination" in the monumental surroundings of the Salle des pas perdus.'[7]

This problem was obvious enough to become the theme of one journalist's feature on the commission. Norman Smith's piece in the Ottawa *Journal* on 27 August 1949 tried to humanize the commission by presenting its members as down-to-earth folks. Entitled 'You Want Money for Culture? Tell Mr. Massey about It,' the piece began:

> First impressions of the Royal Commission of National Development in the Arts, Letters, and Sciences are pretty frightening.
>
> In the first place, the title. Fancy wooing the Muses with a name like that!
>
> And when Rt. Hon. Vincent Massey and his four fellow Commissioners come through a little side door in the reredos of the austere Exchequer Court you rise with everyone else and half expect to hear someone intone 'I am the Resurrection and the Life.'
>
> The panelled walls, the red leather chair, the thick, quiet carpets – and above all those five people raised in solemn judgement! Omar Khayyam would fetch up his book of verse and jug of wine and take Thou the Hell out of there.[8]

Smith went on to describe how this impression was moderated as the personalities and procedures of the commission became apparent. 'See the jovial grin that hovers about the face of the Priest, Most Rev. Georges Lévesque. And that glint in Professor Norman MacKenzie's eye ... And that lady commissioner who heads a University History Department, but looks feminine despite that and asks questions in manner of her sex: twice.' Massey, Smith noted, seemed sincere and attentive, and asked his questions in 'an easy friendly way.' He went out of his way to humanize the chairman, quoting him as quipping to MacKenzie, ' "Well Larry, let's get back to the factory" ' as they finished lunch one day. At the end of the Film hearing, he reported, the commissioners 'hung about, smoked, chinned here and there with witnesses and the press, and we all dwindled out leaving the Exchequer Court considerably shorn of its severity.' Why Smith was moved to present the commission in such a flattering light is not known, but the commissioners themselves could not have commissioned a better piece of public relations work. Despite the supposed informality of the hearings, however, he noted that the public was not storming in to hear them; usually only a handful of spectators were in attendance. In high summer the commission might have attracted a better Ottawa crowd by holding its sessions in the Gatineaus.

As the commissioners grew comfortable with their public role, their sessions became set pieces of theatre. Massey, the director and leading man, could be the soul of cordiality as long as he was interested in the group before him. His deft management of the process was appreciated both by his fellow commissioners and by witnesses. More than one observer was prompted to comment that he was a better actor than his brother Raymond. This did not imply insincerity, but rather a stage sense that ensured smooth and decorous proceedings. There was more to the chairman's work, however, than just play-acting:

> He flung his heart and soul into it, attending every one of the one-hundred and fourteen public sessions, reading each of the four-hundred and sixty-two briefs, poring over the thousands of pages of verbatim testimony. He handled it all with superb stage-craft. His manner was informal without being familiar and he appeared genuinely interested in everything that was said. At the same time, he kept things moving with clockwork speed. His long sensitive hands pulling the glasses down low over his aquiline nose became a familiar spectacle to the hundreds who appeared before him. 'He speaks with those hands,' says his colleague, Father Lévesque.[9]

Massey proved to be a capable chairman of the commission's private meetings as well. In both settings he did not try to dominate, but rather conducted the commission's deliberations as a maestro before musicians. He allowed open and productive discussion, but knew when to intervene to conclude one subject and move on to the next. Lévesque later commented that the old expression 'an iron hand in a velvet glove' aptly described Massey's leadership style.

Norman MacKenzie was 'a relaxed commissioner, with an attitude that usually seemed to hover between the benign and the amused.'[10] He could, however, become very animated and forceful when his pet cause, university funding, came up. Although business at UBC prevented MacKenzie from attending as many sessions as some of his Eastern colleagues, he came to as many as he could, missing only about a dozen. MacKenzie's rival as most amiable commissioner was Lévesque, who maintained a jovial demeanour throughout the hearings. Claude Bissell, who presented a brief to the commission, described his impression of Lévesque in this way:

> The friendly, generous face would light up, the eyes would sparkle with good humour but with a pleasantly distracting hint of irony. The appearance proclaimed the generosity of spirit, but it concealed the crusading ardour which, like MacKenzie, he possessed in abundance. The priest who seemed the very embodiment of pastoral cordiality was also an impassioned social reformer who proclaimed in a speech he gave a few months after he joined the commission: 'The true anti-communists are those who build the new society with justice and love ... nothing will stop us, neither slanders nor threats, no matter whence they come.'[11]

Lévesque often had to attend to duties at the Université Laval but was able to stay in touch with Ottawa and travel back and forth as necessary. Early in the commission's work he became troubled that he was missing nuances in discussions because of what he considered to be the different linguistically based patterns of thought of his anglophone colleagues. By staying at a Dominican house, he missed evenings with the other commissioners at the Chateau Laurier. Lévesque finally moved to the hotel in the hope that informal fraternization would help bridge the two solitudes.

Surveyer, the oldest member of the commission, did not seem to have the time or vigour to put in the same effort as his fellow commissioners over the long haul. He started strongly, taking a close interest in the administrative organization of the commission and recommending that special librarians be employed to keep track of information in a systematic fashion. But he would fade in the stretch as business concerns and ill health kept him away from public hearings, important meetings, and the centre of action in Ottawa. Lévesque and MacKenzie had substantial commitments elsewhere as well but managed to keep involved in the affairs of the commission by pushing themselves to the limit. Even when they were attending to their university responsibilities, they stayed in touch with the core group at the commission's offices in the Laurentian Building in Ottawa. Their connections were closer not just physically, but intellectually. It soon became evident that despite his record of public service, Surveyer was not always on the same wavelength as the other members. He admitted to Massey that he felt inadequate when the commission was 'debating questions which are not familiar to me.'[12]

Neatby's austere public demeanour contrasted sharply with that of Lévesque and MacKenzie, and she could often be startlingly direct and relentless in her questioning. But the commission's tour of the country had a moderating effect on her, forcing her to recognize and respect other ways of life and even bringing her to a grudging acceptance of such alien forms of culture as sports and soap operas. The youngest of the commissioners, Neatby attended all of the commission's sessions and also assumed most of the burden of its day-to-day business. She found the work a welcome change from her teaching routine in Saskatchewan. Unlike her fellow commissioners, she took a leave of absence from her regular job and worked virtually full-time on the commission from the summer of 1949 until January 1951. Only Massey and the commission staff came close to devoting the same amount of effort.

The opening series of public hearings in Ottawa ended in early September, and by early October the commissioners were rattling across the prairies in a private railcar procured by Day to serve as a mobile office for a Western tour that would take them to Winnipeg, Saskatchewan, Edmonton, Vancouver, Victoria, Calgary, and Regina. Unlike the previous set of hearings, these cross-country sessions were not structured around particular themes but covered whatever questions were raised by every interested local, provincial, or national group that wanted to appear. The commission's public hearings in Winnipeg presented a typical slate of representations. There were women's clubs, local arts organizations, religious bodies, private radio stations, a musicians' association, ethnic groups, educational societies, agricultural interests, and a smattering of appearance by individuals: in all, twenty-nine briefs to be heard in three days. Each presentation was accorded between twenty minutes and an hour according to the commissioners' estimate of its importance.

From the start of its tour the commission was reminded of the elitist stigma attached to its work. The Manitoba Region of the Federation of Canadian Artists summed up local attitudes towards art: 'Unless some other factor can be brought into operation, art will continue to have, in the mind of the representative Manitoban, the status of a minor commercial activity having an aura of pretension and operating with quasi-charitable support in an economic sub-cellar. The implication is that artists and their friends are trying to inject some exotic material into the Manitoban way of life.'[13] Similar comments would be made by cultural groups from coast to coast, assuring the commissioners that their initial concerns about the negative associations of culture had been well founded.

As a result, the commission remained wary of associating itself with culture. For the benefit of Vancouver reporters, Massey reiterated the humble intentions of his entourage:

'The word "culture" was wisely not used in the title,' Mr. Massey said in an informal chat with reporters at Hotel Vancouver Sunday. 'It conjures up entirely the wrong idea. As it is, the title is unfortunately long and there's no effective way of changing it.
But it's not a highbrow undertaking at all.'[14]

In Victoria Neatby cultivated a 'just folks' image by presenting herself as a veteran of the Saskatchewan barnyard. 'I'm a real farm woman at heart,' she told the editor of the women's page of the local newspaper. 'I can milk a cow, take care of chickens and I think I could even help with the plowing.'[15] The wisdom of the chairman was also featured in the Victoria press. After the usual disclaimers about culture, Massey again took pains to present the commission's work as a nationalist crusade:

Canada is growing to adult stature in arts, letters, and sciences, Mr. Massey feels.

'We're very conscious of an increased national feeling,' said the author of the widely-read book, 'On Being Canadian.'

'The national note is constantly struck in briefs which are presented to us. There is a feeling of pride in our own achievement. It's not a narrow or artificial feeling – it's an expression of something real.'[16]

The commissioners would continue to pitch this combination of lowbrow pretence and patriotic purpose as they moved across the country.

In session, however, quite a different sort of commission was often evident. Mrs D.M. Ewing of the University Women's Club of Regina engaged in an interesting discussion with Neatby on one of her favourite topics: elevating the masses. Here two members of the cultural elite, talking between themselves, could forget about offending egalitarian sentiments and discuss the dilemma of how to lead the masses to drink deeply of culture without actually shoving their heads into it:

EWING: Of course, Miss Neatby, I think any educationist would think it has to be a gradual process.

Canadian radio is established by the government, and like any government agency it has to take its direction really from the people; but, on the other hand, I think there can be a nice balance achieved between what the critics of the CBC referred to as 'ramming culture down the throats of people' and pandering to the lowest tastes in entertainment.

NEATBY: You think it is the duty of the CBC, as government radio, to give people what they need rather than what they want or think they want?

EWING: I don't think you can put it quite as baldly as that. Adult Educators feel that in any educational process you have to start where people are and any elevation of taste has to be a gradual thing.[17]

The commission would still be grappling with this problem, trying to reconcile liberalism and elitism, months later as it wrote its report.

Social occasions relieved the burden of such weighty considerations at every stop on the commission's travels. Across the country the arrival of a royal commission quickened the blood of society hostesses, and the commission soon began to receive more invitations than it could handle. Usually the local university president and, if it was a provincial capital, the lieutenant-governor felt obliged to entertain them. The social schedule in Winnipeg was typical. On Tuesday evening the commission was invited to the University of Manitoba Faculty Club by President Gillson. Lunch the next day was with the lieutenant-governor and his wife, and Thursday's midday meal was shared with Grant Dexter of the *Free Press*. Another evening party was given for the commission by the son-in-law of Arthur Surveyer, although Surveyer himself had not accompanied the commission on its Western swing. Archie Day, who was either ignorant of his host's identity or else carried away with the festive spirit, chose this inappropriate occasion to mimic Surveyer's deportment while the commission was in session. The parody was unflattering enough to provoke the ire of the host. Day had let his sense of humour prevail over his sense of decorum, and the incident almost cost him his job. René Garneau later summarized the fallout of the incident in a letter to Neatby:

> Il se passe à la Commission des histoires regrettables. Confidentiellement je veux vous dire que M. Surveyer et le P. Lévesque ont écrit à M. Massey au sujet d'une conversation très injurieuse pour les commissaires que mon collègue Day aurait eue à Winnipeg avec des gens chez qui il était invité. M. Surveyer et notre ami dominicain sont très montés. M. Massey a vu M. Day et il est question qui celui-ci retourne aux Affaires extérieures. Pour ma part je ne le veux pas. D'abord parce que j'ai peur qu'on s'imagine qu'il s'agit là d'un coup organisé par la 'race' à laquelle appartiennent le P. Lévesque, M. Surveyer, et moi-même. Ensuite parce qu'il n'est pas sage de changer son cheval au milieu d'une rivière. D'autre part, il faudra que M. Day s'habitue à être plus discret et moins prétentieux.[18]

Fortunately for Day, he had a powerful ally among the commissioners. MacKenzie thought that Day's slip was a forgivable excess of high spiritedness. Like Garneau, he was conscious of how much the commission would suffer from losing its organizational pivot just as it was getting underway. He also liked Day and thought he had indispensable talents. MacKenzie phoned friends such as 'Mike' Pearson and Arnold Heeney, under-secretary of state for external affairs, to get the government on his side. Massey carefully balanced the charges of 'disloyalty' against the practical reasons for keeping Day and decided not to take any action.

In between these distractions and their hearings, the commissioners took the time to do a considerable amount of snooping for themselves. As they recounted in their report: 'we profited from the opportunity to visit universities, local museums, provincial archives, historical monuments, local art centres, exhibitions of handicrafts, private collections of Canadian pictures; to visit broadcasting stations, privately and publicly-owned; to witness television programmes; to attend a typical showing of National Film Board films in a prairie village, the rehearsal of an opera under the auspices of the Canadian Broadcasting Corporation, a programme of local talent at a private radio station, a performance by a Canadian ballet group, a play by a representative amateur company and concerts by two symphony orchestras.'[19] Altogether they maintained a hectic schedule. MacKenzie's thank-you note to one society hostess revealed how busy the commissioners were as well as how some of the entourage relieved the pressure of the commission's work: 'I am sorry that I no longer have the stamina of some of the younger members of the staff, otherwise I would have stayed all night like they seem to have done, but, quite frankly, I have been so busy recently that I do not get much sleep at the best of times and on trips like these with all the extra reading of briefs that has to be done after hours, I find it a great struggle to get any sleep at all, except when I sit as a Commissioner.'[20] With their days and evenings full of hearings, side trips, and social events, the commissioners were hard pressed to find time to read all of the briefs for upcoming sessions.

Interest in the commission was intense enough that excerpts from many of its hearings were reprinted verbatim in local newspapers. In Vancouver one such item demonstrated how the commission dealt with business opposition. The Vancouver Board of Trade's brief had forcibly expressed its laissez-faire principles, including its alarm about government interference in free enterprise through agencies such as the NFB and the CBC. Peter Wright's aggressive counter-attack was recounted at length in the Vancouver *News-Herald*:

> The brief contended that 'in the matter of arts, letters and sciences, the restraining, and often oppressive, hand of government is to be seen ... in many cases detrimental to the public welfare.'
> Mr. Wright asked for examples. Mr. Norris replied that the statement was 'general,' as applying to business.
> 'This isn't a commission on business,' Mr. Wright said.
> 'But those restraints might spread to the arts, letters, and sciences,' said Mr. Norris.
> Mr. Wright replied that the commission so far had heard mostly submissions which said the government had not gone far enough in arts, letters, and sciences.[21]

Wright continued to make Norris look silly for railing against government regulation when there was little government involvement in the arts and letters. Eventually Norris began to wilt under the barrage and tried to distance himself from the brief:

> NORRIS: I am a practising barrister. Let me get that clear. That is all I do.
> WRIGHT: And prepare briefs for the Royal Commission.
> NORRIS: Oh no. I am presenting this brief.
> WRIGHT: You didn't prepare it?
> NORRIS: Well, I had something to do with it.
> WRIGHT: Well, I don't want to embarrass you.
> NORRIS: I am not easily embarrassed.
> WRIGHT: If you don't know the answers to the questions, by all means –
> NORRIS: You see, I am in this position. I should be surrounded by a lot of experts to tell me these things as I present my brief, as I would before the Board of Transport Commissioners or something of that sort, but unfortunately we had a little difficulty.[22]

At this point the courtroom drama degenerated into farce as one of Norris's associates tried to help him out:

COLTMAN: Is it permissible to speak from the floor? It has something to do with the brief, and I thought it might assist.
NORRIS: I am not anxious for Mr. Coltman to intervene. When I want Mr. Coltman's assistance I will get it.[23]

The interrogation progressed, becoming nastier still, until one heated exchange prompted Massey to proclaim 'Order' for the first and only time in the commission's public hearings. Then came the knock-out punch: Wright asked about the Board of Trade's submission to the Aird Commission. Norris, totally unfamiliar with the document, could not believe that it had been in favour of public broadcasting. In the end it was obvious that the Massey Commission's lawyer had pummelled the opposition's lawyer. It was an impressive fulfilment of Massey's strategy of using the commission's legal counsel to ensure that the right point of view prevailed against the self-interested propaganda of business interests.

In Calgary the Calgary Allied Arts Centre provided the commission with a typical example of the problems besetting local arts organizations in Canada. Since 1946 the council had grown from 400 members and 9 affiliated organizations to 1,250 members and 24 affiliated groups. This growth seemed encouraging, but in fact it did not really represent a new Calgarian cultural consciousness. Mr. A.F. Key, director of the council, explained: 'We started purely as a High-Brow organization, a purely cultural organization. After a few months we suddenly realized it was necessary for us to have an audience ... we found that a lot of people in Calgary took the attitude that our place was perhaps alright [sic] for women and children, but we found a dearth of men coming around here.' In an attempt to change this situation the council took in the local Model Trainmen, a group which could use the talents of Calgary artists to paint scenic backdrops for its tiny trains: 'The Model Trainmen have got the attic and are building their little towns and tracks up there and through these people we are now actively interesting our artists in the work they are doing ... We have some young architects in town who are going to design small buildings to go around the tracks and in that way we are tying together our cultural programme with a purely, shall we say, Low-Brow recreational programme and I think it is very effective.'[24] Here on a miniature level was the same subordination of high culture to mundane concerns that the commissioners abhorred in the world at large.

The commission's tour of Western Canada ended in Regina on 3 November 1949. After a break of ten days, hearings in Central Canada began with a five day session in Toronto that opened on 15 November. The highlight of the Toronto hearings was the appearance of Jack Kent Cooke, a local broadcasting entrepreneur whose attitudes epitomized and even caricatured those of private broadcasters across Canada. Cooke obligingly supplied the commission with publicity materials that described him as a 'A Modern Super-Salesman' and credited him with turning a lacklustre Toronto station, CKEY, into a cash machine by introducing novel advertising policies. On the strength of these credentials, Cooke's brief made his pitch for a television licence:

An American is basically the same as a Canadian – motivated by the same impulses, exposed to the same influences of literature, music, the theatre, movies and radio. It is reasonable to conclude that Canadians will like and want television receiving sets in the same proportion as Americans. In the same proportion that Americans buy refrigerators, stoves, rugs, cars, magazines, homes – so do Canadians ... One of the arguments advanced by the CBC against the granting of television licenses to private broadcasters is that: 'On the basis of straight private commercial operation, television would inevitably be primarily a means of projecting non-Canadian material into Canadian homes.' By 'non-Canadian material' the CBC is obviously referring to American material. In the first place, what is wrong with American material? If we are ever to have a Canadian culture, it will come as a result of full exposure to what is undoubtably the fastest rising culture in the world today – that of the U.S.A.[25]

Massey's colleagues claimed that he maintained a poker face throughout the commission's hearings, wincing only once, if imperceptibly, when Cooke made this point in his appearance before the commission.[26] Cooke's assessment represented the businessman's hard-nosed

business said Amer entert (on) liked Amer entert + can't avoid

evaluation that Canadians liked American entertainment and would not be able to avoid its influence even if they did not. But this analysis had little appeal for cultural nationalists who believed that Canada had a distinct identity that was being threatened by the market-driven, free enterprise logic personified by Cooke. Massey unleashed his legal mercenary upon Cooke, and Wright took his time grilling him and carefully skewering his assumptions.

Throughout their hearings the commissioners were also subjected to submissions that had dubious relevance to the arts, letters, and sciences. In Toronto Massey had to tell V.C. Wansbrough, president of Sports College Association, that 'physical fitness has a bearing on most aspects of life, but I do not really think it is anything with which we can be officially concerned.'[27] But Wansbrough pressed on. 'You will be concerned with the educational media by which an organization such as ours achieves its purposes,' he insisted.[28] He had a point there, and the commission heard him out. Perhaps the most tenuous case for appearing before the commission came from the Central Mortgage and Housing Corporation in Ottawa, which justified its appearance with the indisputable assertion that 'it is within their homes and community buildings that people strive to enjoy and practice the arts which are the particular concern of this Royal Commission's deliberations.'[29] Representations such as this were tolerated but not encouraged by the commission.

The commission had more than enough material without these extraneous contributions. The secretarial staff was swamped with work as it tried to prepare transcripts of the hearings. In November more secretarial help was recruited and the salaries of the commission's two overworked court reporters increased. Meanwhile, Surveyer's suggestions about organizing access to information were enacted. A card index that listed the main points from submissions and studies according to subject was compiled under Neatby's supervision by Miss Florence Bissett of the Ottawa Public Library.

Rcm purpose not ignored the RC

As the commission worked its way eastward across the country it drew closer to the potential trouble spot of Quebec. It turned out that Premier Duplessis had decided against a direct confrontation with the commission. Instead, he simply chose to ignore its existence. Quebec nationalists had to turn to other opinion leaders for a cue. *Le Devoir* saw some danger to provincial autonomy and French-Canadian culture from the commission but thought that for that very reason the provincial government and cultural bodies should take an interest in its work. On this basis it rejected a reader's suggestion that the commission be boycotted.[30]

The commission was not without allies in Quebec. The Liberal party and the cultural coexistence the commission represented had substantial support in the French-Canadian press. The universities of Montreal and Laval risked rousing Duplessis's ire by hosting the commission's public hearings. To the great relief of the commissioners, these sessions were typified by enthusiastic dialogue rather than ugly confrontation. They commenced at the Université de Montréal on Wednesday, 23 November 1949, and a staggering diversity of interests appeared over the next four days – symphonies and choirs, scientific organizations, professional associations, a smattering of civic arts groups, and, of course, private radio stations. Never had the commission sat for longer hours, and on Saturday extra time had to be given to the last presentations.

The commission was determined to do all it could to demonstrate to French Canadians that their interests could be protected within the Canadian nation as a whole. Language was the symbolic means by which they expressed respect for French-Canadian culture. The commissioners took pains not simply to recognize French in a token manner, but to operate fully and comfortably in French. MacKenzie recalled that this was a conscious tactic designed to win acceptance for the commission in Quebec: 'We didn't employ interpreters and I think this was the first body of this kind in which this was not done. We asked the witnesses who appeared before us and in the briefs presented to us, to use whatever language, French or English, they were most familiar with and it was assumed that we the members of the committee were competent enough in both languages to be able to understand what was said and to ask intelligent questions based on them.'[31] The commission itself, by its smooth shift from the English-Canadian to the French-Canadian cultural milieu, was to be a shining example of bicultural principles in operation. MacKenzie, in fact, was the only commissioner who seemed less than comfortable with this arrangement. He rarely asked questions in French, and on one occasion when he did, the francophone he addressed replied in English.

But on the whole these tactics paid off with accolades in the French-

Canadian press. It was consistently noted that the commissioners were at ease in French, and consequently the most hostile of newspapers conceded the commission a grudging respect. Even André Laurendeau, the associate editor of *Le Devoir*, wrote after appearing before the commission that Massey spoke the language fluently and that 'one did not have the impression of committing an error by speaking French.'[32] In this way the commission made it difficult for the nationalists to portray it as the vehicle of English-Canadian centralizers bent on the assimilation of French Canada.

The commission's hearings in Quebec were different from those elsewhere in Canada in other ways as well. French Canada's historic struggle for survival had engendered a conscious recognition of the importance of culture, and as a result the commission did not have to deal with the suspicions its subject provoked in English Canada. The fact that French Canadians seemed even more alarmed about American cultural influences than their anglophone compatriots was further evidence of this difference. French Canadians also displayed a keener awareness of the importance of broadcasting in contemporary life and shared the cultural elite's determination to protect it from private commercial interests.

After its hearings in Montreal the commission took a six-week Christmas break before resuming its public sessions on 10 January 1950 at the Université Laval in Quebec City. There the Fédération des sociétés Saint-Jean-Baptiste du Québec presented a classic provincial autonomist rejection of federal initiatives like the Massey Commission. Its brief declared that 'elle croit que l'un des meilleurs moyens de favoriser le progrès du Canada dans les arts, les lettres, et les sciences et l'éducation en général, est le respect de l'autonomie des provinces.'[33] From this position flowed all of the arguments made by Duplessis against the commission and the government it represented, including the major point of dispute in contemporary federal-provincial relations: 'Elle croit que les frictions entre le gouvernement central et ceux des provinces seraient éliminés si ceux-ci recevaient seuls les taxes qui leur reviennent par le pacte de la Confédération. Les provinces pourraient alors accroître leur aide à l'éducation, aux sciences, aux arts, aux lettres et dans les autres sphères de leur domaine, sans l'aide du gouvernement du Canada.'[34] Other provincial rights advocates took different lines of attack. Some argued vehemently that the provincial rather than the federal government should control broadcasting. This sort of opinion received a respectful hearing but had little hope of winning any converts among the commissioners. When confronted with such demands, they politely ignored the fundamental constitutional questions being raised and directed discussion towards subsidiary issues.

The conclusion of hearings in Quebec by no means guaranteed that there was nothing more to fear from nationalist opposition. On 9 March 1950, Lévesque came under fire in the House of Commons from Raoul Poulin, independent MP for Beauce (but, as Lévesque put it, 'pas indépendant de Duplessis!'),[35] after publicly spelling out the commission's attitude towards provincial prerogatives in culture and education. Lévesque's position was reported in *Le Devoir*: 'No one is more anxious than we are to leave exclusively academic education within the purview of the provinces. There remains popular education or culture in general. In this field, the federal government can legitimately play its part.'[36] Throughout its work the commission would rely on this distinction to refute allegations that it was intruding on provincial jurisdiction. For Poulin and other nationalists, however, this hair-splitting was simply the invidious prelude to a wholesale federal invasion of provincial rights. He quoted this statement in the House and objected not just to the principle asserted, but to the fact that a commission supposedly involved in an information-gathering exercise should have such predetermined views.

The commissioners had feared that confrontation with this sort of nationalist opinion would mar their Quebec hearings and cripple their mission. But despite such eruptions of nationalist indignation, French-Canadian opinion in general was remarkably supportive of the commission and its mandate. In fact, almost two-thirds of the briefs received from French-Canadian sources did not question the legitimacy of the commission at all. Instead, they welcomed the opportunity it offered to solicit help for their particular endeavours. The minority which did address the constitutionality of a federal government presence in cultural affairs was split between those that were willing to accept it under certain conditions and those that spurned it outright. The former group was by far the majority. Only about six French-Canadian submissions categorically rejected any federal cultural initiatives.[37]

473
Submiss
only 15
were FC
cuz

There was another notable feature of French-Canadian submissions to the commission. Although the commission received 473 submissions, only about 15 per cent came from exclusively French-Canadian sources. Given the proportion of Canada's population that was French Canadian, this was lower than might have been expected. There were many possible explanations. (1) Perhaps many French-Canadian groups were happy with the representations made by the national organizations of which they were a part. (2) Possibly some French-Canadian nationalists had followed Duplessis's example and boycotted the commission despite *Le Devoir*'s advice. (3) It was also significant that in rural Quebec, community activities still revolved around the church rather than around the type of voluntary associations that were so numerous in English Canada. (4) Finally, the fact that the Massey Commission's tour of the country provided geographical representation more than representation by population must also be taken into account. More time was spent in the West and the Maritimes in proportion to their populations than was spent in Central Canada. The commission's lengthy Ottawa hearings may have offset this somewhat, but they still were not as accessible for most French-Canadian organizations as public sessions held in Quebec.

From Quebec the commission moved on to Fredericton, Saint John, and Halifax, finishing its eastern swing in Charlottetown on 26 January 1950. The Maritime hearings followed the pattern of earlier sessions. It was unfortunate that at the commission's last stop no appearance was made by Mr Thomas H. White. In his capacity as secretary of the Innkeepers of Prince Edward Island, White had earlier submitted a brief that constituted one of the few examples of popular protest registered by the commission:

Please accept this brief in defence of the Common Man. From what I read in the press, this inquiry is to find ways and means to make the common man acquire culture, whether he wishes it or not. Did it ever occur to those presenting briefs to this distinguished body, that perhaps the ordinary individual is quite satisfied with the type of amusement and entertainment that he at present enjoys? Do they dare to think that their way of life is happier than his, or more full of the zest of living? I am sure that the ordinary individual, without the polish that this supposed culture gives him, is happier and leads a life fuller of the homey virtues, such as kindness and tolerance, than his more cultured neighbour ... For such people to try to ram down the throat of the ordinary citizen his own distorted taste is something that savors of totalitarism [*sic*] ... Most of the so-called cultural cult are snobs of the meanest kind. They look down on their fellow men that do not conform to their conceptions of culture ... We are a free and democratic people, and should be allowed to choose our own way of life, and not be dictated to by a group that a very thin coating of the veneer of culture makes, think they are very special in this life.[38]

The brief went on to complain about CBC programming. 'It seems that the moguls in charge of radio feel that they have a great responsibility towards the development of the common man,' wrote White. 'All they really accomplish is to have him shut off his radio, or turn to an American station, where they cater to the common man.'[39]

White would have been pleased by his premier's efforts in the cause of the uncultured. In Charlottetown, a buffet reception for the commission was hosted by Principal McKinnon of Prince of Wales College on the evening of Friday, 27 January. There Massey ended up next to the premier of Prince Edward Island, J. Walter Jones, who confided that 'I can't see why the Commission should bother with Prince Edward Island at all; it doesn't need any culture.'[40] It was fitting that the commission's tour of the country should end with this reminder that culture had elitist associations for many Canadians. But the commissioners also knew from listening to the hundreds of groups that appeared at their hearings that this general suspicion was countered by an active and committed segment of the population with cultural interests, people who would continue to work in their communities towards 'improving' the cultural level of Canadian society.

The commission's public hearings were not quite over, however. A final series of Ottawa sessions was slated to begin on 11 April 1950, and the newly admitted province of Newfoundland had to be scanned for signs of cultural life as well. The final sessions in Ottawa again took on a national character befitting their location as prominent organizations took advantage of their last opportunity to appear before the commission. National voluntary associations – including the Association of Canadian Clubs, the Canadian Arts Council, the Canadian Institute of International Affairs, the Canadian Welfare Council, and the Canada Foundation – again dominated the hearings in the capital. Unlike the first Ottawa hearings, which had been organized largely around special sessions on particular subjects, this time only broadcasting received exclusive treatment. The commission listened for one last time as the CBC, the CAB, and other interested parties rehashed their old quarrels.

But after thousands of miles of travel and interminable hours of serious-minded discussion, the commission's final Ottawa sessions were destined to end on a farcical note. In its last session on the last day of hearings, the commission heard from H.N. Edelstein, helmsman of the local Writers and Players Club. Edelstein had organized the club by phone from his sick bed and informed the commission that he had discovered 'our Yeats ... the Canadian Homer,' a local poet by the name of Wallace Havelock Robb. Robb's 'Thunder Bird,' Mr Edelstein had explained in his brief, was 'the Epic of Canada ... a saga of Canada's far, Heroic Past, of the raw, savage, battle-crimsoned days of its youth. Packed with rich Indian lore; history, legend, and myth; every page throbs with the drama and poetry of that "Homeric Age" of our country.'[41] Edelstein pontificated at length on subjects as diverse as a national theatre, reconstruction, and veterans' housing. He had with him a little tract on the last subject which he offered to read to the commissioners, but the prospect of Edelstein prolonging his appearance stirred Massey to action, and he offered instead to take a copy of 'Homes ... and Homes Fit for Heroes' for the commission's files. Edelstein did not take the hint. With his immediate business out of the way, he felt free to reflect on the pattern of his life, including his emigration and his subsequent discovery of the cultural deficiencies of the colonies: 'In Ottawa ... we have a beautiful city, with beautiful parks, everything beautiful, and I often commune with the flowers and the trees, but there is a great lack for me, who has been accustomed to those cultural beauties as we had in Dublin at the beginning of the century. I knew Yeats – I knew them all. I know the struggles they had.'[42] With this erudite background, Edelstein was not impressed by the Canadian cultural scene. He complained about ' "tripe" writers, who, unfortunately, along with our blockheads, have crushed those who can write in this country.' At this point the commissioners could have been forgiven for suspecting that Edelstein was a comic hired to lampoon the commission's work with a brilliant parody of the artsy dilettante. Massey struggled to regain control of the session, and finally just rudely interrupted and brought the proceedings grinding to a halt. 'Thank you very much, Mr. Edelstein,' he interjected, 'I think we have your views. I do not think we need to ask you any questions – you have stated your views very clearly.' And so the commission's Ottawa hearings ended with the eloquence of Edelstein echoing through the chambers of the Supreme Court of Canada.[43]

Only a quick side-trip to Newfoundland remained to conclude the commission's public hearings. Brooke Claxton flew the commissioners there in July on an air force plane that he was taking to inspect defence installations in the new province. A commission on the arts coming from the air force base must have seemed an odd manifestation of the new federal authority, but Newfoundlanders were equal to the occasion. Premier Joey Smallwood, head of the delegation from the Department of Education, began by putting Massey's reputation in perspective: 'If I may say, Sir, I think that until today, it is perhaps your brother who will be better known to most Newfoundlanders than you yourself. As a matter of fact, he is amongst the few really highly respected screen actors known to the people of Newfoundland. But it would be rather boastful if we were to claim that you in your field of diplomacy, culture and art are as well known to as many people in Newfoundland as your brother would be in his field.'[44] However indelicate such comments, the fact that an expatriate actor was better known than a Canadian who had devoted his life to public service was a vivid illustration of the influence of American mass media in the cultural life of the northern half of the continent. Smallwood went on to provide the commission with a synopsis of the state of culture in Newfoundland: 'the struggle to make a living is still almost as stern as it ever was; and matters of education, art, and culture generally, we must admit very frankly, for the mass of our people these things have been fairly remote. On the other hand, we have in Newfoundland a minority of highly intelligent cultivated people; many of whom are exceedingly well-travelled, well-read, who are greatly preoccupied with that very matter.'[45] To slake the mainlanders' curiosity about Newfoundland culture, the premier sent the commissioners on a tour of a fish-packing plant following the hearing.

The commissioners could be proud of their track record as their hearings wound up. The rival points of view of business interests and French-Canadian nationalists had been met and rebuffed, the former by truculent confrontation and the latter by respect and guile. Moreover, the progress of the commission across Canada had admirably fulfilled the educational and publicity goals which they had set themselves over a year before. Public suspicions of high culture had been reduced, if not by the logic of the commission's case, then at least by its prestige and nationalistic appeal. As one contemporary observer recalled: 'What impressed me perhaps more than anything else was the way in which the commission created its own bow wave of interest, not only looking into needs, but making people think of them, so that by the time of the report's publication the idea that the community had a responsibility towards its art and artists was accepted without serious opposition.'[46] This was no small achievement. With opposition and indifference surmounted, the commissioners commanded the public's attention and could take the initiative by making the case for government-sponsored culture in Canadian democracy.

PART TWO

4

Liberal Humanism

The culture lobby that rallied around the commission as it toured the country was as self-seeking as any pressure group, but its members were also inspired by more than just the hope of advancing their own narrow interests. Many of the submissions to the Massey Commission included criticisms of modern society that stemmed from similar sets of values. Though most clearly expressed by members of the cultural elite, these principles were articulated with varying degrees of sophistication by a wide variety of witnesses. Their comments suggested that however much the culture lobby was the product of good organization, its growth was also the result of true believers uniting behind a cause. In short, it was a movement bound together by ideology as well as self-interest.

In order to understand this ideology it is first necessary to clarify a number of assumptions about various kinds of culture that were displayed by the commission and its supporters. The first was the distinction between culture in its general, anthropological sense and culture as it referred specifically to the arts, letters, and sciences. In their view, culture in the broad sense encompassed the whole range of common influences and experiences which constituted nothing less than the way of life of a people. It implied an entire social and psychological environment which conditioned the existence of those who shared it. In a more restricted sense, however, culture referred to the arts, letters, and sciences that were the focus of the commission's investigations. These conscious creations of humanity reflected and affected the broad culture of their social context, but differed from it inasmuch as they were contrived and selective forms of information, comment, and communication. This distinction between what might be called social culture and creative culture is a familiar one. The commission was interested in encouraging a creative culture that would reflect a unique Canadian social culture.

Within creative culture itself, other distinctions were made between high culture, popular culture, and mass culture. For the culture lobby, high culture encompassed the refined cultural tradition of the artistic, intellectual, and social elite in Western civilization. It was distinguishable from popular and mass culture by its greater degree of analysis of the human condition and by its emphasis upon quality, as determined by the exacting criteria of a discerning audience, rather than by accessibility or mass appeal. Thus an appreciation of high culture required some familiarity with the history and standards of the genre. Although these standards themselves were often radically altered by avant-garde movements, even such revisionism defined itself in terms of established standards, if only to reject them.

The Massey Commission's hearings had shown that the word *culture* was most commonly associated with high culture of this sort. Since the erudite context of high culture was foreign to the uninitiated general public, culture had the negative connotation of undemocratic exclusivity. This also made it an attractive form of snobbery for dilettantes, adding a taint of phoniness to its image problems. People thought of culture not as something available to all, but as an exclusive commodity acquired by the wealthy as a badge of status. Such public suspicions of 'culchah' presented the commissioners with the public relations headache that they tried to ease by using the word as little as possible in their hearings and their report.

For both the commissioners and the culture lobby, however, high culture was in fact anything but elitist, exclusive, or undemocratic. They associated high culture primarily with the acquisition of knowledge and insight. Culture involved a process of exploration, reflection, and intellectual growth through which individuals came to know themselves, as well as the nature of their social existence, better. In this way the otherwise peripheral and suspect commodity of culture was in fact a form of education, a fundamental concern in liberal democratic societies. Indeed, they considered high culture to be thoroughly democratic because it opened to the individual a path of self-improvement leading to intellectual freedom.

A further critical distinction was made between popular culture and the modern phenomenon of mass culture. They thought of popular culture as the folklore, customs, and pastimes that traditionally existed in close relation to a people's social culture. By the middle of the twentieth century, however, the mass media were exposing huge numbers of people to the same entertainment simultaneously and providing the basis of profitable commercial activity in popular print media, film, and radio. Most members of the culture lobby appreciated popular culture in its grassroots forms, for it at least was vibrant, participatory, and directly relevant to the community life of the individual. But mass culture they despised. They believed that its inspiration was purely commercial rather than communal or critical. They feared that its aim of appealing to the greatest quantity of people was achieved at the cost of both the sense of identity provided by popular culture and the intellectual improvement fostered by high culture. In their eyes mass culture was monolithic and menacing; it stultified and then manipulated a gullible public. The ramifications of its continuing growth were a source of great anxiety in a society which entrusted political power to the independent judgments of its citizens.

These assumptions and attitudes about various kinds of culture had great contemporary relevance because of the conclusions thinking Canadians were drawing from their evaluation of world events and dominant trends of the twentieth century. A century which had begun with great promise had instead been characterized by world war, depression, genocide, and ideological schisms that called into question the fundamental values of Western civilization. At the same time many Canadians observed continuing technological change, the growth of the mass media, and the development of the consumer economy with deep ambivalence.

In the decade preceding the establishment of the Massey Commission, Canada, in partnership with other Western democracies, had fought and won a desperate world war against Nazi Germany and its allies, only to have the challenge of fascism succeeded by the threat of communism as postwar tensions crystallized into the Cold War. On one level both Hitler's Germany and the Soviet Union were threats because of their real or perceived expansionism. But fascism and communism also represented systems of government that were ideologically repugnant to Western democracies. During World War II the urgency of winning the war left little time to develop the cause in ideological terms beyond the simple dichotomies of good versus evil and freedom versus tyranny. There was nevertheless a popular recognition that democratic civilization itself hung in the balance and a growing belief that the best long-term defence in a worldwide ideological struggle was to be found in ideology itself.

As Vincent Massey wrote in 1948, 'our peoples need to understand the way of life which they are defending in the war of ideas today so that they can defend it the better.'[1] This was a central tenet of contemporary conventional wisdom. Appearing before the commission on behalf of the Pontifical Institute for Mediaeval Studies at the University of Toronto, Dr Anton C. Pegis summed up a widespread feeling among intellectuals that circumstances demanded a fundamental reaffirmation of the values of Western civilization:

I take it that one of the great cultural problems of the western world today is not just to save itself physically from the A-bomb or the H-bomb, but, even more, to discover its own spiritual character or to discover, in other words, what it is to be a civilization, and what it is to build a culture.

I take it that what we hear from various quarters up and down the North American continent, not to speak of Europe, is precisely that question – that behind the struggle for some survival there is a more serious question, namely what it is that western nations have been living for, and what it is that today they are trying to maintain in existence.

I take it that we are concerned with a little more, something more enduring than just saving ourselves by the skin of our teeth. I take it, in short, that there is the problem of the discovery of civilization today. Its conditions of existence and the spirit which should animate it, and the meaning of law, and the meaning of government, and meaning of man – those are questions which are, so to speak, in the balance today. Perhaps that is more true today than at any other time in history.

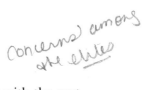

Perhaps the reason for this is that our bonds with the past, and our historical habits, have been so shaken with war, as a civilization, that we have a need to rediscover them, and make use of them for the future.[2]

This desire for a fuller articulation and fulfilment of the beliefs for which World War II and the Cold War were fought spurred the cultural elite to define anew the system of values upon which Western democracies in general and Canada in particular could build a meaningful way of life in the postwar world.

The concerns of the intelligentsia percolated through the ranks of the culture lobby. Since its members generally agreed that the values that underpinned liberal democracy could be found in traditional high culture, cultural questions took on enormous contemporary relevance. 'Truly democratic countries are now rightly stressing moral and spiritual values,' wrote the National Council of Women, 'and the struggle for men's souls today is reflected just as much in literature and films as in world politics.'[3] This belief was so pervasive that even seemingly apolitical branches of the arts were promoted as healthy social influences. The Competitive Festival of Music in New Brunswick, for instance, informed the commission that 'music is *not* one of the trivial things of life ... Those interested in music have a job to do and a part to play in the building of a better world.'[4]

The problem was that just as Canadian society needed it more than ever, high culture seemed to be in retreat before the dominant trends of Western society. The commission heard a litany of complaints about all the phenomena associated with modernization in the Western world, including the consequences of urbanization and industrialization, the consumer economy, the dominance of science and technology, and the growth of mass culture.

The increased affluence and leisure in modern urban industrial life both fascinated and repelled members of the culture lobby. They regretted that the increased leisure time and spending money of the average worker were frittered away on movies, trashy magazines, commercial radio, or sports events. The commission often heard the complaint that these activities involved passive, non-participatory entertainment which did nothing to better the individual. Instead, the development of an interest in culture was recommended as a 'means of improving the mind.'[5]

Many briefs blamed the mass media for this squandering of leisure time. The Discussion Group of Hamilton, an association of concerned citizens formed solely to present a brief to the commission, expressed this widespread distrust:

> ... after a century of popular education, many people in North America are alarmed at the effect of mass production and mass entertainment on the great majority of the population. They fear that the popular culture of the illiterate in past times, in folk tale, folk music, folk dance and popular festivals was more genuinely re-creative than the passive entertainments of today. These critics picture many factory and office workers as engaged all day in work which leaves them fatigued and frustrated because they see no meaning in what they do and no creative result. They seek escape in mass entertainment which also does nothing to satisfy creative instincts, stimulate the imagination, or cultivate the mind – escapist movies, commercialized radio, primitive music, spectator sports, reading which is anodyne rather that stimulus, and so on. The result is mental and spiritual lethargy, an empty life.[6]

In part such condemnations reflected disenchantment. As new means of mass communication had emerged over the previous century, highbrows had hoped that they would help make traditional high culture accessible to all.[7] They were bitterly disappointed to see the mass media become the vehicles of trivial entertainments which titillated the masses, did nothing to improve taste, and in fact threatened to undermine the very high culture they had hoped to see disseminated. Numerous briefs also expressed concerns about the postwar economy's shift to consumerism. No one wanted to deny Canadians the benefits of a better standard of living, but there were deep misgivings about some of the implications of prosperity. Many feared that social values were being shaped not by rational thought or communal concern, but by the commercial imperatives of the consumer economy. In its quest for profits, business sponsored advertising which preyed on desires and fears and exalted the 'false' values of materialism and

selfishness at the expense of more important spiritual, intellectual, and moral concerns. As one witness complained: 'our present commercial system is enveloping every phase of contemporary society with a worship of commercial materialism which reduces public thinking, its hopes and its desires, to a level rarely invaded by criticism, logic, or original analyses.'[8] Instead of developing their individual gifts, modern Canadians were deluded into believing that they could buy identity and happiness.

Leisure, consumerism, and the mass media were all part of the modern menace of mass culture. Advertising linked business and the mass media together in a relationship dominated by the pursuit of profit. Maximum advertising revenue came from reaching the widest possible audience, which in turn meant appealing to human qualities that were most generally shared – or the 'lowest common denominator,' as the popular phrase put it. Time after time the Massey Commission was told that the result was a reduction in the cultural content of the media to a level which made them unlikely means of stimulating any sort of cultural edification.

The rise of mass culture had political as well as cultural implications. In a century which had seen the emergence of serious ideological threats to liberal democracy, the potential for the abuse of the mass media for political ends was evident in their role as instruments of a vacuous mass culture. Propaganda was credited with making a critical contribution to the consolidation of communism in Russia and the growth of fascism in Germany and Italy. Tolerance of the barbarities of totalitarianism from Stalinist purges to the Holocaust suggested that mass persuasion could overwhelm the moral restraint of individuals' consciences. The culture lobby thought that the failure of the media to improve the individual's intellectual and critical faculties left an ignorant citizenry vulnerable to manipulation and exploitation. The Fiddlehead Poetry Society was most eloquent on this point:

Few Canadians go to college: the majority of them do not attend high school ... They have fallen into the habit of accepting with too much credulity and too little critical evaluation the fare which the publishing houses, the press, the films and the radio send them ... Such an attitude of willing suspension of disbelief towards whatever appeals to their desires is dangerous to the suc-

cess of the democratic state. People who in normal times are susceptible to the glib promises of politicians will in abnormal times turn as readily and as uncritically to the Utopias of the Totalitarian Right and the Totalitarian Left. The only safeguard of a democracy is an attitude of intelligent critical evaluation on the part of its citizens.[9]

Otherwise, in the pithy phrase of a contemporary culture guru, 'politically, they are easy dupes of any plausible demagogue who comes along with a slogan and a hillbilly band or its urban equivalent.'[10]

The Canadian Association for Adult Education warned the commission that the mass media should be closely linked to voluntary watchdogs to ensure that they did not become 'a prop for totalitarianism.'[11] This statement exemplified the ambivalence with which members of the culture lobby regarded the media. In the right hands (their own) they offered a superb tool for promoting high culture, public education, and a healthy liberal democracy, and they still hoped to harness them for these purposes. But the modern trend seemed to be towards a commercial dominance of the media which ignored their educational and cultural potential. The general disappointment that these great modern technological advances had failed to bring social progress was overlaid with an immediate fear of their undemocratic potential. Such concerns made broadcasting policy the most important issue on the commission's agenda.

Part of the blame for this predicament was attributable to the intellectual community itself. Many briefs criticized the dominant scientific ethos of modern intellectual life. The Church of England told the commission that only through a renewed emphasis on the humanities could 'the corrective ... be found to the essentially material aspect of other fields of knowledge.'[12] Science provided humanity with the technological advances that underlay modern prosperity, but its ascendancy eclipsed the humanist studies that gave civilization its meaning. The result was epitomized by the paradox of nuclear power, a triumph of science which made the annihilation of humanity possible. The Saskatchewan Council of Home and School Associations told the commission: 'We cannot dare to lag or stumble in the advance of scientific knowledge; and we are grateful for the benefits of the

advance; but some present-day interpretations of science, economics, and technology overshadow, almost overwhelm our world. Will the destructive power of Atomic Energy be the only record of our era?'[13] The amorality of scientific inquiry was just as dangerous as the immorality of capitalism's appeal to material selfishness, for both eclipsed the humanistic agenda which represented true progress. The threat of nuclear annihilation was only the most obvious example of how a society led by materialistic interests alone lacked proper guidance. The technological developments spawned by science had also brought mass production, the mass media, and the consumer economy – all of the major ingredients of mass culture.

The commissioners lent a sympathetic ear to opinions of this sort because they echoed their own convictions. It was, as Lévesque recalled, 'au départ, la philosophie humaniste qui inspirait fortement notre commission.'[14] What precisely did Lévesque mean by humanist? The philosophical values behind the culture lobby were humanistic inasmuch as they addressed such basic human concerns as the Truth and the Good: the real nature of humanity and its existence and the best way for it to live. This required an awareness of, and emphasis on, those factors which made humanity special in creation. Thus humanism focused not upon the material aspects of human existence, but on a person's spiritual, moral, and intellectual character, emphasizing the fulfilment of these capacities as the hallmarks of a fully realized humanity. It followed that people had to be free to realize these innate capabilities.[15]

A number of related beliefs accompanied this central idea. Since the values which distinguished human beings from beasts were first exemplified in the civilizations of the classical world, the study of the classics was central to the humanist creed. Neatby was always ready with a thumbnail sketch that traced the heritage of the humanistic tradition in Western civilization: 'The Greeks contributed the spirit of free inquiry; the Romans the conception of law and discipline; from the Jews came the conception of the intrinsic value and moral responsibility of man, and of the spiritual unity of all mankind. It was long before these truths were fully realized but their germ lies in the Christian philosophy.'[16] Christianity, with its stress on personal salvation, had nurtured respect for the individual, human potential, and learning through the dark ages. The high culture championed by the culture lobby bore the imprint of centuries of Western civilization in which it had been intertwined with the Christian religion.

In fact, the humanism of the culture lobby can be seen as traditional Christian values shorn of their overt religious import to suit a secular political culture. Canadian intellectual historians have described how the Christian consensus that ordered society in Victorian Canada was thrown into disarray and retreat before powerful new modernist forces that emerged in the late nineteenth century. Traditional local cultures fell into decline as new transportation and communications linked the continent. At the same time the rise of industry and big business ushered in an era of unprecedented capitalist greed and class conflict. An increasingly materialistic society seemed to need moral guidance more than ever before, but the rise of science and its empirical method of inquiry, epitomized in Darwin's evolutionary theories, challenged the authority of scripture and traditional religion. New ways of enjoining Christian ethics were required.[17]

Many English-Canadian intellectuals responded to this crisis by adopting from Britain a philosophy known as idealism. Idealism attempted to bridge the gap between religious belief and faith in science, between the ideal and the real, by associating the mind of God with Hegel's logically derived concept of the Absolute Ideal. Since theoretically humankind could, through its capacity to reason, come to know the Absolute Ideal, so too could God and His will be known. Reason itself was a God-given gift that, rather than undermining religious faith, was designed to reveal the divine order in the world. Thus reason and religious faith were complementary rather than incompatible, and scientific progress through critical inquiry could be contained within a framework of Christian values.[18]

Idealism represented an attempt to maintain the authority of religious humanism in an increasingly secular and scientific world. But in adapting Christianity to the times it may have only cleared the way for the triumph of secular values. The rise of the social sciences reflected a growing faith that empirical methods could bring social as well as scientific progress. Humanists fought a rearguard action by arguing for a 'liberal education' that pursued not just facts, but the development of well-rounded individuals with values that would make them conscientious citizens. They even contended that a classical education was the best preparation for modern careers in business and technology.[19] In this way, what A.B. McKillop has called the persistent 'moral imperative' in Canadian thought shed its manifest religious associations and became, by the mid-point of the twentieth century, little more than a humanistic defence of traditional high culture. A humanist sensibility survived despite the dominant scientific ethos of the age because Canadian intellectuals were products of an earlier era of Christian education and social concern.[20] Their ambivalence about the modern world was reflected in society as a whole by a resurgence in religious belief and church attendance during the 1950s.

In French Canada, Lévesque's intellectual formation had been affected by essentially similar responses to the same modern concerns. St Thomas Aquinas was a central figure in the educational tradition of the Université Laval and the Quebec church in general. The Thomist tradition stressed the compatibility of reason and faith, and consequently, individual enlightenment as a means of pursuing both. This position, while compatible with idealism, was not as vulnerable to erosion into secularism because philosophy was kept clearly subordinate to theology. As we have already seen, Lévesque was a social scientist whose scholarship was directed towards Christian humanist goals. Indeed, it was the Western humanist inheritance described by Neatby (in which Aquinas was a pivotal figure) that he believed provided common ground for the French and English cultures in Canada.

Neatby and Lévesque exemplified the compatibility of these cultures on a personal level. They became close friends, in part at least because they shared the same convictions about the importance of the humanist tradition and Christian values. Both believed that society had to be guided by a morality grounded in Christian ethics inspired by faith. It was a view that was strongly reinforced by Massey's nephew George Grant in his special study for the commission on philosophy in Canada. Grant argued that a belief in God was fundamental to the rational pursuit of the good life and made it clear that by 'the good life' he meant not luxurious indulgence but an existence that was wholly informed by a humanism based on faith. 'Men often forgot the need of those disciplines that once had been considered a potent influence in preventing us from becoming beasts,' he warned.[21] But in their roles as commissioners Neatby and Lévesque recognized that it was politically inexpedient to push their religious beliefs on society as a whole. Instead they were content to place their hopes in the traditional high culture that was the best available alternative. As the individual found cultural enlightenment, he or she would absorb the code of ethics that was implicit in that tradition.

The delegations from Canada's major Christian denominations that appeared before the commission displayed a similar faith. The United Church seemed even more conscious of the relationship between cultural development and its spiritual role than its sister denominations. It had its own Commission on Culture which stressed in its brief to the commission that 'whatever will advance our national welfare and cultural development will also advance the interests of the United Church.'[22] This conjunction of interests was personified by one of the United Church delegates, ordained minister and cultural critic Northrop Frye. The presence of Professor Frye was also a reminder of how the churches' interest in culture was related to their traditional concern with education as a central part of an individual's intellectual and spiritual formation.

Indeed, the importance which the culture lobby in general placed upon culture as a form of intellectual training and enlightenment reflected the broader emphasis on popular education in Canadian society, an impulse which shared the goal of developing the intelligent and responsible citizenry deemed necessary to make mass democracy work. This faith in social improvement through education was not limited to formal schooling. The work of organizations like the CAAE in the field of adult education had prepared the ground for the Massey Commission's advocacy of culture, making it easier for the commission to attract the support of a wide variety of voluntary associations. The overlapping of cultural and educational concerns gave the Massey Commission a widespread appeal.

The extent to which the commission was concerned with questions that applied equally to education was demonstrated by the fact that soon after its work was finished, Massey would fund Neatby to write a book on the subject, *So Little for the Mind*, in which she launched a withering attack on modern 'Progressive' educators. In her view Progressive education embodied the same egalitarian heresies as mass culture. Its misguided worship of equality in the name of democracy encouraged a stifling conformity which undermined liberty and denied society the full potential of exceptional individuals. Moreover, the Progressives' promotion of happiness as a good in itself fostered a distorted morality in which self-interest was confused with virtue.[23] *So Little for the Mind* was a postscript to the Massey Report which directly addressed a subject on which constitutional niceties constrained the commission. In essence Neatby was again arguing for the classical curriculum – or high culture – as a source of intellectual standards and moral suasion based on a coherent body of human wisdom.

The humanist critique of modern society was clearly an important distinguishing feature of the culture lobby. It had great contemporary relevance in an era plagued by fears about consumerism, the Cold War, and The Bomb. But it was by no means an exclusively modern or Canadian point of view. Humanism was a natural counterpoint to the influence of capitalism and science in Western society. Concern about mass culture in particular was a long-running and widespread intellectual current in the West that could be traced back at least as far as the eighteenth century when the growth of public literacy began creating a more popular market for literature in Europe. As the mass media continued to grow, diversify, and commercialize, a succession of Western intellectuals from Alexis de Tocqueville to José Ortega y Gasset expressed fears that civilized high culture would be swallowed up in a widening sea of vulgarity. In the period following World War II, fears about mass culture were on the rise. In fact, a lively intellectual debate on the subject was just commencing in the United States. Critic Dwight Macdonald led the way with attacks on mass culture in the *Partisan Review* and other journals, and soon other American intellectuals joined in, producing a spate of similar literature in the 1950s.[24]

The American debate was not altogether home-grown. It was greatly stimulated by the work of the Frankfurt School of Marxist sociologists. Its leading members, including Max Horkheimer, Herbert Marcuse, Theodor W. Adorno, Eric Fromm, and Leo Lowenthal, had been associated with the Institute for Social Research that was founded in Frankfurt in 1923, but had fled to the United States when the Nazis seized power in the 1930s. In analysing what had gone wrong in Germany, they argued that capitalism had been a driving force behind the rise of fascism. They viewed the United States as a monopoly capitalist state with a manipulative mass culture that was a potential breeding ground for totalitarianism. As a result it was critical to preserve the alternative artistic and scholarly perspectives on the margins of American society. The influence of this argument was limited by language barriers; most of the Frankfurt School's writings on culture did not appear in English until the 1960s. But essays like Horkheimer and Adorno's 'The Culture Industry' (1944) were known well enough to have an effect. The Frankfurt School pushed cultural issues to the forefront of intellectual concerns in their adopted country by explicating the political implications of a mass culture that served the interests of industrial capitalism.[25]

One of the interesting features of this debate was the way in which concern about mass culture transcended what seemed to be wide differences in political philosophy. Left-wingers found common cause with conservatives in criticizing the taste of the masses. High culture was their common interest, and fears of its disintegration 'held sway among intellectuals of the liberal left and the conservative right.'[26] Their attacks on the culture of the masses can be seen as a form of class conflict fought on cultural instead of political or economic grounds. But some believed that the real villain was modern capitalism. Economic liberalism had fostered, not freedom, but corporate concentrations of power which manipulated the media in pursuit of profit and thereby threatened individual liberty. These powerful interests used the mass media and mass culture to drill their messages into passive audiences. This view salved the democratic conscience by absolving the people of blame for the poor quality of their cultural fare and implying that if given the opportunity they would exhibit better taste.

As the debate over mass culture developed, serious challenges to this school of thought emerged. Modern communications research suggested that it was both simplistic and pessimistic. Behavioural scientists who had been studying the effects of media on people's behaviour and opinions for the previous twenty years were coming to the conclusion that media messages were filtered through complex channels of peer groups, families, and personal preconceptions before they had any effect on individuals. By 1950 they had not come close to understanding how this process worked, but they were well past perceiving the mass media as omnipotent and manipulative.[27]

The critics of mass culture were also attacked as being arrogantly incapable of either understanding or appreciating the content of mass culture. This counter-argument emphasized that however much the mass media homogenized and appealed to base tastes, they did not operate in a culture vacuum. Of necessity they adapted existing cultural forms into their programming, ensuring that there was a strong strand of the traditional and the authentic interwoven with the glitz and trivialization. At the same time they had a need for novelty which made them quite open to contributions from marginal and grass-roots cultures. As an American cultural historian has noted: 'American popular culture has been continually and powerfully revitalized by the entry of previously alien and isolated cultural groups and forms through modern media. Black and rural white musics, ethnic theatrical traditions, European émigré film producers and directors, countercultural writers and cartoonists – these are only a few examples of marginal cultures that have produced tidal waves in the American mainstream because they were diffused by modern communication.'[28] If these cultures were assimilated somewhat in the process, they gained respect and acceptance in return. Thus mass culture was much more tolerant and pluralistic – and in this sense, more liberal – than traditional high culture. The mass culture critics' inability to recognize these subtleties reflected a narrowness of vision induced by high culture. Their pessimism about modernity, their inability to come to terms with its complex realities, and their adherence to an ideal that was, in contrast, simplistic, elitist, abstract, and moralistic, all combined to give their campaign against the culture of the crowd overtones of class warfare.

But such arguments were only beginning to be heard in the early 1950s. The image of mass culture as monolithic, homogenizing, and authoritarian pervaded the intelligentsia. It is difficult to measure precisely the extent to which contemporary American debate over mass culture affected the Canadian intellectual scene, but there were numerous parallels. Harold Innis was then deeply involved in formulating his famous speculations about the role of communications in the rise and fall of empires and civilizations through the centuries. Innis believed that Western civilization was gravely threatened by the spatial bias of electronic media. The American empire expanded through the power of such media to conquer space and propagate the values upon which consumer capitalism thrived. In doing so it exhibited an insatiable appetite for the ephemeral which eclipsed the enduring moral values perpetuated by time-biased media like books and art, values which any civilization needed to survive.

In 1950 Marshall McLuhan was already showing signs of interest in questions of communication and culture. He synthesized many of the contemporary complaints about mass culture in *The Mechanical Bride* (1951), a critique of recurring icons of advertising in popular print media. McLuhan had previously been a typical academic advocate of traditional high culture as an antidote to mass culture, but *The Mechanical Bride* showed that he had come to believe that the only hope of fostering a critical perspective within the general population was to fight fire with fire. Modern means of mass communication had to be employed to deliver alternative, provocative points of view that would call into question the underlying messages of the commercial media.

McLuhan always acknowledged his intellectual debt to Innis, but there is no evidence that either influenced the Massey Commission. The commissioners were, however, at least peripherally aware of the growing debate south of the border. Neatby and Surveyer sampled the work of Gilbert Seldes, an American broadcasting executive who had written widely on the mass media. Moreover, the commission hired Dr Charles Siepmann, a professor of communications from New York University, to apply the research skills of a social scientist to the study of Canadian broadcasting. But this was not, as it appeared, a case of the commissioners deferring to American expertise. Quite the contrary. Siepmann was an expatriate Englishman, a former director of programs for the BBC who had immigrated to the United States in 1937.

Indeed, when the commissioners wanted intellectual reinforcement, they usually looked to British rather than American sources. In *So Little for the Mind* and in the speeches she later wrote for Massey when he became governor general, Neatby leaned heavily upon the writings of Sir Richard Livingston, Sir Walter Moberley, and other intellectuals involved in the postwar debate about education and social reform in Britain.[29] The planning philosophy of Karl Mannheim, a former colleague of the Frankfurt School sociologists, was a prominent topic in this debate. *Scrutiny*, the journal of F.R. Leavis and the New Criticism, reflected the temper of the times in British literary and intellectual circles. There Mannheim's ideas were debated at length and related to questions about the place of culture in postwar society. Many of the writers associated with *Scrutiny* displayed an antagonism towards modern industrial capitalist society that was inspired by nostalgia for a moral, purposeful, and integrated community that they imagined to have existed in pre-industrial times.[30] The famous American expatriate T.S. Eliot had also just published *Notes towards a Definition of Culture*, which inevitably invited comparison with the writings of Matthew Arnold, the subject of a highly praised recent biography by the American critic Lionel Trilling. Leavis's admiration for Eliot and Trilling was just one of many ways in which *Scrutiny* demonstrated that the intellectual circles of the English-speaking world intersected across borders and oceans.[31]

Clearly the Massey Commission was sitting at a time when concerns about mass culture were intellectually trendy. Canadian highbrows absorbed all the fears of mass culture that were wafting about and turned instinctively to their favourite British cultural authority, Matthew Arnold, for direction.[32] In his review of *So Little for the Mind*, Frank Underhill remarked, 'If I had been writing Miss Neatby's book, I should have taken its title not from John Henry Newman but from Matthew Arnold, and I should have called it Culture and Anarchy in Canada.'[33] Neatby was unapologetic about applying the thought of a Victorian to contemporary problems: 'Arnold may well be condemned as an individualist of aristocratic tastes, and of ideas completely irrelevant to the forward-looking twentieth century ... To do this would be to do him a great injustice, as his own words show. He is, indeed, quite startlingly modern.'[34] Indeed, the presence of a nineteenth-century Englishman in twentieth-century Canadian cultural discourse is not as surprising as it might at first seem. Well-educated Canadians were familiar with Arnold from their school days, for he was a central ornament in the humanist curriculum of the late nineteenth- and early twentieth-century Canadian university.[35] One might have expected Arnold's contemporary, John Ruskin, to have had a similar influence on the commission, since he had stressed the interdependence of aesthetic and moral values and the common man's potential for cultural self-improvement. But however influential these ideas continued to be, Ruskin's reputation declined in the early twentieth century while Arnold remained highly regarded. One of Arnold's favourite terms – 'Philistine' – had, of course, entered everyday speech as a catch-phrase for the boorish bourgeois. But even less common references, such as phrases echoing his injunction to study 'the best that has been thought and known in the world,' were sprinkled throughout the briefs submitted to the Massey Commission.[36]

The members of the culture lobby were indebted to Arnold for more than just inspiring quotations; their views echoed his on a number of fundamental points. Arnold had warned against many of the same social phenomena in Victorian Britain that they abhorred in modern Canada. He criticized his contemporaries for confusing political liberalism with purposeless freedom, economic liberalism with selfishness and materialism, and liberal progress with the triumphs of science over the physical world. In his famous 1869 essay, *Culture and Anarchy*, Arnold argued that progress could only be determined in humanistic terms. Only culture offered a virtuous and enduring source of values; a dynamic liberal society needed such higher ideals to help it decide how to combine the best of the old and the new together in order to ensure that change would be for the better. 'I am a Liberal,' he declared, 'yet I am a Liberal tempered by experience, reflection and renunciation, and I am, above all, a believer in culture.'[37]

It is for this advocacy of culture as a bulwark against anarchy that Arnold is best remembered, but it is important to recognize that he also saw culture as a force which liberated the individual. Culture was a force for freedom because it stimulated the intellectual development and self-awareness that were the true marks of individuality. But even in a free society, freedom had to be qualified by enough authority and communal concern to preserve the social order which protected freedom itself.[38] Culture was also the intellectual and moral training ground in which political judgment and social values could be cultivated. The essential question was how to maintain the proper balance between freedom and authority, and Arnold displayed his fundamental liberalism by placing this responsibility on the individual, trusting that cultural enlightenment would endow him with the necessary critical faculties. This defence of high culture had particular relevance for modern Canadians who saw mass culture as an authoritarian threat to liberal freedom. In Arnold's thought, as in that of the cultural elite, culture was valued for its political effects far more than for its intrinsic merits. There was little advocacy of 'art for art's sake': culture had a role to play in forging the good society.

Arnold's 'liberal' defence of culture sheds a revealing light upon the political implications of the culture lobby's concerns. In attempting to find distinguishing characteristics of a national identity, Canadian nationalists have often presented Canada as a conservative society compared to the United States. Among other things, they point to the British emphasis on authority in Canadian political culture, Canada's reliance on state enterprise in its economic development, and the 'moral imperative' in Canadian intellectual history. Canadian imperialists from the turn of the century provide a good historical example of such attitudes. Carl Berger has shown that the 'tory mind' of the imperialist displayed a concern for community over individuality and a trust in religion as a source of moral authority, accompanied by a contempt for materialism and a disgust with unchecked capitalist greed.[39] Imperialists were disturbed by the restless spirit of the age and focused their sights on some emerging features of modern society that would later be clear targets for the Massey Commission. The personal and intellectual connections between imperialists and members of the commission have prompted at least one observer to conclude that its philosophy reflected a 'profoundly conservative' reassertion of these old values.[40] If George Grant's 1965 *Lament for a Nation* was, as Carl Berger put it, simply a 'depressing footnote' to imperialist thought, then the Massey Commission can be seen as just one more stage in the decline of this anachronistic creed.[41]

cult elite agree with cult lobby

There were many seemingly conservative characteristics displayed by the commission. Its defence of high culture was susceptible to criticisms of being reactionary and elitist. Members of the cultural elite also displayed many concerns that characterized the earlier Canadian intellectual scene. They too attempted to foster a humanistic code of values to guide Canadian society. They looked to the state to offset continental economic forces and encourage Canadian cultural development. Moreover, their fears of an ignorant populace invoked the traditional elitist concern that mass democracy threatened individual liberty.[42]

Whether one defines the commission's perspective as conservative or liberal depends entirely on how the terms are defined. It should

even the cultural elite want to foster a humanistic code of values to guide Canad society

not in absolute terms, but only relative to the United States. Both countries fall within the liberal democratic tradition. The danger in labelling the Massey Commission as conservative lies in the nationalistic connotations of the term. The search for a distinctive and enduring Canadian intellectual tradition can obscure the important ways in which the commission's ideology was shaped by international influences and the unique circumstances of postwar Canada.

The term 'liberal humanist' is perhaps a better way of describing the philosophical position of the Massey Commission and its supporters. If liberalism is associated exclusively with free enterprise and scientific inquiry, then the label would not fit. But it is precisely because it equated free enterprise with monopoly capitalism and scientific inquiry with technological tyranny that the culture lobby opposed them. However much business and technology had been perceived as forces for freedom in the past, their responsibility for mass culture made them appear more as threats to individual liberty than its champions in the present. As an alternative, the cultural elite echoed Arnold's conviction that high culture was a force for individual liberty through self-enlightenment. This position was conservative inasmuch as they sought to 'conserve' traditional high culture, but it was the liberal humanist values in that tradition that were stressed, and they were offered not as a path of retreat into the past but as a guide for progress into the future.

Admittedly, the culture lobby's fear of mass culture was reminiscent of the nineteenth-century tory's warning that too much democratic freedom would pander to mass ignorance and lead to tyranny. But instead of using this fear as an excuse to justify the continuing dominance of an enlightened elite, the commissioners sought to edify the masses to a level where they could exercise their democratic responsibilities competently. But first the individual had to be provided with the means of self-enlightenment: exposure to the traditional high culture of the West. Culture was a necessary part of education for citizenship in a liberal democracy. The naïve idealism of this vision, inspired by the optimistic postwar spirit of nationalism and reconstruction, was in marked contrast to George Grant's disillusioned lament a decade and a half later.

The Cold War had a profound yet paradoxical effect on the ideology of the culture lobby. Its liberalism was particularly conscientious

because the Cold War heightened its awareness of the need to define
and protect the values of Western liberal democracy. At the same
time a theoretical attachment to liberal economic principles prevented
most members of the culture lobby from offering any fundamental
criticism of the capitalist system which had created the cultural conditions they abhorred. Despite the threats it presented to individual
freedom, the liberal capitalist political economy was considered an
integral part of the Western way of life threatened by communism.
Instead of attacking the root of the problem, they could only offer
high culture as a counterweight, a source of values which defined
political freedom in human rather than scientific or capitalistic terms.

Members of the culture lobby displayed a concern for communal
values as well as individual freedoms, but the communist threat made
them sensitive about appearing in the least authoritarian. The secular
temper of modern society also precluded any invocation of religious
authority for their views. High culture may have succeeded Christianity as a source of moral authority, but it was quite a mild authority
compared to its predecessor. It left the ultimate responsibility for
striking the balance between freedom and authority in the hands of
the individual citizen. In this way the cultural elite was more liberal
than its imperialist and idealist forebears even as it echoed their concerns.

The Massey Commission offered high culture as a panacea for the
ills of modernity. This appealed to members of the culture lobby
because it ennobled their cultural interests and cast them as saviours
of the Canadian nation, if not Western civilization as a whole. As their
concerns gained publicity through the commission's hearings, the cause
gained an intellectual and moral dimension that extended its appeal
beyond its organized supporters. The commissioners were happy to
make their commission a vehicle for the articulation and popularization of views that made high culture seem critical to the future of
liberal democracy. Nothing invigorates a cause more than a conviction
of righteousness.

5

Liberal Humanist
Nationalism

*liberal hum of the
cultural elite would become
intertwined with
the nationalist assumptions
+ intel studies*

The cultural elite's pessimism about modern society was crosscut by an optimism about Canada and its prospects in the postwar era. Canadians believed that they had finally emerged from the shadow of Great Britain, and they were enjoying their new-found feelings of independence and international status. It was not surprising that the liberal humanism of the cultural elite would become intertwined with the nationalist assumptions and ambitions that ran throughout the country in the postwar period. Cultural nationalists tended to believe that most problems of modern society originated elsewhere and that with the state's help they could defend Canada's superior national character. Liberal humanism and nationalism combined to form a high-minded and defensive strain of Canadian cultural nationalism.

Despite the strength of its convictions, the culture lobby was aware that on its own it was incapable of offsetting the forces of modern life that it reviled. Science dazzled the populace with its technological wizardry, and business won public favour with bread and circuses. All the friends of culture had to offer was something that, like cod-liver oil, people had little taste for no matter how good it was for them. Given this predicament it was not surprising that the commission and its supporters looked to the state as a means of promoting culture. In demanding state intervention they were in step with modern liberal thought, which had abandoned laissez-faire principles as an outmoded means of fulfilling liberal goals. The Cold War reinforced the elite's case for government intervention by making culture appear to be a matter of central importance in the preservation of the democratic state. As Saint Mary's College in Halifax argued, 'a vigorous cultural life in this age of conflicting ideologies is as important to national welfare as an intelligent armed force.' It followed that 'it would seem but proper for the Federal Government to grant financial assistance to the one as to the other.[1]

However, the threat of communism also gave a new currency to the claims of laissez-faire. Business interests, especially the private radio stations, independent film-makers, and photographers who felt threatened by various government cultural enterprises, equated state-sponsored culture with the threat of communist totalitarianism. The Canadian Association of Broadcasters ominously noted that 'this Commission is sitting at a time when the concepts of individual freedom and enterprise are being destroyed by authoritarian doctrines in many parts of the world.'[2] Since most Canadians thought of democracy simply in terms of freedom, the equation of liberal democracy with free enterprise presented the cultural elite with a popular and potent form of ideological opposition.

The cultural lobby countered that it was powerful business interests represented by the likes of the Canadian Association of Broadcasters that presented the real threat to individual freedom and opportunity in modern Canada. The Canadian Writers' Committee wrote that 'From the commercial sponsor, the advertising agency and the private stations we hear a good deal these days about "free enterprise." They claim they are strong supporters of such a system. But the Canadian writer sees them differently. Their free enterprise is only for themselves.'[3] Private broadcasting in particular created concentrations of power that were intolerable in a liberal democracy. Radio licences were limited monopolies over some of the primary lines of modern communications and thus restricted the individual's free access to information. Far from being impressed with business's invocation of free enterprise ideals, the Canadian Writers' Committee archly inquired, 'Where would industry be in this country without government subsidy?'[4]

Mass culture was an organized and well-financed threat. In response, the culture lobby had organized itself on a national level but needed some supplementary support to counter the strength of its opposition. The state was the only available means of offsetting business power, and it was natural that the cultural elite would look to it to foster the humanistic culture it felt was so necessary to the preservation and enhancement of liberal democracy. The culture lobby was encouraged in its demand for government aid by the fact that there was an established tradition of state intervention in Canada. It was a tradition that probably owed more to the pragmatic need to conquer geography in order to link the country together than to a particular political philosophy. The national railway system was an obvious example of how government subsidy and control were necessary to serve a relatively small population spread across a vast territory, and the national broadcasting system provided a more recent and relevant example of the same logic at work.

The culture lobby appealed to the state for help in promoting high culture on the grounds that mass culture was a foreign threat. In *On Being Canadian*, a book which many members of the cultural elite acknowledged as a classic statement of the Canadian cultural predicament, Vincent Massey had warned that American influences posed a grave menace to Canada. His remarks showed that although he sympathized with like-minded Yankees, in general he identified the republic as the source of many of the banes of modern life: 'Thinking Americans are fighting gallantly against the spiritual dangers which both they and we face: a distorted sense of values, the standardization of life, the worship of mere bulk for its own sake, the uncritical acceptance of the second-rate. But the very size of the United States intensifies these tendencies in that country however they may be resisted, and we in Canada are increasingly exposed to their influence.'5 In the United States, home of Hollywood and all it represented, it was not possible to equate liberal humanist values with national character so unequivocally. But it was in Canada. The economics of mass cultural production, which encouraged centralization of production in the United States, created conditions in which the culture lobby in Canada could argue that mass culture was not a natural part of their society, but something that was threatening Canada from the south.

This point was made time and time again in the commission's hearings. When, as the Canadian Authors Association noted, 'the low-grade literature read in Canada is almost wholly imported,' it was easy to associate high standards with Canadianism.[6] But it was also a necessary means to an end. As Rev. Edward M. Nichols, representing the Co-ordinating Committee of Canadian Youth Groups, told the commission, 'If we are going to have an interest in the arts and letters it seems to me that it will have to be built upon some kind of wholesome Canadian nationalism.'[7] In their bid for government subsidy of their professions and hobbies the members of the culture lobby identified their special interests with the good of the nation as a whole.

This was not necessarily a conscious ploy. Convictions of Canada's cultural superiority were expressed with a sincerity which suggested that they were more than just a cynical means for highbrows to sell high culture to the masses. As both liberal humanism and nationalism were defined in opposition to the tide of American mass culture which spilled over the forty-ninth parallel, they became lumped together in the minds of cultural nationalists. The Comité permanent de la survivance française en Amérique told the commission, 'Le péril le plus grave qui menace l'avenir de cette culture [Canadienne] est ce que l'on appelle "l'américanisme." Depuis plusieurs années, notre pays subit l'influence de son puissant voisin les Etats-Unis. Par le truchement de la presse, de la radio, surtout du cinéma, il emprunte à la riche culture étatsunienne ses éléments souvent les moins humanisants.'[8] Thus the fight for liberal humanism against the banes of modern life became the fight for Canadian culture against foreign influences. The liberal humanism that inspired intellectuals throughout the Western world became a nationalistic cause in Canada.

The culture lobby's call for cultural development was inspired by the faith that if Canada retained some cultural independence, it could build a society more civilized than the United States. This faith in turn rested upon the conviction that Canada was already a significantly different society. No one ever defined exactly what made Canada different, but a firm belief in the superiority of the Canadian way of life was implicit in most of the submissions to the commission. The National Conference of Canadian Universities was atypical only in its explicitness when it bragged that 'our educational system enjoys considerable prestige in many parts of the world, combining the technical competence of the United States with, it is supposed, a less materialistic outlook and a higher regard for true scholarship.'[9] In this and other cases the cultural elite simply defined the Canadian identity in terms of its own liberal humanist values. It was, to twist a phrase, a case of 'la nation, c'est nous,' yet it was a sincere belief all the same.

It was a seductive combination because nationalism and liberal humanism each benefited from the other's strengths. From liberal humanism, nationalism gained a unifying Canadian identity. The natural nationalist impulse to seek unique Canadian qualities in popular culture had been frustrated by a variety of factors. Regional variations in social culture made it difficult to translate grass-roots traits into binding similarities. At the same time, American mass culture was either crowding out or becoming hopelessly entangled with indigenous popular culture. Liberal humanism requited cultural nationalism's desire for identity with a set of moral values and aesthetic standards that were coherent enough to serve as a basis for national unity and distinct enough from those of American mass culture to provide a unique Canadian identity.

From nationalism, on the other hand, liberal humanism gained what it most sorely lacked: popularity. High culture was not exclusive by the choice of its aficionados. The culture lobby was, in fact, suffused with hope for increased public enlightenment through the cultural improvement of individuals. Nationalism offered the perfect vehicle for taking high culture to the people. Facing a common enemy and recognizing the advantages of mutual support, liberal humanism and nationalism joined together to popularize high culture as the best available means of developing a Canadian culture.

Massey perceived the preservation of this unique Canadian cultural identity to be the paramount concern of the commission's work. Conscious that the commission was facing a wide array of seemingly unconnected issues, he made this broad context clear in an early meeting of the commission: 'The main question to be answered had already been proposed by André Siegfried: Could Canadian culture survive as an entity in view of the increasingly strong influences tending to unify the culture of North America? It was the view of the Commission that at the present time Canadian national feeling is stronger than it has been in the past, but also that the pressures upon Canadian life from abroad were also stronger.'[10] Siegfried was a French sociologist who had always paid special attention to Canada as part of his wider interest in the history of nationalism and the character of nations. His *The Race Question in Canada* was recognized as a classic study of

French-English relations. But Massey had in mind a more recent book, *Canada, an International Power*, in which Siegfried had invoked the spectre of continental integration that had haunted Canada throughout its history. Siegfried believed that the east-west axis upon which Canada had developed was quickly being replaced by north-south ties with the United States as the British connection weakened. Canadian nationalism had little economic, ethnic, linguistic, or geographical foundation, he argued; it was a political loyalty that needed cultural reinforcement if it was to exercise any real sway over Canadians. Massey thought the commission's great purpose was to reinforce and expand the unique culture which defined and protected Canadian nationhood. Cultural nationalism was central to Canada's survival. Thus it did not strike the commissioners as silly at all to ask questions such as 'Does this music contribute in any way to an increased consciousness of the Canadian community?'[11]

Cultural nationalism was of particular importance in the postwar period because Canadians thought that their nation was coming of age and defining its mature national character in the process. As the president of the Canadian Federation of Agriculture, H.H. Hannam, declared, 'our nation is now in its formative stage. We are now shaping our national destiny.'[12] The country's growing international prominence further reinforced the urgency of cultural development. Now that Canada was rubbing shoulders on the world stage with older nations with venerable cultural traditions, leading Canadians felt embarrassed by what they perceived to be the poor international image of its culture. Not just promotion of the arts within Canada, then, but cultural exchanges and other means of projecting Canada's cultural image abroad were necessary if Canada was to be recognized as being as civilized as its sister nations of the West.

The amalgam of cultural elitism and nationalism that constituted Canadian cultural nationalism was not, however, without its internal tensions. The popular appeal and Canadian emphasis which nationalism demanded sometimes threatened the critical standards and cosmopolitan outlook of the cultural elite. The claims of nationalism wrestled with those of elitism within the minds of individuals and between different factions of the culture lobby. Organizations that had cultural interests but were not closely linked to the elite tended to be more nationalistic than elitist in their views. Some regarded the elitist emphasis on the broad context of Western culture as a form of colonialism. The Western Stage Society was one of many organizations to make this complaint:

> Canada has a vast sense of inferiority in the Arts. We minimize the skill of our own artists just because they are familiar, and revere our visiting 'experts' just because they come from somewhere else ... If it can be said of any land it can be said of Canada that 'A prophet is not without honour save in his own country and among his own people.' Unlike the Americans we are afraid, and particularly in the Arts, to worship heroes. There is a misdirected domestic and international trade in the arts in which we export our talent and import our arbiters.[13]

For this wing of the culture lobby the solution to the problem was an unabashed nationalistic promotion of Canadian artists and their works. As the Saskatoon Council of Home and School Associations urged, 'Let us press forward, then, to the day when we shall no longer have a thin, shallow, imported, imitative culture – but a culture growing in the hearts and minds of our people.'[14]

The elite leadership of the culture lobby, however, feared that emphasizing nationalism over cultural excellence would breed an inferior and parochial culture in Canada. The Canadian Group of Painters, an outgrowth of the Group of Seven led by Arthur Lismer, appeared before the commission in Montreal. Lismer recalled that the Group of Seven had had a nationalistic purpose, but since then things had changed, probably for the better. 'What is happening today is that ... we all feel that it is not so important that there be Canadian art but there should be art in Canada,' he said.[15] The same position was evident in the brief of the Canadian Writers' Committee, a one-year-old group representing forty-two Canadian writers who differed from the Canadian Authors Association in their distaste for nationalistic boosterism. Its representative, Dr Claude Bissell, told the commission that the group (which included Frank Scott, Earle Birney, Dorothy Livesay, P.K. Page, and W.O. Mitchell) was 'bound together by certain common assumptions. First of all, that in the creation of a national literature we should maintain very high standards, and, at the same time we are aware of our national heritage, we should also be conscious of more cosmopolitan trends around us.'[16] Where one stood on this issue depended upon whether international influences were thought to be evidence of colonial subservience or healthy signs of cultural interaction and critical standards. The 'cosmopolitan or colonial' dispute was a venerable feature of Canadian cultural history. It reflected the inherent tensions within a cultural nationalism which comprised an alliance of elitism and nationalism against the common foe of foreign mass culture.

The strains between elitism and nationalism in Canadian cultural nationalism were also a variation of the tension between popular culture and high culture which generally plagued the Massey Commission's work. Those who had a more nationalistic point of view tended to think of culture in its broad, anthropological sense. It was only through the cultivation of the grass-roots character of the Canadian people, they thought, that a truly Canadian culture could be developed.[17] This left plenty of room, however, for a synthesis of nationalism, with its stress on a national identity founded in social culture, and elitism, with its emphasis on national pride in achieving a high cultural standard. Despite its suspicion of cosmopolitanism, the Western Stage Society recognized the difference between social and creative culture and pointed towards such a resolution in its brief:

A nation's culture is the sum total of what that nation actually is, good or bad, of what it does, and what it aspires to ... That is to say, a nation's Culture and a nation's Art are not the same thing. Art is simply one of the many expressions of and emanations from Culture. Therefore, the development of a nation's Art does not necessarily result in the development of its Culture; but an intelligent interest in the nation's Culture should result in the growth of its Art.[18]

The brief of the University of Toronto Press demonstrated that the elitist wing was just as willing to find a resolution to this dilemma. While insisting that 'scholarship is international,' it nevertheless contended that 'Canada will play its proper international role only when it develops its resources in a truly Canadian spirit to the full extent of its ability.'[19] On the whole, then, the culture lobby was able to resolve its inherent tensions by embracing the ideal of a creative culture in which Canadian content would be combined with elitist form.

Nationalism presented other challenges to the liberal humanism of the cultural elite. The quest for a national cultural identity was rooted in a romantic nationalism which conceived of a nation as a people united by a shared character and goals. In Vancouver this ideal was expressed by Mrs Elsie Graham, who looked forward to the day when all Canadians would share a similar national character: 'Sooner or later, in the historic future, and in much the same way that our progenitors did in the historical past, we shall blend our peoples, in Nationality, speech and literature, absorbing into the blend our separate cultures and heritages and enlarging them to the continuing ascendancy and influence of Our Country and its People ... We desire more than anything to develop a homogeneous Nation of Peoples, enriched and enlarged by the richness of attainment of all its units and sections.'[20] One obvious impediment to this conception of a national cultural identity was the coexistence of English Canadians and French Canadians in Canada. A pursuit of romantic nationalism would require either the separation or assimilation of the French minority.

Recognizing this, most of the cultural elite followed the dictum expressed by the Ligue d'action nationale that 'le Canada est un pays biculturel où il ne peut y avoir d'unité que dans la diversité' and tried to translate this seeming liability into a positive good.[21] Efforts to interpret the unavoidable bicultural fact as a political and cultural asset were made by most groups, both French and English Canadian, who addressed the issue. In the appearance of the Université Laval before the commission, its rector, Mgr Ferdinand Vandry, told the commission that he thought of Canada as two cultures, but one civilization comprising 'les deux éléments ethniques du peuple canadien, une manifestation d'ordre intellectuel et moral par laquelle le peuple de Canada dans son ensemble se distinguera de notre pays voisin, les Etats-Unis, ou les autres pays où on ne trouve qu'une seule culture ... Canada donnera toujours au monde le spectacle d'un peuple qui a réussi à être heureux sous deux cultures différentes.'[22] Here was a definition of a nationalism that qualified the romantic ideal of cultural unity with the liberal principle of toleration and thus reinforced the cultural elite's identification of Canadian nationalism with liberal humanism.

Nevertheless, cultural nationalists still displayed some residual yearnings for the binding similarities emphasized by romantic nationalism. There were frequent references to the similarities of the French and English cultural traditions. Alternatively, there were hopes that the bicultural principle itself might grow into a unifying national ideal and provide the basis for the development of a common Canadian culture. This position even found support in French Canada, especially among those who believed that the best chance for French-Canadian cultural survival lay within a bicultural Canada. The Comité permanent de la survivance française en Amérique wrote that 'au Canada, la culture s'épanouit selon deux modalités distinctes, différentes, plutôt complémentaires qu'opposées. Une partie de la population a emprunté à l'Angleterre ses conceptions de la vie, de l'art, de la science. L'autre les a reçues de la France. Les conditions géographiques, les contingences historiques, les exigences économiques ont modifié ces conceptions, leur ont conféré certains traits de ressemblance qui les préparent à devenir les éléments d'une culture proprement canadienne.'23 Thus it was hoped that cultural interaction and cooperation could foster a common Canadianism which would provide a genuine national unity that respected but transcended each cultural tradition.

The Massey Commission's hearings, however, showed that Canadian cultural development would have to come to terms not just with biculturalism, but multiculturalism as well. Ethnic groups were demanding recognition as new immigration was adding to their size and variety. At the same time the significance of the Holocaust was beginning to sink in, making discriminatory attitudes of the past publicly intolerable. The commission also heard a great deal, especially in the West, about the need to preserve the culture of Canada's native peoples. But the culture lobby as a whole was too concerned about the survival of its own cultural tradition to get worked up about the plights of other minorities. Biculturalism was an accepted fact based on a historic and necessary accommodation, but there seemed to be no reason why new immigrant groups should not assimilate. When confronted with the prospect of extending the logic of the liberal principle of tolerance underlying biculturalism into multiculturalism, the limits of the elite's liberal qualification of romantic nationalism were reached. Massey and others were willing to accept the integration of

*Massey + others
accep the intergration into a
of ethnic cultures into a
distinctive Canad cult.*

ethnic cultures into a distinctive Canadian culture, but the idea of an ethnic mosaic had yet to be translated from an emerging demographic trend into an acknowledged good.[24] Thus each of the two constituent elements of liberal humanist nationalism imposed constraints upon the other. Nationalism limited liberalism just as liberalism qualified nationalism.

Some of the same tensions that ran throughout the culture lobby created strains within the Massey Commission itself. There are numerous testimonials to the good relations which developed among the commissioners, but there did exist significant variations of opinion that would bedevil the commission's deliberations. In his memoirs, MacKenzie recalled that 'we were a very happy group, got on very well together though we did argue betwixt and between ourselves.'[25] The commissioners generally shared a liberal humanist nationalism, but they did not all think exactly alike or wield the same influence within the commission's councils.

Massey is often remembered, and belittled, as an ardent anglophile. In part this was due to his upper-class airs, his fondness for fraternizing with British peers, and the suspicion that he thought of his family as a kind of colonial aristocracy. But there was more to it than this. In his youth Massey had been a member of the imperialist Round Table Movement. His greatest ambition, after being denied elected office, was the post of high commissioner in London, which he finally secured from Mackenzie King and enjoyed throughout the late 1930s and the critical years of the war. In short, Massey's fondness for Britain was undeniable. It has been exaggerated and distorted by many commentators, however, to the point that Massey has somehow been stigmatized as being unpatriotic. The implication has been that the cultural program he pursued for Canada entailed the imposition of the stale affectations of the mother country upon a vibrant young North American democracy.[26]

It has become a common contention in Canadian historiography, however, that Canadian imperialism was but one form of nationalism. This was true in Massey's case. When his social quirks were put aside, there was nothing particularly alien about the intellectual content of his nationalism. The imperialist movement ended a generation before the Massey Commission was formed, and in the interim Massey had adapted to the changing national status of Canada and the evolution of the Commonwealth, keeping step with his country's progress from colony to nation. His record as a left-wing Liberal during the 1930s was more indicative of his mature political thought than the imperialist flirtations of his youth.

The commissioners generally were representative of a generation that had embraced a nationalism of an independent bent as imperialism went into decline in the 1920s. When in the post–World War II era that trajectory threw Canada perilously close to the gravitational pull of the United States, it was time to correct course back in the opposite direction. In the postwar world, emphasizing independence from Britain was no longer as important as it had been two decades before: distinctiveness from the United States was suddenly the key issue. Emphasizing Canada's 'Britishness,' as Massey did, was quite a different thing than it had been in the post–World War I years. Even then, Massey saw Britain, not as a model to be aped and obeyed by servile colonials, but as legitimate source of social and political traditions which made Canada a distinctive society in North America. This was a venerable and fundamental theme of Canadian nationalism.[27]

In fact, Massey's nationalism was sometimes too strong for some of his colleagues. Neatby in particular was leery of the least sign of nationalistic chauvinism. But she ultimately sympathized with Massey's belief that if economic forces were left unhampered they would lead to continentalism and a reinforcement in Canada of all the modern cultural influences she found most threatening. Massey and Neatby were the two members of the commission who had the most time to devote to its work. However, their close collaboration in the commission's offices in Ottawa was based on more than just convenience. Massey discovered not only that Neatby shared many of his views, but that she had the historical knowledge and intellectual acuity necessary to back them up with convincing arguments. The chairman came to depend heavily on Neatby for critical aspects of the commission's work. As Lévesque later told her: 'Je me suis aperçu que M. Massey (soit dit confidentiellement) était complètement effaré à la seule pensée de ne pouvoir compter sur votre présence. J'ai très nettement l'impression que, psychologiquement et intellectuellement, il a absolument besoin de vous pour mener à bon fin cette réunion qui l'effraie un peu. Il veut à tout prix nous voir tous deux à côté de lui.'[28] The relationship of Massey and Neatby was not without its minor tensions. Neatby was very conscious of Massey's foibles, including his self-satisfaction with the correctness of his background, but she found his quirks tolerable. They became lifelong friends.

Of the remaining commissioners, Lévesque was closest to Neatby and Massey both personally and ideologically. He was considered something of a radical in his native province, but his status as a reformer in conservative Quebec was actually based on views similar to those of his English colleagues. A major theme of his writing was the reconciliation of the claims of capitalism, cooperatism, and Catholicism in French-Canadian society. In his work with the Massey Commission, however, he was particularly conscious of the importance of his role as the representative of French-Canadian cultural interests in a federalist context. He saw his first priority to be the defence of French-Canadian culture:

> ... j'avais accepté de participer aux travaux de cette commission plus comme patriote québécois que comme citoyen canadien. Je l'avais souligné à M. Saint-Laurent, comme condition *sine qua non* de ma collaboration. Je ne désirais nullement m'y présenter comme un *Canadian* absolu, mais plutôt assurer la présence de la culture française dans la vie de tout un pays bigarré. J'entendais bien aussi défendre d'arrache-pied les intérêts tout particuliers du Québec. Certes pas à la manière de certains nationalistes qui se contentent de lancer des pierres aux 'Anglais' derrière la clôture inexpugnable de notre province. Bien plutôt en nationaliste présent, soucieux de garder et de prendre ce qui nous revient, tout en apprenant quelque chose de nos frères anglophones, et leur exprimant nos exigences et notre identité.[29]

Lévesque would find that he would have less trouble saving French Canada from English-Canadian assimilators than he would in fighting off assaults by fellow French-Canadian nationalists (the passage above reveals that he was still self-consciously defending himself against such attacks forty years later). The important point, however, is that he was not a Quebec nationalist. He accepted the coexistence of French and English in Canada within the constitutional status quo, and he did not see every federal initiative as inherently threatening to Quebec. Indeed, as an enemy of Duplessis, it was in his interests to counteract provincialism with the federal power as long as French-Canadian interests were well established on that level.

Lévesque's acceptance of biculturalism as the best means of preserving French-Canadian culture was rooted in a liberal humanist outlook. He thought that the unique merit of Canada was its tolerance of various cultural traditions, particularly its historical success in allowing the coexistence of the English-Canadian and French-Canadian cultures. He saw this as the legacy of the common humanism of the two founding cultures. While every Canadian would naturally belong to one or the other of these cultures, it was impossible for the two not to influence each other. The key was to make this a process of mutual enrichment rather than a battle for cultural dominance. In Lévesque's view, the defensive nationalism of the provincial-rights camp was a tacit admission of defeat: 'A strong and vital culture need not be afraid. Neither fanaticism, nor politics, nor money, nor even arms will prevail over it. The only enemy which can vanquish a culture is its own weakness.'[30] This attitude by no means made him any less of a defender of French-Canadian rights. In fact, the fate of French Canadians outside Quebec was a major concern behind his rejection of a French-Canadian nationalism focused on the Quebec state. Lévesque found that Massey shared his belief in cultural coexistence and productive interaction. The two forged a compact based on a bicultural vision of Canada that was accepted by the other commissions as well.

The friendly Dominican was soon on good terms with every member of the commission. As we have seen, Neatby found him to be a man of great integrity, with a lively sense of fun and a sympathetic ear. By 1951, perhaps jesting at their mutual piety and unmarried status, Lévesque was addressing Neatby as 'Ma chère "soeur" ' in their correspondence.[31] Lévesque and Neatby attended receptions for the commission together, 'he referring to her as "my presbyterian boss," her to him as "my catholic padre." '[32]

The inner circle of Massey, Neatby, and Lévesque was not an exclusive ring. MacKenzie was not as intimate a member of this group because of his absences to attend to his duties as president of the University of British Columbia. Yet he was a power in his own right, with political contacts and a publicity consciousness which Massey valued highly. Neatby, however, neither liked nor respected Mac-Kenzie. Part of this dislike was based on a clash of personalities. MacKenzie's down-to-earth bonhomie and boisterous spirit grated against the more puritanical side of Neatby's nature. The differences between the two were best illustrated on the commission's tour of the Maritimes during an evening at Government House in New Brunswick on 18 January 1950. The lieutenant-governor, D.L. MacLaren, was an old World War I friend of MacKenzie's, and dinner evolved into an evening party: 'MacLaren was a good fist at the piano and by midnight, after a fair bit of lubrication, they had begun to work their way through songs ... Larry vividly remembered MacLaren sitting at the piano well into the evening singing with his raucous voice, "Mademoiselle from Armentières"; at the "parlez-vous?" he reached into his pocket and slapped a two-dollar bill down on the piano in front of Hilda Neatby. Hilda was not frightfully amused.'[33] This sort of humour and the general tenor of the evening's entertainment appealed to MacKenzie's fun-loving nature. He was by no means as discriminating as Neatby in eschewing the pleasures of popular culture and the material world.

MacKenzie believed that if culture was to prove itself as a practical good, it could not afford to hold itself aloof from everyday life. An interesting letter he wrote to Neatby suggests that although he embraced the same liberal humanist viewpoint as his colleagues, he thought its esoteric excesses should be tempered with a healthy infusion of populism and pragmatism:

As you no doubt have discovered, I believe very strongly that if the humanities are to count for anything in this day and generation they will have to be associated directly with the lives that we lead and with the lives of our citizens in all walks of life. The ancients whom we now study and admire lived and made their contribution to their contemporary society. Shakespeare and others like him did the same for their period. I would like to think that our humanists, including those in our universities, were doing the same for their society.

It is because of this that I am so keenly interested in encouraging our humanists to keep in touch with their society and with the forces of a cultural kind, even though these be vulgar that are shaping it and influencing it. This need not interfere with their abilities or contributions as scholars and teachers. In fact, I think it will greatly increase their worth in both these respects. It will mean, however, that the rest of the community will realize that they exist and will attach some importance to them, even though they disagree violently with some of the things that they say and do.[34]

MacKenzie was sending brochures describing a lecture series on the arts at the University of British Columbia to Neatby and Massey, perhaps to establish his credentials as a lover of culture with his colleagues.

The differences between Neatby and MacKenzie showed that there were tensions between elitism and populism within the commission itself. Neatby was uncompromising in her intellectual convictions, unrelenting in pursuit of what she believed to be right, and prone to getting a bit carried away by her own moral righteousness. MacKenzie had a deeper faith in the common man and political instincts which bristled at the least hint of any elitist conceit. Neatby may have been the philosophical power behind the throne, but MacKenzie was the commission's populist conscience. He counterbalanced her emphasis on what should be done with a pragmatic sense of what could be done and how to go about doing it. On the whole this would be a creative tension. Neatby's idealistic convictions and moral certainty gave the commission its crusading zeal, while MacKenzie's common sense and political wiles helped it avoid some of the pitfalls into which it otherwise might have blindly barged.

Arthur Surveyer ended up being something of an outsider. He attended fewer public sessions and meetings than any commissioner. In the hearings which he did attend, he showed more interest in concrete problems like community planning that were related to his professional experience than he did in abstract cultural issues. As the work of the commission progressed, however, Surveyer was educated to the issues and began to appreciate the concerns of his fellow commissioners. He is best remembered for his dissenting views on broadcasting, but these ultimately reflected a disagreement, not about the ends espoused by the other commissioners, but about the best means of attaining them. They also showed a mind untrained in the humanities working its way towards an articulation of principles which the other commissioners took as their points of departure. This cultural awakening, however, came too late for Surveyer to play an influential role on the commission. At times his contrary stubbornness on particular issues seemed to stem simply from a proud insistence that his opinion should count.

The differences among the commissioners illustrated the difficulties inherent in judging particular personalities or cultural preferences as highbrow or lowbrow. But nationalism, peer group pressure, and the need to make concrete recommendations moderated these differences. Accommodation in pursuit of a great national goal tended to dissipate Massey's anglophilia, Neatby's puritanism, MacKenzie's populism, and Surveyer's free enterprise principles to a point where compromises were achievable. Even Lévesque, who was at heart a French-Canadian nationalist, believed in Canada insofar as he saw a bicultural federal state as the best means of fulfilling French-Canadian interests.

The commissioners, then, shared the liberal humanist nationalism that characterized the Canadian cultural elite and was influential within the culture lobby as a whole. By integrating its cultural concerns with questions about Canada's future the culture lobby forged a cultural nationalism in which its liberal humanist values became synonymous with the Canadian identity. It was an attractive ideology for Canadians of the day. Their nation was just beginning to exercise its political independence from the British connection, yet already seemed threatened by cultural and economic domination by the United States. The liberal humanist nationalism proffered by the Massey Commission provided some justification and purpose for Canada's existence as an independent nation as it came to terms with both the possibilities and dangers of its new status in the postwar world.

PART THREE

6

The Battle for
the Air Waves

It was primarily on questions of broadcasting policy that the culture lobby and representatives of the commercial mass culture it opposed came into direct conflict. Radio had been one of the wonders of the age for Massey's generation, and in 1949 television was already being developed in Canada. These electronic mass media were critical factors in any cultural policy because they were the vehicles through which every conceivable cultural interest hoped to reach the masses directly and popularize its cause. They were also central to the fulfilment of the cultural elite's hopes for Canadian democracy because they offered unparalleled means for widespread education, information dissemination, and cultural edification. For business interests, on the other hand, they were the key to profits. Private radio wanted to be free to make more money, and business in general saw advertising on the air waves as one of the few ways of selling goods on a scale large enough to support mass production and continued prosperity. Each side had its own vision of what radio and television should be, and all the issues surrounding broadcasting policy came down to a struggle between the cultural interests and the business interests for control of these media. Inevitably, nationalism became one of the weapons deployed in the battle. Since commercialism was associated with continentalism, it was possible for cultural nationalists to portray the struggle as one of Johnny Canuck versus the Almighty Buck.

Given the money and influence at stake in broadcasting, it was not surprising that it became the most important part of the Massey Commission's mandate, attracting more attention and occupying more of the commissioners' time than any other aspect of their work. Debate crystallized around three major issues: regulation, CBC funding, and television development. Radio station owners protested against their status as subordinate parts of a public radio system under the authority of the CBC, claiming that they were unfairly regulated by a competitor. They lobbied for an independent regulatory authority which would allow them to develop as an independent system. At the same time the CBC's chronic financial problems were becoming critical and were aggravated further by the need to begin building a television system. The prospect of television development also raised the stakes in the battle over regulation by introducing the question of whether the national system of broadcasting would be extended intact to an entirely new medium.[1]

The existing broadcasting system had evolved out of the greatest victory of the cultural elite in the interwar years. In the late 1920s, the Aird Commission, appointed by Prime Minister Mackenzie King to advise the government on broadcasting policy, had recommended the establishment of a public radio system. Through the Radio League and its nationwide contacts the cultural elite had lobbied for implementation of the Aird Report, and in 1932 the Conservative government of R.B. Bennett responded by establishing the Canadian Radio Broadcasting Commission. Problems with its funding and administration prompted the Liberals when they returned to power to bring in a new Broadcasting Act, which created the Canadian Broadcasting Corporation in 1936.

The Aird Commission had envisioned the expropriation of existing private stations and the establishment of a system that would be almost entirely under public ownership. Over the years, practical considerations constrained both the government and the CBC from embarking on such a program. Private stations already existed, of course, and expropriating them would have created a political fuss. In any case, the CBC never had the resources to develop a national system of its own stations and was able to provide local service and coast-to-coast coverage only by running its programs through private stations. Instead of disappearing, the private outlets grew in number and influence, comprising 119 of the 136 stations in Canada in 1949.

As the consumer economy burgeoned in the postwar era, the growth of advertising boosted the earnings potential of private radio, and station owners grew increasingly eager to escape the limits which the public system placed upon their profitability. The Canadian Association of Broadcasters (CAB), which would represent 93 of the 119 privately owned radio stations in Canada by 1949, redoubled its efforts to reduce the CBC's powers. It argued that since its stations had not been nationalized, since, in fact, they had grown in strength and numbers, they constituted a parallel private system of radio that should be recognized as being outside of the CBC's domain and regulated accordingly.[2] It was a propitious moment for such a campaign. During the war the impartiality of the CBC had been attacked because of some questionable decisions it had made on political time allotment and other touchy issues. While the reputation of the CBC was at a low ebb, the Cold War lent the free-enterprise rhetoric of the broadcasters added legitimacy.

Along the way the CAB gained some valuable allies in its campaign. Although the Conservative party under Bennett had established public broadcasting, by the mid-1940s it had abandoned its former position and was voicing the CAB's complaints. In 1947 the Progressive Conservative national convention made the creation of an independent regulatory body for radio part of its official party policy.[3] A significant number of newspapers also began changing their positions on the issue. In the 1930s newspapers had generally supported public broadcasting because they had feared competition for advertising from the new medium. Over the years, however, many newspaper owners had acquired interests in private radio stations, and editorial positions correspondingly shifted to support the CAB's demands.

Throughout this period House of Commons committees on broadcasting had resisted the lobbying of the private broadcasters, repeatedly reaffirming the supremacy of the public broadcasting system. Private broadcasters continued to make gains on other fronts, however, becoming more profitable, more powerful, and a proportionately larger part of the national broadcasting scene.[4] Despite repeated rebuffs, the CAB never abandoned its effort to undermine CBC controls. The private broadcasters knew the lobbying game: their case gained credibility through repetition and continued pressure as much as logic. And no matter how many times they heard 'no,' it would only take one 'yes' to change the system irreversibly in their favour.

It was against this background, then, that the Massey Commission opened its investigation into broadcasting policy. During each of its series of Ottawa hearings the commission held special sessions on broadcasting at which the CBC, the CAB, and other interested parties presented briefs. But discussion of broadcasting issues was by no means limited to these hearings; it was an area of concern for practically every organization with cultural interests and attracted comment in hearings right across the country.

The Massey Commission's strategy for dealing with broadcasting issues was to cultivate an aura of magisterial objectivity while supporting and publicizing the principles of public broadcasting and the needs of the CBC as much as possible. The key figure in this plan was its chief legal counsel, Peter Wright. Wright digested the extensive submissions on broadcasting, supplemented them with relevant research, and provided the commissioners with syntheses of issues and appraisals of contending forces. He and the assistant counsel, Guy Roberge, were also responsible for interrogating proponents of the CAB's case.

Even before it had experienced one of Wright's scathing cross-examinations, the CAB had good reason to suspect that the Massey Commission was prejudiced against it. The academic ties, Liberal sympathies, and nationalist sentiments of most of the commissioners made them natural allies of the CBC. Certain commissioners were known to have been strong supporters of the Radio League. Although the CAB had been asking for years for a commission to study broadcasting regulation, this was not the sort of body it had in mind.[5] But the private broadcasters were not overly dismayed, for they knew that no matter how much the cards were stacked against them, they could still gain from the process. The commission's hearings let them parade their views in public, and the seriousness with which broadcasting issues were discussed invested their case with greater credibility.

Wright's strategy for dealing with broadcasting questions became clear at the start of the commission's first public hearing on broadcasting on Monday, 6 September 1949. He opened the session with a melodramatic address in which he invoked the nationalist visions of D'Arcy McGee and Canada First as a prelude to emphasizing the importance of broadcasting to Canada's national identity and unity in the modern world. No one seriously favoured abandoning the existing national goals of broadcasting, he claimed; the issues in contention were just subsidiary questions about how the public broad-casting system could best function.[6] This declaration would pass unchallenged by the CAB, which knew better than to contest its cause on patriotic grounds. Wright had scored a pre-emptive coup for the forces of public broadcasting by establishing premises by which subsequent questions of policy could be evaluated in order to justify public control.

Immediately after Wright's address, the CBC's chairman, Davidson Dunton, presented its brief to the commission. The CBC affected a pose of serene detachment from the sordid squabbling of its unruly underlings. It presented itself as the guardian of a public trust, trying its best to fulfil its mandate in the face of great adversity. Ultimately, however, it could not avoid defending the system with which it was synonymous and painstakingly set out the criteria that made public broadcasting a national necessity in Canada. In the first place, its brief contended, radio frequencies were public, not private property. It followed that broadcasting questions should be decided with the public interest in mind. Furthermore, Canada's small population, strung out along the American border, was not a commercially viable market, which meant that only a public broadcasting system could operate in the national interest. Private interests were subject to market pressures that led to commercialization and Americanization instead of the cultural, educational, and national goals that served the best interests of the Canadian public. The CBC readily admitted that it was in the public interest to have private stations within the national broadcasting system – they filled in gaps in national coverage and provided local service. Their presence was desirable, however, only if they were serving the public system rather than undermining it.

The only problem with the existing system, according to the CBC, was that it had never been given the resources it needed to fulfil its mandate. Now the situation was critical. Costs were rising rapidly as revenues remained fixed. It wanted the radio set licence fees that provided most of its revenue to be doubled to $5. Unless it got this money, it warned, it would be forced to begin cutting back its services. Furthermore, the government's interim television policy had to be confirmed. The CBC felt that the same reasoning which dictated a national system of radio in Canada applied to television as well. To develop television it needed both an adequate television receiver licence fee and government loans to cover capital investment and other development costs.

The Canadian Association of Broadcasters entered the arena on 8 September led by William Guild, manager of station CJOC in Lethbridge and chairman of the CAB board of directors. In its brief the CAB had asserted that there was, in practice if not in law, a 'dual system' of private and public broadcasting in the country and that changes should be made that would recognize this reality. Predictably, its chief demand was for a public regulatory body that would supervise both the CBC and private stations. Guild also wanted modifications to the Broadcasting Act that would legally recognize the existence of private stations and give them the right to appeal regulatory decisions to the courts. All of the CAB's concerns about radio regulation applied to television policy as well, and he promised that private interests would begin developing television immediately, at no cost to the public, if the new medium was regulated under the same terms as the CAB desired for radio.

The CAB's demand for a separate regulatory body rested upon the claim that the CBC functioned as both 'umpire and player' in the radio system. The CBC, it argued, competed with private radio stations, yet was subsidized by them and had the power to set the rules of the game in its own favour. Although the CAB had to concede that the CBC had been a benevolent master, it argued that this was no substitute for free enterprise, which it took pains to associate with democracy. 'It is our contention,' concluded the CAB brief, 'that such a situation as exists in radio broadcasting in Canada today is undemocratic.'[7]

The CAB took care not to challenge the fundamental principle of public control directly. But despite its attempts to frame the issue entirely in terms of democratic rights, its demands could not help but arouse nationalist apprehensions. Many private stations were less circumspect than the CAB and openly expressed their desire to form private networks or to link themselves to American networks.[8] Among defenders of public broadcasting this business calculus prompted concern that any concession to the CAB's demands would effectively destroy the public system. They feared that the establishment of an independent regulatory body would make the private broadcasting sector equal to the CBC instead of a subordinate part of a public broadcasting system. Private broadcasters would then proceed to erode the audience coverage and commercial revenues of the CBC.

The CBC itself countered the CAB's argument by pointing out that in a public system that was designed to serve the national interest, the CAB's concerns about equality of status and free enterprise were irrelevant. Instead, 'in any question between private or local interests and national interests, the national interest must prevail.'[9] Surveyer seemed impressed with the 'umpire and player' analogy, however, and questioned Dunton closely on this point. Dunton reiterated the CBC's stand that the private stations were intended to be subordinate parts of the national system and could not expect to be treated as equals.

As the commission moved across the country, the broader pattern of support for the CBC and the CAB became clear. Private radio stations, boards of trade, chambers of commerce, radio manufacturers, and advertisers generally supported the CAB's case. On the other hand, local and national voluntary associations in the culture lobby were staunch, if not uncritical, defenders of the CBC. Organizations representing rural Canada were particularly strong supporters of the CBC, one of the few cultural services available outside urban areas. The opinions of private citizens or other neutral parties were heard only rarely; instead, the commission's hearings became a battleground in which these two contending interest groups clashed.

The voluntary associations were freer than the commission itself to criticize the CAB, and they often did so virulently, questioning its motives and its tactics and denouncing its campaign as a plot against the national interests of Canadians. Their attacks focused on the character and effects of the type of programming carried by the private stations. On one level their disdain for private radio stemmed from a simple aversion to what they perceived to be the low quality of private stations' programs. Many criticized commercial programming on grounds of taste alone, deriding shows such as 'soap operas, sports broadcasts, "boogie-woogie" and other forms of dance music, so-called "light" music, popular French songs (on the French stations), childish playlets, quiz programmes, give away shows and other forms of infantilism [that] flourish in private stations' broadcasts.'[10] The 'infantilism' of private station programming was commonly attributed to the increasing commercialization of the medium. The Association of Canadian Radio Artists explained to the commission that 'art for culture's sake is a serious heresy in commercial centres. The primal urge is to exploit, not promote art.'[11] Soap operas in particular were flagellated for their lack of any artistic standards. But the effects of commercialization were most evident in advertising itself, which was deemed to be increasingly raucous and overbearing. The Prince Edward Island Adult Education Council complained that 'when those big national firms come along, they go hammer and tongs at you, until you cannot bear it and you shut off the radio.'[12] There was also widespread disapproval of commercials which stretched the boundaries of good taste. References to 'B.O.' and other such subjects, however disguised, were thought crude and vulgar. (It was telling that Massey did not even know what 'B.O.' meant when the term was used by a witness.)[13]

Many organizations were so outraged by the content of some radio shows that they advocated censorship. The Federated Women's Institutes of Canada told the commission that 'programs depicting violence and crime, especially those given for children, are causing much concern among right-thinking people' and that 'rigid censorship will be required to eliminate undesirable types of pictures' in television.[14] Even the Calgary Business and Professional Women's Club, otherwise a supporter of the CAB, thought that there should be more censorship to ensure 'truth and good taste.'[15] Such demands represented an arbitrary and illiberal response to the excesses of modern mass culture that was recognized as such and eschewed by the more thoughtful elements of the cultural elite.

Instead of this subjective aversion and repressive reaction to 'inferior' forms of culture, the elite had a more rational critique of private radio programming and a more democratic solution to the problem. It aimed at eradicating demand for such fare rather than outlawing its supply. This approach was inspired by the belief that the electronic media offered an unrivalled means for educating the public. As Dr Robert Newton, president of the University of Alberta, put it, 'radio vies with the press and the movies for first place as an instrument of public education.' It followed that 'the public has an interest in educational instruments at least equal to that of any private enterprises which operate them.'[16] The problem with commercial programming was that its emphasis on attracting the largest possible audience catered to the 'lowest common denominator.' Neither individuals nor society as a whole could be culturally enriched on a diet of soap operas and B.O. ads.

The great question confronting the cultural elite was how to initiate the public into the joys of culture without arbitrarily imposing its own taste. Dictating taste was illiberal both in means and ends: not only would it involve authoritarian propagandizing, but the brainwashed products of such a procedure were exactly the opposite of the independent and free-thinking citizens considered essential to the successful functioning of a liberal democratic state. The answer lay in providing education without coercion. High culture could be dangled in front of individuals in the hope that their better instincts would prompt them to take the bait. Once they were hooked, their edification could then proceed through self-enlightenment. The Public Affairs Institute of Vancouver noted that the British experience offered hope that the masses could be elevated in this fashion: 'it can be proved that public taste can and does change remarkably over the years. A recent B.B.C. listening survey in England shows a general upgrading in taste over a 15 year period, with every segment of the population moving "up" – if you can call it that – in taste, as regards musical, dramatic and informational programs.'[17] In order for this process to take place, high culture at least had to be made available to the public. Private stations were criticized because they made little effort to offer such alternative cultural fare; their pandering to base instincts had a stultifying effect on society.

The cultural elite looked to the CBC to provide the type of programming that could improve public taste over the long term. Instead of simply catering to common, but lowly, interests, the CBC declared that 'we believe radio has the responsibility of "leading" the listener to a certain extent.'[18] It mixed enough light entertainment to hold its audience with enough serious culture to tempt people to explore better things. Thus its premiere programs were aimed squarely at educational and cultural goals. 'Wednesday Night' was then the jewel in the crown of the crown corporation. Its 1949 schedule presented evenings which mixed classical music, serious theatre, readings of poetry, short stories, and talks. Included were shows such as 'A Layman's History of Music' which were geared specifically towards making culture accessible to the common man.

Among the most innovative of the CBC's shows were interactive programs such as the 'National Farm Radio Forum' which fostered discussion groups across the country in order to encourage grass-roots debate on a wide variety of political, social, and economic issues. Here was a working example of the cultural elite's ideal of how the mass media could be used to stimulate and strengthen democracy. The 'Citizen's Forum' promotional brochures summed up the idea of the program on their covers. 'Here's a good way for Canadians to meet the challenges of our times,' they began. 'We can read the facts, listen to the experts, talk it over together, make up our minds, act with our neighbours.'[19]

The culture lobby believed that private radio stations underestimated the intelligence of their listeners. On the other hand, there were limits to how far and how fast audience taste could be developed. The manager of CFAR in Flin Flon told the commission of the disastrous consequences of its experiments with high culture:

> For a good number of months, the station carried nearly all programs of a cultural nature ... And what were the results?
>
> Our station lost touch with the communities it serves and its effectiveness was severely challenged. We were compelled to slash the CBC Symphony, The Opera, nearly all of the Distinguished Artist Series, Recitals and Concerts, and replace [them] with light shorter-length symphonic programs, Hit parades, popular orchestras, American transcribed programs, listeners' choice programs, special events series, ball games, fights, etc. And we have begun to receive the reward of comments such as ... 'your station has certainly picked up' ... 'there's some life in your station now,' ... 'Thank God, you've cut some of that cultural tripe!'[20]

Significantly, the CFAR manager was not opposed to cultural fare but warned that the commission should 'consider the capabilities of the individual Canadian for absorbing radio content of a cultural nature,' for fear of inducing a backlash against high culture that would hurt cultural development in the long term.[21] Few private stations openly disputed the premise that edifying the masses was a good thing. The CAB and its members avoided challenging this sacred cow just as they avoided disputing its bovine associates, nationalism and the public interest.

Since a concern for democracy was on everyone's mind in the midst of the Cold War, the battle between the culture lobby and the private broadcasters was largely fought in terms of who had the more 'democratic' approach to broadcasting. Private broadcasters recognized that the problem of how to change popular preferences democratically was a vulnerable part of the elite's case and emphasized the authoritarian implications of any attempt to dictate taste. They continually equated free enterprise with democracy and claimed that their programming was democratic because it directly reflected audience preferences. Since competition for profit made private stations strive to win the largest possible audience, their programming was necessarily popular and, therefore, more democratic than the arbitrary creations of a bureaucracy like the CBC.[22] This conviction was summed up in the credo that they were simply 'giving the public what it wants.' A number of audience surveys were put forward by private broadcasters to demonstrate the popularity of commercial programs over CBC productions, suggesting that a democratic majority supported private radio more than the public system.

Advocates of public radio countered with their own public opinion polls, yet on the whole there was no denying that commercial radio was more popular than the CBC. The cultural elite resorted to different arguments which transcended the numbers game and questioned the validity of the 'giving the public what it wants' maxim as a basis for democratic broadcasting. If programming always catered to the majority, they pointed out, significant portions of the population would never be served. The Canadian Writers' Committee also complained in its brief that the CAB approach curtailed artistic freedom. As it pointed out, 'the public did not want *Hamlet* till Shakespeare created it.'[23]

But the fundamental justification for public broadcasting was to be found in the educational purposes of the cultural elite. It was an approach that focused on the individual rather than the mass, and measured success in terms of effect instead of mere contact. The value of a program had to be measured not by the quantity of listeners it received but by the quality of the impact it had upon those who heard it. A talk by Dr Arthur L. Phelps on the first 'Wednesday Night' program on 3 December 1947 was included in the CBC's enclosures with its brief. It clearly expressed the underlying faith of the cultural elite in the potential of the individual: 'The CBC ... is ... under fire in this country ... because its underlying philosophy goes dead against some of the basic assumptions of continental North American society ... Its theory, like that of education and the church, and great art, is a faith in the long-run human potential, held with zeal and patience against appearances and even against the listener ratings ... Basically, for all of us, it's a matter of belief or disbelief in the human potential: belief or disbelief in people.'[24] The cultural elite rebutted the CAB's simple equation of democracy and mass popularity with a contrasting vision of a pluralistic, individualistic, and humanistic political order. It was the difference between democracy and liberal democracy.

The cultural elite might have had a more sophisticated concept of liberal democracy, but the broadcasters had more of the public on their wavelength. Their association of free enterprise with democracy had a simple plausibility that won extensive public support in the increasingly chilly climate of the Cold War. Mr Walter Elliott, president of Elliott-Haynes, Ltd, the private stations' favourite audience-polling firm, gave the commission an audio-visual presentation on how public opinion was measured in his work. Significantly, the issue which was addressed in the sample poll he presented to the commissioners was what he called 'the attitude of the Canadian people toward the principle of socialization – that is, socialization of industry, as such, but more particularly the socialization of the radio broadcasting industry.'[25] Elliott's figures showed that sympathy for public radio in 1944 had been at 31 per cent as compared to a 48 per cent level of support for private radio. By 1949 there had been a significant shift in favour of private enterprise; the figures were 20 per cent versus 58 per cent. Elliott explained the reasons behind this change for the benefit of the commissioners: 'The swing to the right has been occasioned by many things, one of which was the espionage trial at Ottawa. That had a profound effect on the thinking of the people in Canada. It was not so much a swing to the right because of a pull to the right; it was because of a push from the left. Also the stiffening attitude of the Western Nations towards Russia has an influence.'[26] The increasing prosperity of business in the postwar era, and its success in avoiding the anticipated stigma of wartime price-gouging, also worked in its favour, Elliott added. Free enterprise was associated not just with freedom, but with prosperity and progress – a correlation which the CAB also took care to reinforce.

One of private radio's arguments that best exploited the Cold War climate was the assertion that the CBC's regulatory powers restricted freedom of speech. The CAB was less strident on this theme in its presentations to the Massey Commission than it had been in previous years. In the past it had argued that the CBC was potentially a partisan instrument of the government of the day which could arbitrarily decide what Canadians 'may or may not hear.'[27] The implication of this line of argument, of course, was that the CBC represented the kind of state tyranny that laissez-faire guarded against. This time the CAB was careful to let this rest as an implied threat, avoiding any direct complaints or examples of such abuses. But extremist elements in the private camp were less circumspect. Station CFCY in Charlottetown told the commission that the argument that radio licences were public property was a cover for the takeover of radio by left-wing groups for their own propaganda purposes. Many businessmen were convinced that the CBC gave leftist organizations and labour unions a platform from which to espouse their views while muffling the voice of business. Newsletters put out by the public relations firm Johnson, Everson, and Charlesworth for private radio interests included material such as an editorial which argued that 'the Pinkishness of the State-owned radio system is indicated by the slanting of the subjects.'[28]

The private station owners' concern about the CBC's advocacy of a particular viewpoint did not prevent some of them from doing the same with their own stations. There were numerous reports of private stations advocating their side of the broadcasting debate on the air. The Massey Commission was shown a copy of a memo from the Alberta manager of the CBC that reported on a program called the 'Voice of Radio' that he had heard on CJCA in Edmonton in March 1948. Unlisted and unintroduced, the 'Voice' followed the evening newscast, and in 'an unctuous soothing delivery which is devilishly clever' gave a commentary on radio subjects which criticized the public system. One such broadcast complained about CBC hockey coverage and ended with the moral: 'That's government in business – that's umpiring the ball game when you belong to one of the teams – Good night.'[29] This sort of activity provided the cultural interests with evidence that privately owned media constituted a greater threat to democratic freedom than state enterprise.

This danger was exacerbated by the fact that there was clearly a trend towards concentration of ownership in Canadian radio. For example, one enterprise, All-Canada Mutually Operated Radio, held shares in eleven privately owned stations, ten of which were in the Canadian West. It also controlled All-Canada Radio Facilities Limited, which sold pre-recorded radio programs to stations that were in turn sold to advertisers. Nor was the trend towards monopoly limited to the medium of radio. Thirty-nine members of the Canadian Daily Newspaper Association were owners of private radio stations. It would hardly be healthy for democracy to have the air waves controlled by a handful of opinionated capitalists. The commission heard from a radio station manager who opposed newspaper ownership of radio on the basis of his own experience of its dangerous consequences. G.S. Henry had lost his position as manager of CJCA Edmonton in 1948 when he had protested against the efforts of the station's owner, who also published the Edmonton *Journal*, to repress news and union advertising about a strike at his newspaper.[30] Wright made a point of questioning private station representatives closely about their ownership and never hesitated to suggest how the trend towards concentration of ownership might be detrimental to the public interest.

The cultural elite's concerns about concentration of media ownership were reinforced by the fact that it was the larger radio interests which were most solidly behind the CAB's efforts to emasculate the public broadcasting system. The CAB position was strongly supported by about twenty stations that appeared before the commission. Seven of the other fifteen stations that made representations were quite happy with the existing system. CKVL Verdun, for instance, told the commission that 'we have no complaints with the CBC at the present time. As a matter of fact, we have done so well under the present system that we wouldn't dare have any complaints. We are very happy.'[31] J.J. Gourd, a Montreal lawyer and owner of three private radio stations, concurred. In his view, the existing system offered small businessmen in radio some protection from being absorbed by larger interests in the inexorable progress of monopoly. He sent a copy of his brief to other private stations, asking for their endorsement.[32] The CAB was alarmed by such independent thinking and dispatched a telegram to all of its stations, telling them to ignore his brief and to endorse the CAB position instead.

In this manner the battle over which form of broadcasting was the most democratic shifted back and forth. It was not the only ground, however, on which the fight for the air waves was contested. The culture lobby also made much of its contention that only a public and national broadcasting system could operate in the public and national interests. Although the private broadcasters had a weaker prima facie case on these points, they were not about to concede any ground without a fight. They countered criticisms of their excessive commercialization, for instance, by portraying advertising as a public service. Advertising was an essential part of modern economic life: it lowered unit costs by raising demand, creating mass markets, a higher standard of living, and greater leisure.[33]

Private stations did their utmost to refute the accusation that they were only out for profit by filling endless pages of their briefs with evidence of their services to their communities. For the most part these consisted of free time and publicity given to local charities and fund-raising events. A station in Moncton, for instance, tried to impress the Massey Commission with evidence of its public-spiritedness by noting that its trade character, 'Lionel the Lobster,' had been given an honorary life membership in the local Kiwanis Club in recognition of his contributions to the community.[34] This probably made a dubious impression on the commission; Massey's ideal Canadian cultural ambassador was not some clown in a crustacean costume. Critics of the private stations countered their attempts to appear public-spirited by noting that this sort of activity provided both good public relations and cheap programming.

Debate about the 'public interest' often overlapped with its nationalistic variant, the 'national interest.' This was another motherhood issue that the CAB did its best to appropriate as its own. It claimed that since the private stations operated at the local level, they collectively represented the nation better than the CBC. In this way they expressed not just the national political will, but the Canadian cultural identity as well. The private stations fostered cultural development at the grass-roots level, the only place where a truly Canadian culture could be expected to originate.

The culture lobby was staggered by the audacity of this claim. One of its most common criticisms of private broadcasters was that they failed miserably to develop culture on the local level. 'The private stations were doing absolutely nothing to develop talent unless it was on the basis that salvation is free,' claimed a musicians' union.[35] Their request that private stations use 5 per cent of their gross revenue to employ Canadian artists had been ignored by the CAB. Wright picked up on such criticisms and asked every private station that appeared before the commission how much money it spent on developing local talent. CFQC Saskatoon complained that such attacks were unfair because 'as soon as we develop talent here it moves elsewhere.'[36] Nevertheless, cultural interests generally credited the CBC with being almost single-handedly responsible for the development of Canadian talent over the previous decade.

The development of local talent was a critical issue because it provided the Canadian content that the nationalism in liberal humanist nationalism demanded. Many of the cultural interests which supported public radio in Canada did so because they thought that it was only under such a system that a distinctly Canadian culture could be developed. As the Canadian Congress of Labour put it, 'If we want a genuinely Canadian culture to flourish and grow strong, we must preserve our genuinely Canadian radio.'[37] It was not just the quality of private radio that was feared, but its tendency to depend on American programming. Cultural interests perceived American programs as unfair competition, produced more cheaply for the massive American market and extended to Canada at a further discount that could not be matched by domestic production. Simple economics meant that commercial radio led inexorably to American radio. But William Guild dismissed as pure conjecture allegations that private broadcasters would increase American programming if they had the chance. Besides, being a neighbour of the United States was part of the Canadian cultural experience; it was neither possible nor desirable to raise an Iron Curtain along the border. Like Jack Kent Cooke, Guild argued that free cultural interchange between the two countries would in fact promote the development of a distinct Canadian cultural consciousness.

Like it or not, it was indeed impossible to seal off Canada from American radio. Border stations beamed signals into the most populous areas of Canada, ensuring that Canadian radio, private and public, was in competition with American radio. And even the most avid nationalist had to admit that American shows like 'Fibber McGee and Molly,' 'Bob Hope,' and 'Lux Radio Theater' were extremely popular in Canada. CKOC in Hamilton presented an audience survey to the commission that recorded a massive switch of Toronto and Hamilton audiences to a Buffalo station when the Jack Benny show began to be broadcast there.[38] Even the CBC had to run popular American shows to keep its audience share.

Although they were stalwart supporters of the CBC in its conflict with the CAB, the cultural interests were not uncritical of the public broadcasting corporation. They were, in fact, very concerned about the increasing commercialism of the CBC itself. The CBC had been running more and more commercials on its national networks in an attempt to make up its revenue shortfalls. Not only did this put it in the unfortunate position of appearing to compete for advertising with the private stations, it also compromised its commitment to serve minority audiences and elevate taste. The CBC justified its use of commercial programs by maintaining that some such programming did fit its mandate and that it needed the revenue to maintain its other more noble pursuits. But the voluntary organizations were not happy with the trend. 'It would be a tragic day in Canadian history if our chief Federal claim to National Good Taste – the CBC – were to fall victim to commercialism,' warned the Arts Centre of Greater Victoria.[39] The private owners, jealous of their ad revenues, were quick to echo this criticism. Here at least was one issue upon which the private broadcasters and the culture lobby could agree.

There were other issues on which the CBC would find itself isolated. Its proposal for increasing radio-set licence fees, for example, met with general disapproval. This attracted more public attention than other aspects of broadcasting policy because it would have had the most direct impact upon most people. CKEY Toronto presented the commission with a public opinion poll that showed that 84 per cent of Canadians opposed the idea of increasing the licence fee, with only 4.4 per cent in favour. The Conservative party had come out in favour of abolishing the licence fee entirely. The press generally concurred.

An editorial in the Vancouver *Sun* argued that now that nearly everyone had a radio, it made more sense to fund the CBC out of general revenues.[40] Friends of the CBC warned that the resentment that would be created by raising the fee would offset any financial benefit to be gained. Other countries had higher licence fees, but they did not live next door to the United States, where private stations provided Canadians with 'free' programming. If Canadians had a clearer understanding of what the CBC did, they would not resent paying the fee, but under existing conditions it was regarded as a nuisance tax.

The drawbacks of this source of funding were offset, in the view of the CBC, by the fact that it provided an independent source of revenue which kept it free from political control. To meet this concern a number of alternative ways in which the CBC could be funded without being subjected to political influence were suggested. Some briefs recommended that the CBC be given a statutory grant, while others thought the answer was to direct all revenue from radio customs, excise, and sales taxes into the CBC's coffers.

The culture lobby criticized the CBC on other issues as well. French-Canadian groups complained that the CBC offered better service in English than in French. French Canadians in Quebec wanted a second French-language network, while those outside of Quebec wanted an extension of bilingual radio service nationwide. A number of other groups protested the CBC's failure to provide any radio service at all to their parts of the country. The CBC told the commission that it was in sympathy with these complaints but that it simply could not afford to provide coverage in some marginal areas. The CBC was also plagued by regional jealousies. Its main production centres were in Montreal and Toronto, and other parts of the country naturally resented this centralization. They griped that broadcasting, like every other important institution in Canadian life, was dominated by an Eastern urban bias. Centralized production also bled local talent out of smaller communities into the centres where work was available.

All of these concerns about radio applied to the new medium of television as well. Great excitement was building about the advent of TV. 'Canada in Range of Television Now!' trumpeted an article in the *National Home Monthly* for May 1949:

A recent Duane Jones survey in the United States reveals how much change there has been in the family life of America among television set owners. Of 1,580 respondents, 92.5 per cent said they listen to the radio less than they did before buying T/V: 80.9 per cent said they went to the movies less: 58.9 per cent said they read fewer books: 48.5 per cent read magazines less: 23.9 per cent read newspapers less.

Conversation and bridge are disappearing, but visiting is increasing. T/V set owners report that 72.1 per cent more children are visiting their homes than before, and after mother has called to pick up Junior, father apparently drops in on his neighbour to watch the fights, for 76.8 per cent found that they had more adults visiting their homes than before T/V. The increase in the consumption of Coca-Cola and Orange Crush is reported to be considerable.[41]

The author's declaration that 'if you have $400, you can buy a television and revolutionize your way of life overnight' epitomized the hype that whetted the public's anticipation of television service.[42]

Under the glare of such curiosity the CBC maintained for television the same basic considerations that determined its radio policy. In its brief the CBC pointed out that the Canadian Broadcasting Act of 1936 applied to television as well as radio. In the national interest, public ownership and control were desirable. And again, adequate funds, through loans for capital expenditures and development costs, then licence fees to carry operating costs, were needed. Indeed, the biggest difference between radio and television was that 'because of higher costs detrimental tendencies in commercial sound broadcasting would be intensified in television.'[43] Concern about American domination of television was even more acute than in radio because the United States already had numerous television stations in operation.

Canadian authorities had been delaying television development in the hope that they could learn from the mistakes of others and minimize the huge start-up costs involved. The Massey Commission was told that to build, equip, and maintain just one television station in Canada would require at least $500,000 for the first year, and that programming would cost about the same amount on top of that. It would take a long time to recoup this investment: reportedly no U.S. television stations were yet in the black. In the face of such daunting financial hurdles, Dunton and his board had decided that it would be necessary to extend the licence-fee method of financing to television. They concluded that a $10 fee would be necessary but hesitated to advocate this before the Massey Commission for fear of a public outcry.[44] Still, they thought it the only fair method of funding because only those who received service would pay during the long period before coast-to-coast coverage was provided.

In the meantime the CAB was exploiting the public's interest in the new medium by claiming that it could provide television service right away and at no expense to the taxpayer. It could do so, however, only if a regulatory set-up similar to the one it wanted in radio was established for television. But the CBC already had the government's blessing in its plans for television development. The interim government policy on television, announced in March 1949, had allowed the CBC to go ahead with the establishment of production centres and transmitters in Toronto and Montreal. Late in 1949 the government lent the CBC $4,500,000 to meet initial capital and programming costs. The CBC was also empowered to grant private licences on the condition that private operators would use its national programming.

Television development would parallel that of the radio system, and the CBC would retain the same controls over television as it did over radio. Numerous applications for television licences had already been made, but the CBC decided to defer any decision on them because it had doubts about the quality of service that these applicants were capable of providing. Instead it suggested that applicants pool their resources with other broadcasters in order to achieve the capital base necessary to support such an expensive undertaking. Needless to say, private broadcasters were not pleased with this decision or the general direction that government policy was taking. Many private interests confessed to the commission that they had serious doubts about having the CBC involved in the new medium at all. A number of private radio stations feared that competition from television would put them out of business and thought that because of this possibility it was only fair that existing radio licensees should be given the first crack at television licences.

Whether the issue was television or radio, it was not hard for interested observers of the commission, including the CAB, to tell that the commission was leaning in favour of the CBC. The culture lobby's arguments made the commission comfortable with its own prejudices, and the commission's own studies only reinforced its opinions. Throughout its public hearings the commission had Dr Charles Siepmann, chairman of the Department of Communications of New York University, analysing commercialization and Americanization of Canadian radio. Early in January 1950 Siepmann submitted a preliminary report to the commission. His conclusions essentially confirmed the culture lobby's suspicions that the profit motive made private stations poor vehicles for cultural development and Canadian content. It was his estimate that many private stations grossly abused their responsibilities within the national broadcasting system by providing 'inadequate and unsuitable' programs.[45] On the other hand, he thought that the CBC largely fulfilled its mandate to produce balanced programming and encourage Canadian talent.

In July 1950, with the controversy of their public hearings behind them, the commissioners gathered at Batterwood, Massey's estate near Port Hope, Ontario, for a series of meetings that included their first extended consideration of broadcasting policy. MacKenzie suggested that the guiding principle in their deliberations about radio should be 'control by the people of Canada of a medium so powerful to affect the opinions and the attitudes of Canadian citizens.'[46] There was general agreement about the need for both private and public radio in Canada, he argued; the problem was determining where to draw the line between the two. This made the question of an independent regulatory body – for both radio and television – the single most important broadcasting issue.

It was at this point that the first ominous signs of disagreement among the commissioners on this central question became apparent: 'Mr. Surveyer expressed his belief that the country as a whole was in favour of the establishment of an independent body to regulate both private stations and the C.B.C. Since the C.B.C. had increasingly become a commercial business, it was clearly in competition with the private stations, yet at the same time it could control its "competitors" to their disadvantage.'[47] MacKenzie immediately attempted to paper over this crack in the unanimity of the commissioners by conceding that Surveyer had a good point but temporizing that the CAB had not given a clear idea of how such a regulatory body would be organized. But the regulatory issue was so fundamental that the breach soon broadened. There was a reasonable case to be made for a separate regulatory body, but friends of the CBC viewed the proposal as a heretical attack on the principle of public broadcasting. Massey, Lévesque, and Neatby lit into Surveyer with a barrage of arguments which echoed the pro-CBC case from the hearings.

Since the CBC's increased dependence upon commercial revenue bolstered the CAB's case for an independent regulatory body, the commissioners tried to find ways of reversing this trend. They conceded that the CBC had to carry some commercial programs to balance its offerings and that it also had to serve advertisers who wanted national coverage. If other sources of revenue could be found, however, they would prefer the CBC to carry these shows without advertising. Davidson Dunton had been summoned to Batterwood to address this issue. He reported that about one-third of the CBC's commercial revenue came from American shows. It would be impossible, however, to get American commercial programs without their advertising content. If the CBC cut out commercial advertising altogether, he continued, it would suffer a devastating loss of revenue, lose popular American programs that attracted audiences to its stations, and have to devise inadequate replacements of its own at great expense.

Despite these apparent constraints, the commissioners maintained that cuts in advertising should be made in any areas where they were at all possible. They felt that the CBC should abandon local commercial business, except in areas not served by private stations. They agreed that as compensation the CBC would need greater assurance that it would have enough revenue to fulfil its plans for the future. Where would the money come from? The commissioners were sensitive enough to public opinion to recognize the danger of hiking licence fees, but at the same time they were reluctant to abandon the existing fee because they felt that the user-pay principle was not only fair but encouraged a healthy direct relationship between the CBC and its listeners. To make up the difference between revenue from existing licence fees and the CBC's needs, they decided that a grant based on the number of home radios in the country should be made from the federal government's consolidated revenue. A formula could be worked out that would lower this grant as advertising revenues rose, thereby removing any financial incentive for the CBC to accept advertising.

Discussion then moved on to less contentious radio and television problems. By the end of the Batterwood meetings the general lines of the commission's broadcasting policies were clearly established; they would be refined and shaped into specific recommendations as the commission worked on its report in the months that followed. During the same period the split between Surveyer and his fellow commissioners would continue to widen despite continued efforts to salvage some sort of consensus on one of the most important questions facing the commission. With this one exception, however, the commission's approach to broadcasting questions resoundingly endorsed the culture lobby's stand against the private broadcasting interests. For those with educational aims and nationalistic sentiments, broadcasting was the single most important means for promoting these interests throughout Canadian society. The private stations would be thrown a few sops by the commission, but for the time being they had again been beaten back by the one-two punch of cultural improvement and the national interest.

7

From Scholarships to University Funding

In an era of jurisdictional disputes and squabbling over taxation powers between the federal and provincial governments, it was not surprising that the Massey Commission would be criticized as an intrusion by the federal government into the provincial domain. The danger of the commission's foundering on provincial recalcitrance was most acute in Quebec, where the provincial government jealously defended its role as guardian of French-Canadian culture. The federal government was prepared to concede the provinces an exclusive sphere of influence in education, if not culture. St Laurent's fears of protest in Quebec ensured that the financial problems of the universities were not among the subjects included in the commission's terms of reference. The order in council which established the Massey Commission instructed it to conduct its investigation 'with full respect for the constitutional jurisdiction of the provinces,' and the commission's only duty that had anything to do with formal education was to advise the government on 'methods by which research is aided including grants for scholarships through various Federal Government agencies.'[1] But a striking thing happened between the time these orders were issued and the commission reported. The Massey Commission decided to recommend federal funding for universities, a major federal initiative in a traditionally provincial field.

There were a number of factors that made it difficult for the Massey Commission to avoid educational questions. Not the least of these was the proclivity of the cultural elite to think of culture as a form of education. Although the commission tried not to extend this connection beyond informal or adult education, the close association between the two made it difficult to ignore formal institutions. Indeed, it was natural that a commission staffed and supported by academics would regard the university, rather than the artist's studio, as the real centre of cultural life in Canada. It was the universities that conserved and disseminated high culture, and the severity of their financial crises eventually lured the commissioners across the blurred line between culture and education.

At the start of their inquiry, however, the commissioners dutifully set out only to recommend improvements to existing federal scholarships and research grants. This in itself was a matter of great concern to the academic community. The Social Science Research Council had published a gloomy overview of the subject by J.B. Brebner in 1945, and things had improved little in the intervening years.[2] Here at least was an open field where much good could be done.

Day was instructed to survey deputy ministers and heads of government agencies who had experience in the area to see how they thought improvements could be made.[3] These bureaucrats appeared at the commission's special hearings on scholarships in Ottawa on 16 and 17 August 1949. The picture they painted was not pretty. With the exception of the National Research Council's semi-independent domain, there existed only a hodge-podge of offerings derived from the needs of particular government departments or the demands of certain vocal constituencies. Most of these civil servants were happy to provide the commission with informed proposals for improvements.

As the commission held hearings across the country, numerous briefs offered opinions on the topic as well. Naturally, universities were the most interested and informed on the subject. One after another they told the commissioners what they already knew: a lack of money excluded some of Canada's best students from higher education. In Prince Edward Island, Saint Dunstan's College made this point in a more vivid fashion than most when it noted that 'enrolment is directly proportional to the prices of farm produce.'[4] The professoriate argued that the federal government should provide not just funding for research at the graduate and postgraduate levels, but a system of undergraduate scholarships that would ensure a steady stream of talent for these higher levels to draw upon. Such scholarships would represent a significant federal initiative in education, but as always, they could be justified on nationalistic grounds. It was argued that the nation was not benefiting from the talents of its best young people because they were blocked from attending university by financial barriers.

The commissioners were receptive to such pleas. As far as they were concerned, the question was not whether scholarships should be improved, but how, and by how much. In the summer of 1949 they established a Special Committee on Scholarships to investigate the subject in detail. MacKenzie's interest in university issues made him the natural choice for chairman, and its roster was soon filled out with a collection of well-known academics and civil servants. Included were Dr George Brown (University of Toronto), Dr Léon Lortie, vice-president elect of the National Conference of Canadian Universities (Université de Montréal), Dr C.J. Mackenzie (chairman of the National Research Council), Dr R.G. Trotter (Queen's University), Dr David Thomson (McGill University), Mr Léon Mayrand (Department of External Affairs), Mr Paul Tremblay (Department of External Affairs), and Dr John Robbins (Dominion Bureau of Statistics). René Garneau, the commission's associate secretary, was the administrative liaison between the sub-committee and the commission.

Although the committee was composed for the most part of university men whose stake in its work was obvious, its other members represented critical interests as well. C.J. Mackenzie was there to look out for the National Research Council (NRC) and to provide the committee with the benefit of its extensive experience with funding research and scholarships. Dr John Robbins was a fixture on any national undertaking related to education in this period; in his work at the Dominion Bureau of Statistics he had for many years been the only government official in Canada with a nationwide view of the subject. The Department of External Affairs was there because it was interested in promoting international student exchanges and scholarship programs. Canada was not offering anywhere near the same number of scholarships to students from other countries as were offered to Canadians from abroad. But there was more to the department's interest than an effort to balance this inequity. It was anxious to establish a system of scholarships in Western Europe to help absorb several million dollars of Canadian credits that were trapped there by currency regulations.

At the first meeting of the scholarships committee on 22 August 1949, MacKenzie quickly outlined the administrative questions that the committee would have to wrestle with in devising a scholarships plan. He wanted to find a method of administering awards that would minimize federal-provincial power squabbles. MacKenzie and other university presidents were more than eager to get the federal government involved – they had toiled too long under the unenlightened parsimony of provincial treasurers. On the other hand, too much federal control would provoke fears that the central government was intruding on provincial turf. The answer, MacKenzie suggested, was to invest administrative responsibility in a third party. With this in mind, he posed another important question for the committee:

a) would it be better to appoint a Council representing humanities, social sciences, arts and music, and to ask the National Research Council to administer the scholarships granted by this humanities and social sciences Council, or b) to organize a completely separate body, a kind of Humanities and Research Council, which would take charge of administering scholarships to graduates and under-graduates in humanities and social sciences?[5]

MacKenzie favoured the first proposal, but the multiple responsibilities proposed for such an agency attracted interest from so many different groups that its final form would remain controversial for months to come.

MacKenzie also set out some other basic questions that would have to be dealt with in devising a new system of government scholarships: 'How many students should be assisted on each level? ... What proportion of scholarships to Humanities and Social Sciences? What proportion to Sciences and Research?'[6] Here were the two fundamental issues that would most preoccupy the committee. To begin addressing them, MacKenzie put committee members George Brown of the University of Toronto and John Robbins to work on a preliminary report on scholarships in humanities and social sciences and assigned David

Thomson of McGill and C.J. Mackenzie a similar task for research and scientific studies.

Later, at the urging of the commission, MacKenzie asked Brown and Robbins to examine research in the humanities and social sciences as well. This request reflected the commission's conviction that science was in less need of aid than other areas of study. Neatby and Lévesque pointed out that simply increasing existing funding would do nothing for the humanities, which were almost entirely ignored by both the federal and the provincial governments.[7] The neglected state of the humanities in an age of science was, of course, a hackneyed theme within the culture lobby.[8] The commissioners, however, were in the unusual position of being able to do something about it. Their determination to take decisive action was reinforced by their public hearings. The Humanities Research Council of Canada, for example, presented a lengthy list of problems facing scholars in the humanities in Canada: inadequate libraries, heavy teaching loads, insufficient time for study, inadequate funds for publishing, as well as a paucity of postgraduate scholarships.[9]

There was agreement that the scholarships situation reflected the general malaise of a modern world which ignored the humanities at its peril. Even scientists appearing before the commission conceded this point. The vice-president of Mount Allison University, Dr Harold McKiel, an engineer by training, was asked by Neatby whether he thought that the sciences promoted international cooperation more than the humanities:

MCKIEL: ... after fifteen years as Dean of the Faculty of Science, I can say that I do not believe that. I believe that the only possible solution to international problems, the only basis on which international understanding can be attained, is an adequate knowledge of your fellow man. And that comes from the humanities and social sciences and not from science ... it's too highly technical, too highly restricted, without providing an adequate understanding of the world in which we live.[10]

Léon Lortie told the commission that 'in the present state of the world, and in order to cope with the terrible situation that science has borne upon us, we need students and graduates in the social sciences and the humanities.'[11] Despite his background, Surveyer also agreed that the humanities were neglected and deserved special attention.[12]

This recognition of the sad plight of the humanities at a time when the world needed them most created a situation in which a commission ostensibly responsible for the arts, letters, *and* sciences concentrated almost entirely on the first two and paid little attention to the last. The sciences seemed to be doing well enough without any help from the commission. C.J. Mackenzie, president of the NRC, told the commissioners that the council was already able to fund every promising graduate and postgraduate student in the sciences. 'We have never felt embarrassed because of lack of money for scholarships,' he reported.[13] The commission's MacKenzie asked him whether there was a need for more undergraduate scholarships to attract more students into the sciences, but C.J. maintained that they were already getting the numbers they needed. The commissioners respected C.J. Mackenzie and were happy to leave science to someone who knew something about it. They preferred to concentrate their attention on getting the same level of funding for their own interests.

A lack of pressure from the scientific community made it easy for the commission to follow this tack. There were demands from various sources for projects such as a national botanical garden, a national zoological garden, and a national aquarium. Some scientific organizations also appeared before the commission to call for better funding and better coordination of research among sponsoring bodies. But these appeals were not nearly as numerous or as agitated as those that came from interests representing the arts and letters. The commission trimmed its sails accordingly; at a meeting on 9 September 1949 it elected to make its special studies in the sciences fewer in number and more general in scope.[14]

The commissioners found it easy to agree that the humanities were in greater need of help than the sciences. But the other major point originally raised by MacKenzie – 'How many students should be assisted on each level?' – provoked a spirited debate that arose out of fundamental differences in their views on the role of the university. The controversy hinged on whether national scholarships should be unapologetically elitist and provide substantial funding for the very best students, or whether it would be better to spread the same amount of money among more students to ensure wider access to university education. It was, in short, the old question of whether to emphasize quality or quantity.

The commission questioned knowledgeable witnesses closely on this point. In a typical exchange, Massey asked President Kirkconnell of Acadia University whether he thought that scholarships should be selective and based on outstanding merit, or widespread and aimed at encouraging every capable student. Kirkconnell replied that scholarships should be what their name indicated – a recognition of intellectual quality. From the commissioners' table came an echo of agreement from Hilda Neatby. Major General E.L.M. Burns of the Department of Veterans' Affairs took a utilitarian view of the federal government's interest in the area and came to the same conclusion: 'While it may be desirable that in a democratic society all young people who have the "wit and will" should have a university education, it is assumed that the State is most vitally concerned in securing the interests of a relatively small percentage of candidates of outstanding potentialities and that at the outset the proposed National Scholarships would be awarded primarily upon "capacity" rather than "need" – on a quality rather than quantity basis.'[15] Arguments were also made that Canada should specialize and concentrate on quality in particular areas because it was too small a country to aspire to universal excellence.

On the other hand, Dr W.P. Thompson, president of the University of Saskatchewan, favoured spreading scholarships around like manure to see what would spring up. Dr A.E. Kerr, president of Dalhousie University, agreed: he was fed up with geniuses, he told the commission, and wanted more merely capable students to get scholarship money. The salutary effects of the Direct Veterans Assistance (DVA) plan were often tendered as evidence of the rewards that could be reaped from a generous system of scholarships which would send to university young men and women who otherwise had no hope of postsecondary education.

Since the scholarships question divided the cultural elite into elitist and populist factions, Neatby and MacKenzie were destined to clash over the issue. Although both believed that elites were not undemocratic if based on a meritocracy accessible through equality of opportunity, their disagreement hinged on the degree to which the door of opportunity should be swung open. Conflict on this point first became apparent at a meeting of the scholarships committee on 17 March 1950, at which the first concrete proposal for a system of undergraduate scholarships was discussed. Brown and Robbins presented a scheme which provided for a few prestigious scholarships and a large number of lesser awards. This scheme would recognize outstanding young scholars while providing considerable support for about 20 per cent of Canadian university students.[16]

Dr R.G. Trotter of Queen's criticized the proposal, preferring a few unconditional scholarships combined with a generous loans scheme for the lesser lights. Lortie was of the same mind, although he favoured a few scholarships of nominal value instead of widespread loans. As it happened, MacKenzie was unable to be at this meeting because of business in Vancouver, and Neatby had attended to keep the commission informed of developments in his absence. She plunged into the fray in support of Trotter's point of view. The result, as Robbins later told MacKenzie, was that the 'Scholarships Committee has run into "heavy seas." '[17] It was only with difficulty that Brown and Robbins were able to pilot their proposal through the committee, and Neatby stirred up enough opposition to indicate that stormier passages lay ahead.

At first Massey was not opposed to the Brown and Robbins plan. Garneau informed MacKenzie that the chairman liked the idea of having two types of undergraduate scholarships. He was worried, however, that the bursaries and loans proposal was a bit too extensive.[18] Massey's initial response would soon change, however. Robbins reported to MacKenzie that 'Miss Neatby reported the outcome [of the meeting] to Mr. Massey and apparently frightened him off completely.'[19] Neatby feared that wide access to universities would do more to lower their educational standards than to raise the level of public intelligence. She managed to raise serious doubts in Massey's mind, and the chairman decided that the whole idea of undergraduate scholarships should be put aside on the grounds that it was outside the commission's terms of reference.[20]

At the same time MacKenzie was criticizing the scholarship proposal for entirely different reasons. He was not unsympathetic to Massey's concern that the proposal was too ambitious, but his apprehension on this count rested on the more practical concern that the cost involved might scare off the government. He thought that a more flexible proposal would stand a better chance of being introduced because it could employ whatever amount of money the government was willing to put into it. But the real basis of MacKenzie's opposition to the scholarship proposal was exactly the opposite of Neatby's objection to the plan. As he put it: 'The main issue ... is whether this scheme is to be a democratic one ... providing opportunity for a number of young men and women of good ability who might not otherwise be able to attend a university, or whether it is to be based on ... the aristocratic principle ... Personally, I am very strongly in favour of the first ... on the basis of my own experience ... I am absolutely certain that the second scheme would not be acceptable to the majority of Canadians.'[21] It was typical of MacKenzie that his response was based on a pragmatic assessment of public reaction as well as principle. The public wanted access more than excellence, and there was, he thought, room for both. 'The principle of making such a limited number so eminent is wrong, I think,' he noted in the margins of the scholarships proposal, 'and may kick back.'[22]

With Massey planning to drop undergraduate scholarships and MacKenzie hoping to keep the scheme but scrap its elitist elements, it appeared that a nasty clash was ahead. In a letter to Robbins in early April, MacKenzie hinted that this incipient breach was indicative of a larger rift that divided the commission on other issues as well. This time, however, he was prepared to take a stand if Massey tried to drop the entire proposal at Neatby's instigation:

I am not surprised at what you write, in view of the temperament and the experience of the individuals concerned. Technically, they probably are right, in that I imagine our terms of reference were limited in their conception to the scholarships and research already undertaken by the Federal Government. However, my interest in this Royal Commission is largely centered on expanding this field. My own view, therefore, is that those of us on the Committee should go ahead and prepare a very strong report and present it to the Commission. It will then be their responsibility to use it in any ways that they see fit.

...

P.S. I would not be too worried about the views of either Miss

Neatby or the Chairman in respect of our own report. If necessary, I am prepared to put in a minority report on this issue. I would like to have the Committee's memorandum as a basis for this.[23]

Both Massey and MacKenzie were planning to attend the next scholarships committee meeting, which was scheduled for Monday, 10 April 1950. There the issue would be decided.

MacKenzie arrived in Ottawa the Saturday before to allow himself time to confer with his allies and scout the ground. His efforts were not in vain. When the meeting convened and Massey raised the question of undergraduate scholarships, it became apparent that MacKenzie had gotten to him beforehand and arranged a compromise. Instead of ruling out the possibility of a broad scheme, Massey limited himself to warning that 'the greatest care should be taken to avoid giving ground for controversy with respect to the Commission's Report.' But he added: 'the Commission might draw attention to the fact that it had been urged from a number of quarters that something should be done to take the place of D.V.A. – to help students from rural areas and others handicapped by lack of means, and to aid universities – but that these things should be said in such a way as to avoid creating a controversial atmosphere.'[24] MacKenzie leapt at this opening, reinforcing Massey's tentative acceptance of the proposal by commenting that he 'questioned the wisdom of adopting a legalistic interpretation of any part of the Terms of Reference as it might limit the whole Report.'[25] MacKenzie and Massey had also found common ground in their concern that the government might be frightened by too ambitious a scheme. MacKenzie told the committee that no definite numbers of students or amounts of money should be mentioned; instead, basic principles alone should be set out. The crisis averted, a relieved committee went on to discuss other business.

For anyone knowledgeable about university finances it was a small step from scholarships and research grants to a consideration of direct federal funding for universities. University representatives invariably punctuated any discussion about scholarships with the observation that sending more students to university through an improved scholarships scheme would only increase the financial burden upon universities. Like many other members of the cultural elite, Léon Lortie wore many hats. He appeared before the commission in Montreal as a representative of the Association canadienne-française pour l'avancement des sciences. In an interchange that seemed to have been staged for the benefit of the public, Neatby asked him whether federal scholarships should not be supplemented by direct grants to the universities: 'LORTIE: We entirely agreed on this because we are all University Professors here, and we know ... every time a thousand dollars is received by a University in grant or for a fellowship it actually costs three hundred to the University to maintain this man or this project in operation.'[26] To offset these expenses the universities wanted the government to pay them a supplementary grant for each scholarship as it did under the DVA plan. Supplementary grants were not enough to meet the universities' wider needs, yet they set a precedent of federal funding that made the prospect of direct federal grants to the universities seem less radical. In this fashion, scholarships led to supplementary grants, which in turn paved the way for direct federal funding.

The financial pressures that were squeezing Canadian universities were described to the commission in great detail. Partly because of an influx of war veterans, university enrolments in 1949 were more than double their wartime levels. The government's Direct Veterans Assistance plan was scheduled to end by 1951. In the short term this meant that the universities would have to bear the fixed costs of investments made in larger staff and facilities as enrolment and tuition fee revenue dropped. In the long term enrolment was expected to equal and surpass existing levels, but then it would not be accompanied by federal supplementary grants as it was under the DVA plan.

The universities contended that funding from the federal government was their only hope. There were no other obvious sources of revenue available. Provincial contributions seemed to be at their limit, given the onerous demands upon the limited budgets of provinces in the postwar period. Endowment revenue and private donations might be increased somewhat through shrewd management and successful fund-raising campaigns, but not enough to cover escalating costs. Student fees had already been raised, and to increase them would only further limit access to universities on the basis of economic status.[27]

The commissioners' sympathies on this issue were not hard to predict. All except Surveyer and Massey were university teachers or administrators by profession. Massey, of course, had taught at the University of Toronto as a young man and was currently its chancellor. Neatby was on record as supporting federal funding for universities. MacKenzie was identified with the cause even more closely – in fact, he was an active collaborator with the university lobby. As president of the National Conference of Canadian Universities (NCCU) for 1947–8, he had been a leading advocate of federal funding for universities. He stayed in touch with the current NCCU executive and helped it plot strategy and plan its brief for the Massey Commission.

There was never any question in the minds of the commissioners about whether the federal government should fund the universities. The question was whether it could, given the political dangers involved. At first Massey was very careful to respect the prime minister's wishes and not overstep the commission's terms of reference. When the NCCU appeared before the commission on 23 August 1949, for example, Massey began the proceedings with a gentle warning that 'we have to limit the subjects on which we make recommendations to the Government to those which are specifically mentioned in our Terms of Reference.'[28]

The universities recognized the constitutional difficulties which made the Canadian government hesitate to grapple with their problem. They pointed out, however, that the federal government was already involved in education and a beneficiary of the work of Canadian universities in areas such as defence, scientific research, resource management, health and welfare, vocational education, and the DVA plan. They also justified presenting their demands to the commission on the grounds that Canadian universities were the institutional bastions of the nation's cultural life. The NCCU quoted John Stuart Mill's declaration that 'a university exists for the purpose of laying open to each succeeding generation, as far as the conditions of the case admit, the accumulated treasure of the thoughts of mankind' and went on to comment that

this is particularly true in Arts and Letters for from the faculties and schools in which these are studied and practised come the citizens with trained minds, liberal and informed opinions, good taste, and critical judgement without whom a national civilization is impossible. It is in these university departments, too, that the rare creative minds, the future Canadian writers, musicians, artists, and architects find the ideal environment for maturing their techniques and both opportunities and encouragement to produce. Moreover there are no alternative nurseries of a truly Canadian culture.[29]

The NCCU made it clear that Canadian universities would not be able to continue to play this role if some sort of financial help was not forthcoming. It believed that constitutional quibbles about federal funding could be overcome by devising a 'no strings attached' formula for administering university grants. The NCCU also suggested that the federal government should give money only for technical and professional education, areas where direct federal benefits were clearly evident. Then the universities could shift the funds freed by this subsidy into support for the humanities, which were most closely associated with the educational prerogatives of the provinces under the British North America Act.

The NCCU's pleadings brought the issue of federal funding for universities to public attention. Its presentation was reported by major dailies across the country. 'Universities Face Financial Crisis without Federal Help, Inquiry Told,' warned the headline in the Toronto *Globe and Mail*.[30] Lévesque recalls that the emergence of this issue caused consternation in the highest levels of government. St Laurent, for example, was quite alarmed by the NCCU brief. Spying Lévesque on the street in Ottawa, he buttonholed him and demanded to know what was going on. 'Pourquoi touchez-vous à cette question?' he asked. 'Nous avions pourtant assez de problèmes sur les bras.'[31]

St Laurent was of course most worried about the impact of this proposal in Quebec, where provincial control over education was traditionally guarded as a critical line of defence for French-Canadian culture. The commission got an idea of French-Canadian nationalist opinion on the subject in its Montreal and Quebec City hearings. The Chambre de commerce de Québec, for instance, argued that the universities' problem was not provincial parsimony but the federal appropriation of taxing powers. The federal government should give the provincial governments back the tax money they needed to do their jobs.[32] Nevertheless, opinion in French Canada was by no means unanimously opposed to the proposal. Although some organizations rejected the idea outright, others supported it on the condition that money was given without interference in provincial control over education. The Comité permanent de la survivance française en Amérique, for example, told the commission that while it felt the provinces had exclusive control over education, the federal government could give education grants if there were no strings attached. Support for such proposals came from other groups, including the Association canadienne des éducateurs de la langue française:

> La commission royale d'enquête à reçu les recommendations les plus variées et les plus généreuses concernant l'aide aux institutions d'enseignement, aux professeurs et aux étudiants. L'Acelf trouve la plupart de ces recommendations très heureuses et parfaitement justifiées ... L'idéal serait que chacune des provinces puisse répondre adéquatement à ce double besoin puisque ce sont elles qui ont dans notre pays la mission immédiate de suppléer les parents dans l'éducation des enfants et des futurs citoyens. Et si les provinces ne peuvent suffrire, pourquoi l'Etat fédéral ne leur viendrait-il pas en aide en leur accordant un subside spécialement destiné à l'éducation, mais administré exclusivement par les provinces.[33]

The commission made sure that the prime minister was aware that opinion in French Canada was not as irreconcilably opposed to federal funding for universities as he had supposed. Garneau sent St Laurent copies of briefs from French-Canadian organizations that had shown sympathy for the idea. As the months passed, Pickersgill also ensured that St Laurent heard about the support that the universities' proposal continued to receive in the commission's hearings.

There was little serious opposition to the idea in English Canada. Indeed, in many provinces there was a clamour for not just a federal bailout of universities, but for federal funding for public schools as well. Ministers of education from disadvantaged provinces asked for money to ensure 'more equitable educational opportunities for all Canadian children.'[34] Saskatchewan's Woodrow Lloyd added the by now familiar 'education for democracy' argument:

> Historically despotisms were based on slavery, fear and igno-

rance. In the modern world dictatorships, making use of terror methods, controlled press, denial of information to the people and subordination of the thoughts and actions of the masses to the purposes of individual despots or ruling cliques, have essentially the same foundations. Democracy on the other hand rests on the emancipation of the human spirit, on individual freedom, and on education for private living and social participation. No one in the Western World today would deny that education is the very life blood of free institutions.[35]

The Canadian Teachers' Federation and numerous provincial teachers' associations were even more outspoken in demanding federal aid for public school education. Many areas in Canada were suffering a severe teacher shortage, and teachers saw federal funding as the only possible help in sight.

Supporters of federal aid for public schooling realized that their proposal would face even greater resistance on constitutional grounds than funding for university education. To surmount this barrier they used all the arguments employed by advocates of federal funding for universities plus a few new ones of their own. One of their novel contentions was that the constitution should evolve along with society. Strict conformity with the letter of the BNA Act, argued the Alberta Federation of Home and School Associations, was unrealistic as social needs changed over time: 'Believing that government policies should be revised from time to time in accordance with the needs and changing conditions, we ... are convinced that national implications and the vastly increased cost of education merits [*sic*] grants from a government which didn't exist when the present system of financing education was established.'[36] The Alberta Teachers' Association went even further, suggesting that the provinces had defaulted any rights in the area of education because they had not done their job under the BNA Act. The Canadian Teachers' Federation recognized that federal aid was 'a need born of a shift in taxation' but, unlike French-Canadian groups that perceived the same problem, thought that the answer was a larger federal role in education rather than a transfer of taxing powers to the provinces.[37]

Years before, Brooke Claxton had declared in a speech that 'the constitution does not prevent the federal government from giving substantial assistance to education. Direct assistance might be given in several ways.'[38] This comment from a prominent member of cabinet had bolstered hopes that the central government might be able to help public schools. But there was little chance that the Massey Commission would recommend federal aid for public education. Such an initiative would represent a far more serious intrusion into provincial jurisdiction than university funding. Besides, the commissioners identified more with the universities and were personally affected and alarmed by their financial problems. They could also find more justification for taking an interest in university finances on the grounds that the universities played a direct role in fostering the arts and letters. In short, helping the universities held greater rewards and fewer risks. There is no evidence that the Massey Commission ever seriously contemplated recommending federal aid for public schooling; funding for universities was radical enough, and even a recommendation in this area was by no means certain.

It was becoming more likely, however, as the universities lobbied the media, the commission, and the government. In June 1950 the NCCU's representatives were back in Ottawa, this time to pressure the commission in private. NCCU president F. Cyril James argued that the universities had become the commission's problem whether they liked it or not: 'Principal James ... pointed out that unless there is some clarification of the responsibilities of this Commission in connection with Federal aid to Universities, the public and government will assume that this problem has been solved, if the Commission's report should be silent on this matter.'[39] By this point the commission, torn between respect for its terms of reference and its desire to help the universities, was in a quandary. James kept pushing. 'The entire question of Federal Aid to Universities is supposedly under review by this Royal Commission,' he insisted; 'if relief is not given, the Canadian Universities will face grave embarrassment.'[40]

But was the question the commission's responsibility or not? MacKenzie thought that James should talk to St Laurent and remind him of the uncertainty about the commission's mandate in this area. Massey agreed:

The Chairman suggested that if the Prime Minister and the Government decide that Federal aid to Universities is a direct responsibility of this Commission, this Commission will undertake to make recommendations. The Chairman suggested that it would not be at all improper for the delegation to the Prime Minister to suggest that the present obscurity be clarified, but he pointed out that this Commission must be careful not to put an excessive interpretation on its Terms of Reference; this whole matter of Federal aid to Universities was charged with emotion, but it was evident that a strong case had been made by the visiting presidents for including the present plight of the Humanities and all appropriate remedial measures within the Terms of Reference of this Commission.[41]

In fact, the NCCU had been lobbying the government in general, and St Laurent in particular, throughout the commission's tenure. That very month the prime minister assured James that help would be found 'by some means or other.'[42] He later told James privately that it would make it easier for the federal government to satisfy the NCCU's requests if the universities continued to generate public support for their proposal.

Evidently the prime minister was preparing to alter the government's course on this issue. St Laurent was sympathetic to the universities' plight and eager to help them out if he could, and it now seemed that some sort of aid was politically possible. The Massey Commission's hearings had made a difference by showing that most of the country was strongly in favour of federal funding for universities and that even in French Canada there was guarded acceptance of the proposal. This impressed St Laurent and others who had formerly feared that such a move would trigger a bitter constitutional controversy. It was evident that there was political support across the country, including Quebec, which could offset whatever problems Duplessis might create. Moreover, the opposition parties in Parliament were coming out in favour of such a move.[43]

At a series of discussions on university issues in mid-July the commission continued conscientiously to avoid the subject of direct aid, concentrating only on scholarships, research grants, and their administration.[44] But in early September Massey wrote to MacKenzie that 'Miss Neatby and I have come to the conclusion that we can and should recommend Federal Aid to Universities.'[45] The prime minister made the government's approval of this change public in a convocation speech at the University of Toronto in October. With Massey, as chancellor, on the podium, St Laurent declared that 'many of us recognize increasingly that some means must be found to ensure to our universities the financial capacity to perform the many services which are required in the interest of the nation.' He then turned to Massey and told him that he hoped that his commission would 'be able to help us find a proper solution to that difficult problem.'[46] Thereafter in the House of Commons St Laurent fielded inquiries about federal aid for universities with the reply that the report of the royal commission would be awaited before action was taken.

Everyone was concerned about the implications of such a decision for Lévesque, who would be the target for most of the flak that a federal initiative in education would draw in Quebec. Massey diplomatically offered him a veto over the proposal: 'We are all agreed on the subject. But we realize that because of the special situation in Quebec, Father Lévesque will, as a consequence, face painful and hard opposition. As our mandate does not specifically request us to concern ourselves with this question and as we have always respected the particular responsibilities of each of us, I propose that we set aside this particular recommendation if Father Lévesque does not consent to it.'[47] Lévesque went along with the proposal 'même si j'entendais déjà éclater les tonnerres dans le ciel québécois.'[48]

He was not simply caving in to pressure from his anglophone colleagues. Lévesque had good reasons of his own to desire a federal presence in university funding, for he had personally experienced the dangers inherent in a situation in which universities were entirely dependent upon the favour of a provincial premier. Just that spring he had written to MacKenzie describing the pressures exerted upon academic freedom by Duplessis, pressures brought to bear on him personally in revenge for his opposition to the premier:

Notre gouvernement provincial est pratiquement devenu une dictature. Il exerce tout particulièrement sa pression politique, même sous forme de chantage, sur l'Université. En fait, il contrôle déjà de façon partisane l'Université de Montréal. Et depuis quelque temps il veut réduire l'Université Laval à la même situation. Je pourrais vous en donner de multiple preuves et exemples concernant plusieurs Facultés. Qu'il me suffise de vous citer le cas de notre Faculté des sciences sociales.

M. Duplessis a récemment annoncé au recteur, Monseigneur Ferdinand Vandry, que notre octroi annuel de $50,000. serait coupé de moitié. Pendant ce temps, ses principaux lieutenants répètent à qui veut l'entendre que les $2,000,000. qui restent à donner par le gouvernement en vertu de la souscription de $4,000,000. votée au Parlement, ne seront versés qu'à la condition que le Père Lévesque quitte l'Université. En plus de ce chantage financier, le gouvernement exerce contre nous une pression morale visant à discréditer l'enseignement et les professeurs de la Faculté que le prime minister lui-même a publiquement accusé de propager l'*'erreur.'* Ils semblent avoir juré d'obtenir particulièrement la tête du professeur Maurice Lamontagne et celle du doyen. Inutile de vous dire qu'un des griefs qu'ils ont contre moi c'est ma participation à la Commission royale.[49]

Vandry had until then resisted the pressure of the government, but Lévesque feared that money troubles and continuing government coercion might soon force him to capitulate. With this on his mind, it was hardly surprising that Lévesque would support federal funding for universities.

Once the commission had decided on this recommendation, there still remained the problem of devising a method by which federal aid could be given with the least possible appearance of federal intrusion into provincial jurisdiction. One suggestion was a system of direct grants per student per annum similar to the means by which DVA funds had been awarded to the universities.[50] But Jack Pickersgill had what he thought was a better idea:

I recall pointing out to Larry [MacKenzie] that a per càpita grant based on the provincial population would serve as a rough measure of equalization since, generally speaking, the poorer provinces had fewer students in proportion to their population. But I insisted that the stronger argument was that such a formula would be entirely automatic and could not possibly be construed as discriminating among provinces or institutions, and that any other formula was certain to be attacked as an invasion of provincial jurisdiction.[51]

This proposal was accepted and recommended by the commission.

The fact that such a major recommendation as federal funding for universities was not foreshadowed in the Massey Commission's terms of reference has over the years raised suspicions that the commission was operating on a hidden agenda designed to foist a federal appropriation of new constitutional prerogatives upon an unsuspecting public. Although Claxton's and Pickersgill's original hopes for the commission and MacKenzie's scheming with these government insiders and the NCCU executive lend support to such a conspiracy theory, the real reasons for the commission's adoption of the university funding proposal were neither very secret nor exclusively elitist. To a large extent they represented the response of a politically sensitive democratic government to its perception of popular will. Massey scrupulously followed St Laurent's wishes to avoid involving the commission in questions regarding formal education until the prime minister himself changed his mind on the issue. When that change did come, it was in response to the universities' lobbying efforts, but these efforts were backed up by evidence of broad public support that emerged in response to the publicity received by the universities during the commission's hearings. If St Laurent had not believed that federal funding had changed from a dangerous imbroglio into a winning political issue, he would not have instructed the commission to pursue the matter.

The reasons that federal funding for universities became a feasible political initiative are more difficult to define. It was, however, the type of policy that fit the postwar mood of Canada. Canadians were coming to expect that the state would play an active role in bringing about the better postwar world everyone anticipated. This expectation was strongest in an area such as education where there was no conflict between state intervention and private interests as there was in broadcasting. Education itself was considered one of the prime agents of the progress that was popularly envisioned for the postwar world. Although culture was suspect, Canadians knew the value of education – it paid off with tangible rewards like better jobs with higher salaries. Finally, the nationalist mood of postwar Canada opened the way for an extension of the central government's role. Time and time again the Massey Commission heard arguments which justified a federal role in education on the basis of the national interest.

Behind all these factors was the plain fact that it was the federal government alone that had the money necessary to maintain, let alone improve, Canadian university education. The scholarships and direct funding recommended by the Massey Commission can be seen as simply an extension of the DVA plan and other existing federal programs in the field. As such they represented another case in which the wartime powers and tax appropriations of the central government were translated into a permanently expanded federal role in peacetime. Pushed and jostled by these various dreams and realities, the Massey Commission went stumbling rather than sneaking towards one of its principal recommendations.

8

Hand-Outs for
Longhairs

Twentieth-century Canada had not been the most hospitable environment for the nurturing of the arts. Most Canadians had been too distracted by war and depression to improve themselves with poetry and painting or to support their local theatre or symphony. Even at the best of times Comstocks and Boetians stalked the land. The Vancouver Little Theatre's description of the tribulations it had endured through the years gave the Massey Commission some indication of the perilous nature of the average cultural organization's existence over previous decades:

> Through depression, war (even Pearl Harbour [*sic*] blackout) floods, street car strikes, fog, blizzards, lack of public interest, falling off of its membership, near loss of its theatre building through threatened bankruptcy, being turned out of its rented workshop buildings and moving four years in a row to often most inadequate rehearsal space because it was all that could be found, the Vancouver Little Theatre has kept these years of unbroken performance through the loyalty and determination of a small number of its members, many of whom have been associated with the organization since the beginning and are still either active or audience members.[1]

Many similar enterprises had not managed to survive such hazards at all. In the late 1940s, however, the cultural community was confident that these years of trial were behind it.

The Massey Commission was told that there was a new spirit in the land, that interest in the arts was quickening as Canadians settled into a new era of peace and prosperity. The Fredericton Art Club reported that the arts were being accepted more widely as the nation moved beyond the pioneer stage of its development: 'We know that art has been regarded as a sissy thing and not something done by a strong, healthy people. In recent years this view has changed. Art is now considered one of the more important factors in healthy development. Art is now considered as something that contributes to the preservation of our democratic way of life.'[2] The dedicated few who had tended the flickering flame of civilization through barbarous times expected to see their stewardship rewarded as interest in the arts rekindled throughout the country. They were also determined to capitalize on the new spirit in the land by putting in place institutional and financial supports that would ensure that a high level of activity in the arts would become a permanent feature of Canadian society.

A parade of witnesses testified that a new burst of enterprise was evident in every area of cultural activity. Mrs Margaret K. Hall, who was questioned on literary developments by Massey in Fredericton, gave a typical assessment:

MASSEY: We gather from what various people tell us that there are more books being read in Canada now than there were ten years ago. Is that in keeping with your experience?
HALL: A great many more, Mr. Chairman. We are selling more and more every year. Last year was our big year.
...
MASSEY: Would you say that Canadian books are being read to a greater extent than they used to be?
HALL: Yes.
MASSEY: And that there are more of them?
HALL: Yes.[3]

The Canadian Music Council's Dr Ettore Mazzoleni noted a similar development in his field, testifying that 'there has grown up in Canada in the last ten years a very active and vital body of young creative talent in music.'[4] The same kind of flowering was reported not just in music and literature, but in painting, drama, arts and crafts, and even ballet and opera.

Some even went as far as to declare that a cultural 'renaissance' was underway in Canada. The Discussion Group of Hamilton thought that the increase in cultural activity represented the dawn of a new era. It saw

> an unprecedented stirring in Canadian mental life. The output of Canadian books has increased as well as the popular response to them, a genuine Canadian literature is beginning to emerge, an extraordinary number of people are trying to paint, dance and act. Art exhibitions, the Dominion Drama Festival, the Ballet Festival, better support for libraries, the radio forums, the more frequent performance of Canadian music, even if it cannot yet profitably be published, are all evidence of new intellectual life in this country, signs that we are passing out of pioneer and colonial conditions and becoming an independent, mature society.[5]

Perhaps this was less a renaissance than a return to levels of cultural activity that might be expected during a period of peacetime prosperity, but cultural nationalists, excited about signs of progress elsewhere in natural life, liked to think that the nation was making great strides culturally as well. Some credited the CBC and the NFB with precipitating this change; others attributed cultural growth to the work of national voluntary organizations. But the metaphor describing the change as part of Canada's 'growing up' from a crude pioneer society into a civilized mature nation was by far the most common way of explaining the new vitality in the arts.

Despite the impression conveyed by such reports, Canadians were not yet donning tutus *en masse* and taking to the streets to prance and pirouette to the strains of the lute. The culture lobby admitted that the 'renaissance' had yet to percolate throughout society. Reports from the grass-roots suggested that a significant amount of voluntary cultural activity was still oriented towards lowbrow forms of leisure like hockey. In fact, the cultural community's postwar plans for encouraging the arts through the construction of community centres had run head-on into this reality. Professor Alan Klein, vice-chairman of the Canadian Welfare Council, regretfully informed the commission that hockey alone stimulated energetic local action and support: 'in communities where the interest began in a community centre in which you would have a wide range of participation in leisure time activities, in arts, crafts, music, and drama, including sports, the concept ... got warped ... because the strong and well-organized group, the group with financial backing, largely was a hockey interest. [What] started out to be a War Memorial Community Centre ... ended up in very many cases in Canada as glorified hockey – with one activity.'6 The Northern Ontario Art Association confirmed the dangers of losing control of the community-centre movement to sports organizations. 'The athletic interests have been very aggressive,' it reported. 'Sometimes a community centre has begun as an ideal among the cultural people and it has been taken over by the athletic interests and made into a sports palace.'7

Similar admissions of the precarious status of culture came even as its defenders emphasized the new vigour evident in the arts. The contradiction between these different portrayals was not hard to explain: it was a posture calculated to justify government subsidy. Canadian cultural activity had to be made to look promising, but not so promising that it could make it on its own. Conversely, it had to appear beleaguered, but not beyond saving. The object was to make a government rescue operation seem both necessary and worthwhile.

These criteria alone, however, were not enough: an appearance of crisis was also necessary to spur the government into action. To this end the cultural interests argued that Canadian cultural development was at a critical turning point. The future of the arts in Canada hung in the balance: they could either flourish or collapse, depending, of course, on whether or not aid from the federal government was provided. In drama, for instance, the commission was told that although there were as yet no significant professional playwrights, actors, or facilities, there was enough energy, talent, and enthusiasm to develop serious theatre in Canada. Miss Dorothy Somerset, an English professor at the University of British Columbia, claimed that 'theatre has reached a critical point in its development in Canada. There is a quotation which I cannot complete at the moment, but it is something to the effect that "There is a tide in the affairs of men ..." and I feel that tide is here in Canadian theatre.'[8] The commission was told that nothing more than a limited amateurism could ever be expected from Canadian theatre unless new financial support was forthcoming. Calls for aid were framed in similar terms by musicians, dancers, painters, and writers.

When arguing for arts subsidies the culture lobby also chose to downplay indigenous competition from popular obsessions such as hockey and instead blame its problems on external threats to the nation's cultural life. It maintained that Canadian culture needed state support to counteract market forces which otherwise allowed the country to be dominated by international mass culture. In literature, for example, cultural development was not just a matter of writing books – it required coming to grips with the economic factors which hampered Canadian publishing. The Book Publishers Branch of the Toronto Board of Trade pointed out that the development of Canadian literature was limited by Canada's small population, large territory, two languages, diverse regions, pioneering areas, and cultural variety. Neither Canada as a whole nor any of its regions constituted an economically viable publishing market. 'We are almost a multitude of small islands of culture in a large sea,' the publishers concluded.[9] Stranded on these islands, Canadians read more foreign books and periodicals than any other nation in the world. The free market constantly undermined any efforts to build a nationalistic Canadian culture.

Cultural nationalism went hand in hand with anti-Americanism because it was easy to associate mass culture with the United States. The Vancouver and Mainland Branch of the Canadian Authors Association, like many representatives of the culture lobby, blamed American cultural imperialism for Canada's problems: 'For years we Canadians have been flooded with American moving pictures, American radio programs, American magazines, American books. Something should be done before the Canadian viewpoint is lost entirely. We have become unsure of anything Canadian in concept, just because it is Canadian and therefore unheralded and unknown.'[10] The consensus was that Canadian culture was beaten down and starved out by the economic clout of the United States. The Canadian Arts Council claimed that as a result it was impossible to make a living as a full-time artist in Canada.

This was somewhat misleading. Many commercial cultural enterprises were surviving, and even thriving. It was the type of highbrow culture that the cultural elite associated with Canadian culture that was struggling. The commercially successful Theatre Under the Stars company in Vancouver told the commission that when first building an audience it had learned to avoid the words *Canadian* and *artistic* in publicizing a performance:

> If the leading man in a popular show were an American, his achievement in the United States would be heavily publicized, while the Canadian leading lady playing opposite him would be publicized on the basis of her qualities but without reference as to where she had been born or where she had performed ... Any ideas or even phrases which might be considered 'long-hair' were deleted from advertising and publicity, even to the extent of calling operettas 'Musical Comedies.' The curse of the 'art' label was, and still is, combatted by inserting at least one modern-clothes musical into the season's repertoire.[11]

This suggested that Canadian culture was unpopular because the general public made the same association between Canadian culture and high culture as the elite, and stayed away from anything that had the least whiff of either. But most witnesses before the Massey Commission preferred to blame Canadians' lack of interest in indigenous culture as a mark of colonialism or the famous Canadian 'inferiority complex.'

Others concluded that Canadians were simply dazzled by commercial razzmatazz and that all Canadian culture needed was more American-style salesmanship. Promoting culture was just like selling a consumer product such as a radio, according to Mrs Fingarson of the Vancouver and Mainland Branch of the Canadian Authors Association. In its brief her organization had elaborated on this point: 'Sell Canada to the Canadians. Every Canadian wants to be proud of his nationality, but at present it is a nebulous thing. Radio, screen and publications should be employed to tell about our wonderful country, our history, our heritage. If this one job is done thoroughly, we feel that many of the existing ills will cease to be. Soon Canadian writings will be demanded and proper recognition and remuneration will fall into place behind ... this educational program will take time.[12] But the idea of flogging Canadian culture like any other product in a competitive market-place did not sit well with the more elitist members of the culture lobby. In their minds, a commercial Canadian culture would be little better than the commercial American culture it displaced. Instead of lowering Canadian culture to the level of the masses, the masses should be edified to a level where they could appreciate indigenous high culture.

The culture elite did not interchange the words *educate* and *sell* as freely as Fingarson and other boosters in the culture lobby. In the liberal humanist glossary, education was not a matter of converting the subject to a particular cause, but a process that awakened individuals to a fuller range of cultural possibilities, enabling them to exercise free choice. But even this process was associated with nationalism, for the development of such a citizenry was seen as a possibility in Canada but not in the United States.

The elite's refusal to go commercial meant the problem of how to promote Canadian culture remained. Making a living as a 'serious' artist was hard elsewhere as well, but not impossible, since most other countries could sustain at least some highbrow culture in their larger cultural markets. Moreover, in older, wealthier countries, private foundations or rich individuals often functioned as patrons of the arts. In Canada, however, it seemed that the government was the only entity with the money and mandate to do the job. In the postwar period the chance of obtaining such aid seemed to be better than ever before as the government contemplated new social programs. The culture lobby's emphasis on the effects of market forces on Canadian culture reflected the growing acceptance of the idea that the state should compensate for the shortcomings of the capitalist economy. In this case government intervention was justified by more than just a concern for the social good; it was a matter of national sovereignty as well. Numerous briefs emphasized that the development of a national identity was impeded by foreign mass culture and that national unity and international prestige suffered as a consequence. In this way nationalism was used to invoke the state's sense of responsibility for its own jurisdiction and survival. The idea of the nation had to be backed by the strength of the state; government aid was required if Canadian culture was to flourish.

The projection of Canada's image abroad was often cited as a way in which cultural development served the interests of the Canadian state. As Joseph Whitmore, chairman of the Canadian Ballet Festival Association, told the commission: 'we are concerned with ballet in Canada not only for itself but, as we state in the first page of our brief, as a national medium of artistic propaganda. We feel, as expressed there, that the ballet can do a great deal for Canada and the Canadian Government.'[13] The example of Britain's Sadler's Wells Ballet, which had recently completed an international tour to great acclaim, was often cited to demonstrate the benefits a country could reap from cultural diplomacy. Cultural relations abroad were a natural concern for Canada, which had suddenly found itself thrust into the international spotlight without much time to prepare, or much confidence in its manners. The commissioners worried about the fact that Canadian diplomatic missions did not have qualified staff for cultural relations and publicity work. Nor were there any support systems to help artists, scholars, exhibitions, or performing arts groups travel abroad. The inclusion of such responsibilities in the commission's terms of reference reflected the concerns of internationalists in the government like Lester Pearson; indeed, the Department of External Affairs was looking forward to receiving advice from the commission on the subject.

The question of cultural relations abroad was related in turn to the issue of Canada's role in the United Nations Educational, Scientific and Cultural Organization (UNESCO). Educational and cultural groups had been lobbying for a national commission for UNESCO ever since Canada signed the treaty which created it in 1946. In the wake of World War II, UNESCO's commitment to the premise that international peace could only come through mutual understanding among the world's nations was an attractive if fuzzy concept that inspired pious enthusiasm in many quarters of the culture lobby.

It was an idea that Neatby found revoltingly naïve. When a representative of the Canadian Teachers' Federation, which had been lobbying the federal government for a national commission for UNESCO, told her that UNESCO's purpose was the 'promotion of peace through understanding,' she pounced: 'You should not agree with the statement that perhaps the better people understand each other the more likely they are to fight? ... The countries that have fought in modern times have been the ones where the scientific, educational, and cultural associations have been the most close and intimate.'[14] Neatby repeated the attack whenever supporters of UNESCO appeared. 'Do you think the recent war was due to misunderstanding on our part of what Hitler wanted to do?' she asked Mr Tom Parker, president of the Nova Scotia Teachers' Union. 'Isn't it our job to teach the children to tolerate the tolerable and not to tolerate the intolerable?'[15] Lévesque had to intervene to save the well-meaning witness from a continued assault.

Despite Neatby's doubts, the UNESCO problem was indelibly inscribed on the commission's agenda. The enthusiasm of voluntary associations would have ensured its prominence even if it had not been included in the commission's terms of reference. Day had noted earlier that implementing UNESCO programs in Canada and nominating the Canadian delegation to the annual conference constituted a problem which 'always has aroused great heat in Canadian literary and artistic circles and which has been a source of embarrassment to the department [of External Affairs].'[16] Although this was quite a different question from arts subsidies, it was an area in which the government was already involved with voluntary associations and wanted the commission's advice on how to manage its relations with them. Since these same voluntary associations were deeply involved in the country's artistic life, the UNESCO issue pulled the government one step closer to assuming responsibility for sponsoring the arts.

The idea that the government should subsidize artists provoked serious opposition from outside the culture lobby. The question of federal intrusion into a sphere of activity rightly belonging to the provinces arose in the realm of culture just as it had in the area of federal aid to education. Indeed, Quebec premier Maurice Duplessis saw the entire mandate of the Massey Commission as an affront to provincial rights. Massey did not have the same scruples about federal support for culture in the broad sense, however, as he maintained about aid for education. The culture lobby naturally shared his view on the subject. The Manitoba Drama League presented a typical opinion:

In conclusion, the Manitoba Drama League would state that while acknowledging that under the Art of Confederation [*sic!*]

education is a provincial matter, the general status of the arts in
Canada and in Manitoba in particular needs the subvention of
the Dominion government, in the matter of funds and in the
clear evidence of a sympathetic understanding of the position of
the artist in Canada. Unless the subvention is forthcoming, the
League feels convinced that the current stagnation of the arts in
Canada will continue until all that is left is a degeneration into
artistic barbarism.[17]

A number of reasons were given for seeking federal rather than provincial aid. Provincial governments were not as enlightened about
culture as the federal government, it was thought, and were less likely
to give money. Nor did they have as much money to contribute. Even
if they did donate, it would be for reasons that would no doubt be
tied to provincial interests, and this would hardly satisfy the pan-
Canadian vision of cultural nationalists.

Most of the limited number of briefs received by the commission
from individual Canadians were inspired by opposition to the idea of
government subsidies for the arts. A certain Mr J.S. McMahon felt
that the culture lobby was a privileged group bent on promoting its
special interests at the expense of the general taxpayer: 'I am an
ordinary citizen and taxpayer. I have no culture and as I seldom listen
to the CBC I am afraid I will never have any. I feel that the trouble
with the intellegenzia [sic] is that they are not willing to pay for their
own pleasures. If a man enjoys football (which is a form of art) he is
willing to pay $2.00 per seat to see a game and support his team, but
if a man, or woman, enjoys a symphony orchestra, he thinks it should
be supported by the taxpayers.'[18] Such criticism did not trouble the
members of the cultural elite greatly. Most did not think of themselves
as a self-serving clique: their cause was justified in terms of the social
good and the national interest – as they defined them, of course.
Those who did think in terms of interest-group politics no doubt
considered themselves as worthy of subsidy as other interest groups
already favoured by government policies.

There were other criticisms of the idea of government cultural
subsidy which troubled members of the cultural elite even less. In
some quarters of Canadian society, the prospect of government aid
for culture was perceived as evidence of socialism, if not totalitari-

anism. One particularly right-wing version of such criticism was published with more conviction than syntax:

> Royal Commission on cultural affairs continues to collect magnificent samples of loose thinking. Association of Adult Education, mildly leftist, but including a few ardent Socialists, demand that there should be set up a Government Commission to direct cultural affairs in Canada. The consequence would be the sort of control of public thinking so well described in the book, '1984.' The reformers hate freedom of thought, as well as of speech and action. Free men might not fall in with their ideas.[19]

The cultural lobby was not impressed with such simplistic denunciations because it saw cultural development as the only way in which individuals could be raised to a level where they could fully exercise their democratic rights and freedoms.

This attitude reflected the modern recognition that liberal goals could only be achieved through positive action rather than a detached reliance on laissez-faire principles. David Smith, a friend of Neatby's from Saskatchewan who was involved in adult education and sat on the Saskatchewan Arts Board, expressed this view eloquently:

> I have sympathy with the intent and the emotional flavour of the feeling for voluntary effort. Implicit in these statements are ideas about the democratic tradition of freedom from arbitrary government and the opportunity to act on one's own initiative. Unfortunately our thinking on these matters is still back at the time when we were fighting to escape from arbitrary government. We still talk of freedom as though it were freedom *from* some outside control. We need to move on to consideration of how the freedom *to* is to be organized. Our definition of freedom is negative rather than positive. This is understandable if we are fighting to get out from under restrictions or controls but our society suffers seriously from the notion that elbow room is all that is required for freedom to bear fruit.[20]

The intelligentsia, the electorate, and even the government had come to accept positive liberalism in the realm of economic and social programs, but extending it into the cultural arena aroused fears of state control over free thought. As another submission pointed out, however, mass culture itself had that effect. 'The development of mass productive methods in the fields of cultural entertainment has tended to discourage individual initiative,' wrote the Calgary Allied Arts Centre.[21] By providing alternatives to mass culture the government would in fact be stimulating individualism. These types of analyses turned the tables on the standard laissez-faire critique of government intervention, making commercial mass culture the real authoritarian threat and government intervention a means of promoting individual freedom.

The advocates of state subsidies for the arts were confident that whatever dangers it involved could be avoided through careful planning and management. Although they dismissed the spectre of cultural totalitarianism as a right-wing bogey, they did admit the danger that government funding could degenerate into a quagmire of political patronage and undue influence. The same problem applied in the field of public broadcasting, however, and could be avoided by creating a body like the CBC which was independent of the government in its operations and financing.

Another critic warned that by mixing nationalism with socialism the culture lobby was creating a particularly potent concoction which had had dangerous effects in recent memory. 'Hitler tried it, with very destructive results,' he warned. 'The Russians are trying it.'[22] Such warnings from isolated individuals made little impact, however, compared to the dozens upon dozens of submissions which demanded federal aid in the cause of cultural nationalism. Members of the culture lobby saw Canadian culture as beleaguered, not bellicose; they wanted to restore it to health, not transform it into a monster. Moreover, the fundamental political and cultural values that they associated with Canadian nationalism made it intrinsically antithetical to fascism and communism. Not only was Canadian culture associated with democratic ideals, but the principle of tolerance arising out of the bicultural fact made any mutation of Canadian nationalism into a monolithic creed unlikely. In fact, the cultural elite felt that Canadian nationalism could provide a salutary example to the rest of the world of how such dangers could be avoided.

Quite apart from the dangers of an activist state, the cultural elite was faced with questions about the compatibility of bureaucracy and creativity. These were expressed forcibly by David Brock of Vancouver, another one of the handful of individuals who submitted a brief critical of the culture lobby's goals. He ridiculed the idea that a culture could be created by government decree:

> ... the painful fact remains that most art is the product of inner conflict and even agony. Happiness imposed by act of parliament or from a full ice-box will never produce a single work of art. It is the opinion of Christopher Morley that if you had given John Keats free access to enough doughnuts and chicken wings and other snacks at midnight, you could have prevented him from writing any poetry at all ... poetry of sane men is beaten hollow by poetry of madmen. This is probably true of all the arts, as far as a certain purity and a certain ultimate magic are concerned. Has the Commission been urged to give Canada a greater supply of lunatics, and to become, as it were, a commission-in-lunacy in a strange new non-legal sense? ... The song of Beauty and Art and Love is indubitably a stinking song when composed and sung by the kind of self-conscious beauty-lover and culture-lover now imploring your aid ... In fact (and here lies a great danger) the government will surely have to establish an artistic quarantine station in order to determine which artists are healthy and deserving of encouragement, and which must be excluded from our truly and typically Canadian scene ... Can you foster a national culture by design, not accident? And if you can, is it bound to be a good thing?[23]

Here was a question that was troubling the cultural elite. The liberal humanist creed balanced its belief in traditional high culture with the liberal notion that a culture could develop only as the spontaneous creation of voluntary effort. There was no question that a culture created under centralized direction would be an artificial monstrosity that would be worse than having no national culture at all. No culture at all, however, was exactly what was expected if decisive steps were not taken to promote Canadian cultural development. Again, the benefits of government aid for the arts outweighed the risks, especially since the risks were recognized and could be guarded against.

The way to avoid all of these related dangers – totalitarianism, politicization, patronage, excessive nationalism, or artificiality – was to find a means by which government aid could encourage but not direct cultural activity. Not all of the proposals made to the commission met this criterion. The idea that the government establish a ministry of culture, attractive for the prestige and power it would bring to the field, was rejected because it would place too much control over the arts directly in the hands of a faceless bureaucracy controlled by political masters. On the other hand, suggestions such as improving prizes for distinguished works or encouraging arts festivals involved no interference with the creative process, but were not comprehensive enough to promise any real improvement in cultural activity.

The community centre concept was very popular with certain cultural interests. The centres were often promoted as war memorials since the cultivation of the arts had a central place in the vision of the better world for which the sacrifices of the war had been made. The Orchestre symphonique de Québec was one of many organizations to underline this connection: 'nous exprimons le regret que les deniers dépensés pour l'érection de monuments de tous genres en hommage aux héros des deux dernières guerres n'aient pas été employés plutôt pour la construction de centres civiques servant à la fois de points de ralliement où notre population aurait constamment sous les yeux le souvenir de ceux qui sont morts pour la patrie, et de centres d'éducation populaire destinés à stimuler toujours de plus en plus le goût du bon et du beau dans tous les domaines.'[24] Drama groups, which needed elaborate facilities more than other arts organizations, were particularly enthusiastic about community centres. The centres were also envisioned as facilities for instruction in the arts and for the display of touring art exhibitions. However, some of the support for the idea derived more from civic boosterism than from an interest in culture, and detractors argued that buildings alone provided no guarantee that the arts would flourish. It was pointed out once again that amalgamating high culture with other interests in community centres might only ensure that the less popular pursuits would be squeezed out.

By this time the community centre idea was in any case losing out to the concept of a quasi-governmental council for the arts. It was not much of a surprise when this suggestion was made during the hearings of the Massey Commission: it had long been bruited in cultural circles. Lord Keynes's writings on the Arts Council of Great Britain were very influential at the time. The cultural elite looked to the British council as a model of how the worst dangers of state intervention could be circumvented. Massey himself was on record in *On Being Canadian* as supporting such a plan:

> It [the Arts Council of Great Britain] now carries on these activities on a permanent basis and all its money ... comes from the British taxpayer, although in its administration it preserves independence from civil service control. We would do well to study such a successful experiment in state aid. If offers us a useful model. We need public money for the encouragement of our cultural life, but we want it without official control or political interference. That is why a Ministry of Fine Arts or a federal department of National Culture would be regrettable. The very phrases are chilling. The arts can thrive only in the air of freedom.[25]

The arts council idea was attractive to the cultural elite because it satisfied all of their concerns about the negative potential of state aid. Here was a body at arm's length from the government to allow subsidy without bureaucratic control or political interference. Unlike community centres, it was also at arm's length from the public in order to protect it from the tyranny of popular taste.

From the very beginning of their work the commissioners had considered it probable that they would recommend the establishment of an arts council. They discussed the possible functions and composition of such a council during their first meetings in May 1949. Informed observers also expected that an arts council would be one of the commission's principal recommendations: it was mentioned in 102 submissions to the commission and discussed in four of the commission's special studies.

In fact, the recommendation of an arts council was generally regarded as a *fait accompli*. This was illustrated by the character of discussion on the subject in the commission's public hearings. The commissioners' interest was focused on how such a body should be composed rather than on whether it should be created in the first place. Concern with such details put them well ahead of the culture lobby as a whole, whose briefs made only vague suggestions that it should be patterned after the Arts Council of Great Britain or, less frequently, the NRC. The commissioners had specific questions on whether the council should be composed of artists, lay people, or representatives of the voluntary associations, and they often had to pump witnesses to get the kind of opinions they wanted.[26]

In the summer of 1950, with most of their public hearings behind them, the commissioners held extensive and detailed private discussions on the arts council proposal. They concluded that it should be composed of lay members, but stipulated that 'there should be mandatory consultation between this Council and the Cultural Agencies.' The 'Canadian Council for the Arts and Letters,' as they tentatively titled the body, would report to the prime minister and have no formal connection with any departments of government. Its 'fundamental purpose' would be 'to stimulate and to help existing voluntary organizations of proven competence.'[27]

The range of functions that such a council should assume became a matter of extensive debate as the commission's work progressed. Should there, for instance, be a council for the arts as well as a council for the humanities and social sciences? It would make sense to have bodies in each of these different areas to play the role performed by the National Research Council in the sciences. A similar problem arose regarding Canada's external cultural relations. In Britain the Arts Council of Great Britain handled domestic cultural matters, while the British Council was responsible for cultural relations abroad. Should they recommend a similar division of responsibility between two councils in Canada? If so, should the council concerned with external relations also serve as a national commission for UNESCO, or should yet another separate body be created? If a UNESCO commission was established, should it handle all relations between Canada and the United Nations and its various agencies?

Massey's preliminary thinking on this subject was that an UNESCO commission might 'share also something of the functions now performed by the British Council or by the Arts Council of Great Britain.'[28] A letter from Archibald Day to MacKenzie's assistant, Geoffrey Andrew, affirms that at the beginning of its discussions on the issue the commission was thinking in terms of creating one agency which could provide domestic arts subsidies, manage Canada's cultural relations abroad, and serve as a national commission for UNESCO: 'From what I can gather in preliminary conversations, it seems very likely that this Royal Commission will give some thought to the establishment of a body similar to the Arts Council of Great Britain, which would serve also as the Canadian equivalent of the British Council, and could also undertake the much less important duties of a National Commission for UNESCO.'[29] Such early ruminations were by no means conclusive. At this point, for example, the idea of a council for the humanities and social sciences had not yet come up; it would emerge later out of the work of MacKenzie's scholarships committee. The commissioners picked up the issue again once their public hearings had concluded more than a year later. MacKenzie, Lévesque, and Neatby discussed it during meetings in Ottawa from 12 to 17 July 1950. The strength of demands made in public hearings for action in each of these areas had convinced them to abandon Massey's original idea of an omnibus agency and recommend the establishment of separate councils for the arts, external cultural relations, and UNESCO. The UNESCO commission would, however, be part of a committee responsible for UN affairs in general.[30] Since neither Massey nor Surveyer could attend these sessions, it was agreed that these conclusions would be tentative and subject to the approval of the commission as a whole. The following week, the entire commission gathered at Batterwood for the intensive series of meetings that would settle its policies on major questions. Massey quickly set about reversing the trend towards a proliferation of agencies. This time the commissioners agreed that the Canadian Council could handle both domestic and foreign cultural affairs. For the time being a separate humanities and social sciences council and a separate United Nations council remained in the plans. Ultimately, however, the commission would decide that these too should be absorbed into a single multi-purpose council.

There were many reasons for this decision. There was some concern that several bodies with related jurisdictions would create wasteful duplication of effort. The commissioners were also sensitive to the danger of appearing to be reckless bureaucratizers to a public which would not be familiar with or convinced of the need for government initiatives in each of these areas. But the consolidation of functions into a single council was a policy that was largely based on the commissioners' assessment of the political prospects of their recommendations. They decided that it would be much more difficult to get the government to set up a number of councils than it would be to persuade it to set up a single agency. The probability of the establishment of an omnibus council would be enhanced by the greater importance it would gain from its many functions. If such a body was created, it could always spin off different councils with specialized functions later on.

It was for its recommendation for the creation of the Canada Council that the Massey Commission would be best remembered. Indeed, the commissioners themselves regarded this as the single most important proposal to come out of their work.[31] There were good reasons for this sentiment. In areas such as broadcasting, university education, or federal cultural agencies, the commission was wrestling with established institutions and policies; it found itself involved in constitutional controversy, sordid squabbles with private interests, or tedious administrative questions that would continue to rankle long after it finished its work. The arts, on the other hand, were a field that they had almost entirely to themselves. Here there was the chance to create something new, something unsullied by the claims of rival factions or established interests, something that could significantly change the Canadian cultural scene.

The issue of subsidies for the arts inspired the purest expression of the beliefs and goals of both the commissioners and the culture lobby in general. In making its claim for arts subsidies, for example, the culture lobby clearly set out the connections it saw between its interests and the interests of the Canadian nation. In order to recruit the national government as a patron for the arts it took pains to emphasize issues of national sovereignty and downplay popular cultural preferences. By inferring that the popularity of lowbrow culture was the result of American influence, the culture lobby again reinforced the association of Canadian cultural nationalism with high culture.

Even the mechanism suggested by the culture lobby for the dispensation of aid to the arts spoke volumes about its leadership and goals. Like the cultural elite, the arts council was to be well connected to the government and well insulated from popular influence. Critics may have seen this bastion of high culture as a privileged enclave for a special interest group, but the cultural interests saw it as a base of operations for the improvement of the masses and of Canadian liberal democracy. Care was taken to ensure that the government itself would not be able to use the council to control cultural development. Again, the cynic might think this gave the cultural elite the best of both worlds: government money without accountability. But the culture lobby did not think of the council as a means of directly aggrandizing its own power. The council was supposed to encourage rather than direct cultural development. This stipulation was rooted in the liberal conviction that a centrally directed culture would be both politically dangerous and culturally artificial, but it also reflected the nationalist imperative to create an indigenous culture with popular appeal. Suspended somewhere between government and the people and belonging wholly to neither, the arts council proposal was the bureaucratic embodiment of the cultural elite and its liberal humanist nationalism.

9

Cultivating the Hinterland

The sorry state of the handful of cultural institutions that the federal government had acquired over the years had supplied part of the pretext for establishing the Massey Commission. Here was one area in which the federal government's cultural role was largely unchallenged, if unfulfilled. As the commission's work progressed, other aspects of its mandate stole the show. Nevertheless, institutions such as the National Gallery, the Public Archives, and the National Museum also had their parts to play in the commission's emerging cultural strategy.[1] Ideally these institutions served cultural nationalism in three ways. Their primary function was to be central bastions of national culture. From this base they could also act as national leaders in their fields, setting standards and offering services across the country. Finally, they also served as national status symbols that adorned the nation's capital by posing as monuments to Canada's heritage, learning, and taste. This last role was a matter of image more than substance and gave federal cultural institutions a value to the nation that extended beyond their service to particular cultural interests.

These were the ideal roles of these institutions. In reality, they were too underfunded to take the lead in national cultural life and too rundown to impress tourists. They were sources of embarrassment rather than pride for many Canadians. The exception was the National Film Board, which excelled at serving the country as a whole and had won international recognition. The NFB also suffered from the handicaps endured by its sister institutions, but instead of collecting artefacts it produced a product that could be easily distributed around the country. The Massey Commission wanted to see all federal cultural institutions acquire the resources necessary to exert a similar national influence to the fullest extent possible in their fields.

Discussions about federal cultural institutions were somewhat dull compared to the policy battles being waged in other areas. Invariably they involved estimating what was required in funding, staffing, accommodation, and administration to fulfil each institution's existing mandate and to extend its influence and prestige. Once again the National Film Board was the exception. The NFB's critics charged that it was an agency packed with profligate longhairs, bureaucratic despots, and 'commie' spies. This attack launched a lively dispute that generated almost enough excitement to compensate for the tedium of discussions about the national importance of improving the curatorship of rock samples at the National Museum and other such arcana.

The general problem affecting every federal cultural institution was a lack of money. The National Museum, for example, had a budget of $177,500 for 1948–9. With this it was supposed to gather and hold natural history material of scientific and economic interest, conduct research in the natural sciences, and 'educate the public concerning the Natural History and resources of Canada.'[2] There simply was not enough money to fulfil this mandate, museum officials complained, comparing their funding to that of other natural history museums to underline their point. The American Museum of Natural History, with a budget of over $2 million, had more full-time scientists at work in its Insect and Spider Division than there were on the entire National Museum staff. If the much greater population of the United States was taken into account, this budget was not all that disproportionate on a per capita basis. But in a field where a city museum like the Chicago Natural Historical Museum had an annual budget of $1.1. million, Canada's National Museum was obviously in the minor leagues. When museums outside the natural history field were also taken into account, Canada came off looking still worse: it spent $30,000 on museums for every million citizens; the corresponding figures for Great Britain and the United States were $80,000 and $100,000 respectively.[3]

The most visible evidence that federal cultural institutions had too little money could be seen in their accommodations. The National Gallery provided a good example. It was housed in a wing of the National Museum's Victoria Building that was cramped and inaccessible. Gallery officials told the commission that what they needed most was a new building in which the gallery's paintings could be properly stored and displayed. There were no environmental controls in the Victoria Building to protect valuable paintings from deterioration. The fact that the gallery began at the back of the museum's dinosaur collection was thought to aptly represent the place of art in the government's priorities, if not in national consciousness. Those who listened to gallery officials describe their building as a fire-trap sitting on a geological fault could have been forgiven for imagining that at any moment the gallery might burst into flames and sink slowly into the underworld as a judgment of the gods upon a race of Philistines.

The federal government had never paid much attention to its cultural institutions. It had acquired most of them in a haphazard manner that was aptly illustrated by their administrative arrangements. The National Museum of Canada was a bureau of the Mines, Forests and Scientific Services Branch of the Department of Mines and Resources, a situation that derived from its establishment by the Geological Survey in 1841. The Historic Sites and Monuments Board was part of the National Parks Service of the same department. The National Gallery, on the other hand, was under the Department of Public Works. No wonder Brooke Claxton had hoped for the consolidation of all of the government's cultural functions under the management of one branch of government.

A few submissions to the commission recommended the creation of a cultural ministry for this purpose. However, this proposal competed with the idea of creating a government mechanism for arts funding and, as we have seen, ultimately foundered on fears of institutionalizing excessive government interference in culture. This left the administrative problems of federal cultural institutions unresolved, and the commission continued to receive recommendations that they should at least be grouped together and placed under the Secretary of State or some other minister. The commissioners had given some consideration to such a recommendation earlier on. They were genuinely interested in finding some way of ensuring better coordination and cooperation between government cultural institutions. Ultimately, however, they decided that bureaucratic tinkering would only distract attention from the underfunding that really crippled these institutions. Their debate about administrative questions was subsequently limited to considering whether the National Gallery and the National Museum needed boards of trustees to shelter them from direct control by government departments that were insensitive to their special needs.

The Public Archives proposed a different type of administrative reform that would affect the entire government. It wanted to see the establishment of a comprehensive records management system that would provide for the automatic and compulsory transfer of inactive government files to a public records office. Such an office would enforce access restrictions and could turn over files of historical interest to the Archives. A memorandum prepared for the commission by the new Dominion archivist, Dr Kaye Lamb, emphasized that if given the necessary resources the Archives itself could play the role of a public records office. Lamb also wanted to see the Archives get enough money to launch a more active acquisitions policy.

The culture lobby generally supported officials of the cultural institutions in their demands. It was not content, however, merely to see the existing institutions strengthened: it wanted to see new government cultural institutions established as well. Various briefs suggested the creation of a national orchestra, a national theatre, and a national opera. Massey himself was a strong advocate of a national portrait gallery like the one in Britain, which he thought would be a popular attraction. From the science community came pressure for the establishment of a national botanical garden. Disparaging comparisons were made between Canada and South Africa, which had one, Australia, which had four, and even British Guiana, which had two. Other science interests wanted a museum that would cover more than just natural history. The commissioners themselves regretted that the National Museum was predominantly a museum of natural rather than human history. The only museums of the latter type operated by the federal government were the ramshackle historical collection at the Public Archives and the War Museum of the Department of National Defence. A variety of proposals for new museums were made, and it soon became clear that the commission had another complicated issue on its hands.[4] A Special Committee on Museums was set up in August 1949 to look into this and related matters.[5]

One new federal cultural institution – a national library – was already in the works as the Massey Commission deliberated. Plans for the library were nothing new; it had been promised by successive governments since John A. Macdonald's day. But this time something was finally being done. The Canadian Library Association (supported by the Royal Society of Canada, the Social Science Research Council of Canada, the Canadian Historical Association, and the Canadian Political Science Association) had submitted 'A Joint Brief on a National Library for Canada' to the government on 18 December 1946. The brief included an appendix full of resolutions in support of a national library from voluntary bodies across the country – a display of solidarity among cultural interests reminiscent of the Radio League's successes years before. The government was finally prodded into action. On 9 June 1948 the House of Commons Joint Committee of Both Houses on the Library of Parliament passed a resolution which called for the establishment of a bibliographic centre as a first step towards creating a national library. The resolution was approved by the House of Commons on 11 June 1948, and soon work was under way in compiling a bibliography of Canadiana. The government seemed committed to going ahead with the project.

The commission established a Special Committee on Libraries and Public Records to look into issues concerning the Public Archives and the proposed library,[6] and soon this committee was debating the question of the proper relationship between the new library and the Archives. By its second meeting, disagreement on this point had divided the committee into opposing camps: 'It was pointed out on the one hand that the work of the librarian is very different from that of the archivist and entails a different method and a different viewpoint; and on the other, that physical proximity is highly desirable, that an archives must have a working library, and that division of existing collections between the two institutions would present some difficult problems. After considerable discussion and the expression of a number of divergent views it was agreed to differ.'[7] This issue simmered unresolved for almost a year. Eventually the commissioners came to support the idea of a combined archives and library building in which the two institutions could exist autonomously yet benefit by sharing information and services.

The culture lobby followed the gestation of the national library with interest: over a hundred references were made to it in briefs submitted to the commission. This attention showed how federal cultural institutions were increasingly important focuses for the activities of different cultural interests on a national level. Just as the development of the national library was followed closely by the Canadian Library Association, the Public Archives was a special concern of the Canadian Historical Association. The National Film Board was avidly supported by film councils across the country. Each federal cultural institution had its own particular constituency of support within the cultural elite and the larger cultural lobby, and these constituencies themselves were gaining new support from the increasingly educated and affluent public of the postwar era.

There was general agreement on the library's purpose: it should concentrate on collecting Canadian materials and making them available nationwide through an inter-library loan network. Like every other federal cultural institution, it was faced with the challenge of providing a centre of excellence and decentralized services at the same time. These dual roles were especially daunting in a country of Canada's vast physical size and scattered population. But the culture lobby would not countenance national cultural institutions that were only central bastions of culture. It demanded touring exhibitions or loans programs that would circulate their resources around the country. As the Saskatoon Archaeological Society pointed out, the National Museum's claim that it was 'centrally located and readily reached by the streetcar' betrayed the sort of centrist bias that regional cultural interests were trying to overcome.[8] An equitable sharing of federal cultural expenditures required some presence for these institutions outside of Ottawa.

The different interests of the national cultural elite and local members of the culture lobby were reflected in this issue. National pride and elitist standards demanded centralized excellence; national unity and the encouragement of local cultural activity necessitated decentralized services. Both demands were based, however, on something more than just unvarnished greed for special favours from the government. Each cultural interest was convinced that its particular area of concern was an important aspect of national cultural development. The desire for improved services in these areas also served the idealistic goal of bringing the advantages of high culture to the Canadian people. It was only proper for a democratic nation to make these cultural resources available to as many of its citizens as possible.

The National Gallery provided an example of how this was already being done. H.O. McCurry, its director, told the commission that its loan exhibition system made it an international leader in this field. The program's beginnings aptly illustrated the maxim that necessity is the mother of invention. When fire destroyed the Parliament Buildings in 1916, the House of Commons and the Senate temporarily moved into the National Gallery, which literally had to take its show on the road. Touring exhibitions had been part of its programming ever since. Gallery officials readily admitted that there was a need for more travelling exhibitions, but the lack of safe local facilities for the display of paintings and uncertainty about whether they would be handled and shipped properly while on tour restricted the quantity and quality of tours that could be sent out. In the meantime, they offered other types of extension work, including art films produced in cooperation with the NFB, educational radio programs made with the CBC, and the distribution of small reproductions of Canadian paintings through schools.

Although the commission would note that 'the briefs are unanimous in urging the extension of National Museum services, including travelling exhibitions, expert lecturers and increased publications,'[9] it became apparent that the National Museum was not as interested as the National Gallery in serving local institutions. Dr F.J. Alcock, chief curator of the National Museum, was disillusioned by his experience of past experiments with the idea: 'There has been the odd time when we have made, more or less, permanent loans to them but we find it is a somewhat dangerous policy because, if it gets around that one museum is getting stuff from the National Museum, they all want stuff, all our things are listed and catalogued, and are really there for study at our Museum.'[10] Like McCurry, Alcock fretted about untrained boors in the hinterland trashing precious parts of his collections. He professed to like the idea in principle but thought that a reasonably extensive and even-handed program was out of the question with the budget the Museum had or was likely to have.

Similar activities were expected from the Public Archives and the National Library. But as the gallery and museum directors had indicated, there were obvious limits to how many physical artefacts could or should be circulated from these central collections. The theme reached a bathetic climax when John R. Kidd, secretary of the Canadian Citizenship Council, declared that the Public Archives and the National Library should be taken to the people. Others thought it was ridiculous to consider sending irreplaceable original records on tour, and doubted whether the average Canadian would care about seeing them. In subsequent discussion Kidd conceded Neatby's rejoinder that in the case of the archives, at least, professional intermediaries might be necessary. Nevertheless, new technologies offered compromises. When the commission subsequently asked Dr Kaye Lamb, Dominion archivist, about the possibilities of 'a wider national use' of the Public Archives and the National Library, he described a number of new services that could be provided for the public: filmstrips, photostats, microfilms, pamphlets, and publications of documents. And there were ways in which federal cultural institutions could play a national role aside from providing access to their collections. Across the country community libraries, galleries, archives, and museums told the commission that they needed help with their problems of unsuitable space, underfunding, and inadequately trained staff. They wanted technical aid and advice as much as touring exhibitions from federal institutions.

Some of the other areas of inquiry assigned to the commission were even less susceptible to popularization. St Laurent had written to the commission on 25 April 1950 to ask that it make recommendations in three additional areas: honours and awards, the provision of information about Canada abroad, and the preservation of historical monuments. The last two matters fit in with existing concerns of the commission and had already been discussed by many submissions. Honours and awards, however, were a different matter. Some of the commissioners shied away from the idea of instituting them in Canada because they thought the concept inherently undemocratic. Massey disagreed; in fact, he maintained that the point of such awards was to honour the humble for their contributions to society. Eventually a compromise was reached. To spare the commission the elitist stigma attached to such a proposal, it was resolved that Massey would submit recommendations on the subject privately to the prime minister. There would be no mention of honours and awards in the commission's report, even though this involved falsifying the official record by expunging the reference to them in the prime minister's letter as it was reprinted in the report's opening pages.[11]

The federal cultural institution that was most popular with Canadians was the one that was able to offer its services most widely. The National Film Board worked in a medium which, like radio and television, enjoyed mass popularity. As a result, many of the same issues which vexed broadcasting policy plagued the NFB. Like the CBC, the NFB was involved in a field where commercial interests pursued profit. The dominance of the American film industry paralleled the great popularity of American radio, and, as in broadcasting, the private sector of the Canadian film industry complained bitterly about the government's role in their field and lobbied hard for restrictions on the NFB. There was, however, one significant difference between the NFB and the CBC. While the CBC controlled the entire field of broadcasting, the NFB produced only educational and documentary films, leaving the lucrative and popular field of feature films to the Americans.

The NFB was also a much more vulnerable target than CBC. When its role as a wartime propaganda agency ended, the NFB had trouble finding a new purpose to justify its peacetime existence. At this critical juncture its reputation was smeared by allegations of communist infiltration. The revelations of Igor Gouzenko, the Soviet cipher clerk who defected with evidence of a communist spy ring in Canada in 1945, had implicated a former secretary at the NFB. Newspapers followed up this lead with allegations that tainted the entire organization with communist associations. The royal commission investigating Gouzenko's revelations never got to the bottom of the matter, and a cloud of suspicion was left hanging over the NFB.

At the same time the Canadian commercial film industry began to turn against the NFB. Private film producers had worked well with the NFB during the war, but at its end they hoped that the NFB would be reduced to an advisory role that would leave government production for them. When this did not happen, they began to complain that the NFB was a government monopoly competing against them unfairly. They supplemented their attack with charges that it was ineptly managed – a prime example of bureaucratic waste and inefficiency in an area where private enterprise could operate more efficiently and at no cost to the taxpayer.

In this poisoned atmosphere, Ross McLean, government film commissioner, appeared for the commission's special session on film on 24 August 1949. McLean argued that the NFB did not compete with other branches of the industry. Indeed, the NFB was a stimulus to film work in the country because its distribution system provided an outlet for Canadian films. He admitted that 'sometimes they do not feel that we allocate enough production work to outside producers' but claimed that 'that is determined partly by the limitations on our budget and partly by the fact that we have a plant and a technical capacity which should be economically used.'[12] One of the central demands of the NFB's brief was that it be made a crown corporation like the CBC. McLean thought that corporate status would help counter accusations of mismanagement by enabling the NFB to conduct its affairs more efficiently and allowing it to enter into contractual arrangements on a more businesslike basis.

Like the CBC, the NFB played a special role in rural Canada, where its film nights were a popular diversion. As McLean put it: 'we feel a particular responsibility towards all farming communities in Canada and all outpost communities which do not normally have the same channels of communication with, shall we say, interpreters of a national purpose, that urban audiences have.'[13] The NFB's base of support in rural areas had been further broadened during the war through its distribution of government industrial and propaganda films. This function ceased with the end of the war, however, and its distribution network was cut back. The void could not be filled entirely by the NFB's new Rural Field Projection Service, which continued to be reduced by financial constraints over the next few years, and so the NFB encouraged the formation of local film councils. Films that were first shown on the NFB's rural circuits were later given a wider showing through these voluntary associations. In the late 1940s, provincial federations of the local councils and a national federation were formed. Not surprisingly, these organizations were staunch supporters of the NFB and ensured that support for it was voiced often and fervently in the commission's hearings.

There were, however, many voices of criticism in the hearings as well. From French Canada came complaint that anglophone interests predominated in the film board and that too few films were produced in French.[14] The NFB was careful to counter these accusations by projecting an image of bicultural impartiality. With some exceptions, McLean declared, 'we consider that anything emanating from the Government of Canada as special information ought to be published in both languages.'[15] Paul Theriault, executive officer of French programs for the NFB, told the commission that the NFB was careful to respect the cultural autonomy of Quebec and did not try to impose a federal distribution system, but rather worked through existing local and provincial networks.

Private film interests were a far greater threat to the NFB's future. The brief of the Association of Motion Picture Producers and Laboratories of Canada (AMPPLC) questioned the wisdom of what it described as a government monopoly of a sensitive industry. The AMPPLC argued that the NFB, originally intended as a coordinating agency, had only become a producing body because of the war and was now a bureaucratic monster that refused to shrink back to its proper size and function. It suggested that 'the Board's objective is the establishment of a grand ministry of culture and information as independent from the Government as necessary to allow it elbow room for competing with private industry, and as close to the government as necessary to achieve security for its members during both employment and retirement.'[16] The AMPPLC also complained that the NFB was able to underbid its members for contracts outside the federal government because it was government subsidized. The NFB was duplicating facilities already available in the private sector and using them to underprice private business at taxpayers' expense, they told the commission: 'Our whole position is that it is in the buying and selling market in competition with us. We say that we can contribute to the arts and culture just as well, and we think you will agree when we show you some of our pictures.'[17] The commission dutifully trooped off to a screening of The Loon's Necklace, an award-winning privately produced short film.

The NFB faced opposition not only from film-makers, but from commercial photographers, who also felt that they were in competition with a government-subsidized organization. Throughout the fall of 1949 the Commercial and Press Photographer's Association of Canada (CAPPAC) was mobilizing its membership by asking for statistical and anecdotal evidence of competition from the NFB's still-photo service. It was also encouraging members to launch a campaign of letter writing to members of Parliament. CAPPAC and its supporters received rough treatment from the commission's legal counsel. Wright attacked their assumptions that private enterprise was more efficient than government enterprise and that it was government subsidy that lowered NFB production costs. On the whole, the commission treated CAPPAC's claims as exaggerated and self-serving and paid them little heed.

The NFB was the subject of much behind-the-scenes political manoeuvring throughout the commission's tenure. Massey had decided before public hearings commenced that an investigation of the Board by a third party was advisable to combat the private sector's allegations of bureaucratic inefficiency and waste: 'The Chairman summed up the discussion in expressing the wish that an impartial, intelligent and competent person, not necessarily connected with the production of films, be appointed to report on the Film Board to the Commission. He suggested that an eminent personality like Mr. Walter Gordon, C.A., be requested to do the survey. This survey would restore the morale of the N.F.B. personnel which, in the opinion of the majority of the Commissioners, should be one of the first steps to be taken.'[18] The commission wanted to avoid getting itself entangled in administrative questions so that it could concentrate on the NFB's cultural role. Massey's suggestion was eventually adopted by the government, and the management consulting firm of J.D. Woods and Gordon was hired on 15 November 1949.

A few days later, the *Financial Post* published a sensationalistic article headlined 'Film Board Monopoly Facing Major Test.' The full-page story chastised the NFB for its impertinence in asking the Massey Commission for corporate status, more money, a role in television, and a wider mandate in film at a time when it was under severe public criticism. The most damaging part of the article, however, was its revelation that the Department of National Defence had been routing its film work elsewhere because it had security concerns about NFB personnel.[19] Apparently Film Commissioner McLean had asked the

RCMP six months earlier to do a security check on NFB employees to settle the issue of whether the Board harboured communist sympathizers once and for all.

The leaking of this news upset the NFB's board of governors so much that they did not renew McLean's contract after it expired in January 1950. Altogether, it was a demoralizing period for the staff of the NFB. The public was presented with the image of an agency inundated with red ink, red tape, and Red spies. Presumed guilty until proven innocent, it was being investigated by Woods-Gordon for competence, the RCMP for communism, and the Massey Commission for Canadianism. At the same time it was under attack in the House of Commons. Conservative MP G.K. Fraser (Peterborough West) had chosen the Film Board as a *bête noire* that could carry him into the political limelight. He charged that it had made recommendations in its brief that were not in line with government policy. He also backed up the private photographers' complaints about government infringement upon their business and reiterated allegations about the existence of communist sympathizers among NFB employees. Fraser was encouraged by the fact that Robert Winters, who was responsible for the NFB as minister of mines and resources, had publicly dissociated himself from the NFB's brief to the Massey Commission because its demands for corporate status and new legislation had not been government policy. But now Winters responded with positive reports on the yet-to-be-completed investigations of the Film Board and declarations of his own confidence in the NFB's work.[20]

By early 1950, however, the NFB's trials were almost over. The government appointed Arthur Irwin, formerly editor of *Maclean's* (and therefore, interestingly enough, from Maclean-Hunter, the same firm that owned the *Financial Post*), as the new film commissioner. That winter Irwin received a list of thirty-six 'suspicious' employees from the RCMP. After further investigation and discussion with the Mounties, Irwin managed to chop this list down to just three employees, who were then dismissed. Not content to have his organization simply cleared of the taint of communism, Irwin appeared determined to compensate for the NFB's alleged sins by converting it into an aggressive Cold Warrior. In November 1950 he provided the commission with a memorandum entitled 'Summary of Preliminary Proposals for the Use of Film in Psychological Warfare,' which proposed to make the NFB a propaganda machine for the West in its international ideological battle with the Soviet Union.[21] The commissioners were uncomfortable with this proposal. Even in a just cause, propaganda undermined the very independence of judgment that was essential to liberal democracy. In the end they discouraged Irwin's plan.

In the meantime the Woods-Gordon Report was submitted to the government and proved to be very sympathetic to the NFB. It attributed the Film Board's administrative problems to the exigencies of wartime expansion and the unorthodox nature of its work. It felt that the NFB in fact needed more independence from government control to become efficient but thought corporate status too autonomous, since government ties were essential to its operations. While the report recommended a general tightening up of administrative practices, it also called for changes in the Film Act to eliminate legislative impediments to the organization's efficiency. Most of the NFB's problems – its lack of working capital, permanent staff, and centralized accommodations – were not of its own making.

The government benefited from the Massey Commission's advice but did not wait for its report before implementing many of the Woods-Gordon recommendations in a new Film Act in October 1950. Allegations of communist sympathies and mismanagement were finally put to rest; it remained for the Massey Commission to deal with the private film-makers' accusations that the NFB was a government monopoly in the film business. The commissioners thought that this charge was exaggerated, but they worried about the poor relations between the NFB and private producers that the controversy reflected. They believed that the NFB had every right to produce any films it desired, but they also wanted it to let out more contracts to private producers. The need for documentary films on Canadian subjects, they thought, was far greater than the NFB could fill, and to meet the demand it should be assisting private producers in every way possible. At the same time the commissioners strongly supported the Film Board's role as a film producer and urged that it should be particularly active in experimental and research work.[22]

It was hardly surprising that the Massey Commission would support the NFB in this controversy. Next to the CBC, it was the most influential agent of cultural improvement across the country. Unlike the CBC, however, the NFB was restricted to documentary and educational work which constituted only a small portion of activity in its medium. As MacKenzie observed the squabbling over the NFB, he could not help but think that the main problems facing film in Canada were not even being addressed. More than any other commissioner, he was concerned about the dim prospects for developing a Canadian feature film industry. Noting that the distribution system in Canada was either owned outright by U.S. film interest or tightly affiliated with them, he began to wonder whether a quota system for Canadian content in Canadian theatres or some other type of subsidy was necessary to establish a Canadian presence in the market. Mr E.C. Wood, vice-chairman of the Canadian Chamber of Commerce, was one of several witnesses MacKenzie questioned on this point:

> MACKENZIE: You think they can compete with Hollywood? Do you think they can deal with the monopoly control of movie houses and that sort of thing?
> WOOD: I am afraid I am not qualified to answer that, sir. That is a pretty big order.
> MACKENZIE: It is one of the things that seems to me to be almost incapable of dealing with or meeting, unless somebody is subsidized to do it, the magnitude of competition is so great.[23]

MacKenzie's concerns were echoed by many voluntary organizations that were interested in film. But on the whole the culture lobby viewed movies as a threat rather than a medium for the expression of Canadian culture. The equation of high culture with national identity held firm.

The commission itself would make no recommendations on the subject. Instead the commissioners limited themselves to recommending that the NFB devote more effort to improving and expanding its distribution system. The commissioners still tended to think of radio and film as means for the dissemination of traditional high culture rather than as media that engendered new forms of cultural expression. Movies were not art. They recognized that Hollywood had a powerful and, they thought, debilitating effect on Canadian culture, yet they were not accustomed to dealing with mass culture on its own terms. All they could offer was the antidote of high culture.

The NFB was invaluable because it was educational; through its documentary films it could make people accept doses of high culture that
they would have trouble swallowing straight up.[24]

At the same time the commissioners were determined that straight
shots of high culture should be available for those who could develop
a taste for them. This made them very sympathetic to the culture
lobby's demand for the decentralization of the services and exhibits
of traditional federal culture institutions. Massey told one witness that
'one of the important questions we want to get information about as
we move around the country is how far can these national institutions
in Ottawa serve the community as a whole, because they belong to
Canada as a whole, not only to Ottawa.'[25] Decentralization was merely
a geographical expression of the culture lobby's general interest in
popularizing high culture. As such, it was accompanied by the usual
questions about the democratic ethics of attempting to change popular
taste. Nowhere was this more obvious than in the consideration of
proposals that the National Gallery offer more touring exhibitions.
A.J. Hazelgrove, president of the Royal Architectural Institute of
Canada, was one of many witnesses who doubted that Canadians were
ready for what passed as avant-garde art: 'Take, for example, an
exhibition of modern painting. These exhibitions go to certain places
and people are simply floored. They do not understand them. They
do not understand the background or the development. The average
person regards them as something slightly crazy.'[26] As always, edifying the masses involved the risk of breaching democratic principles
by dictating taste. The policy of extending federal cultural services
was susceptible to the criticism that it was a form of authoritarianism
which imposed centralist and elitist cultural norms upon popular preferences and distinctive local communities.[27]

The cultural elite fully recognized the risks of appearing to dictate
cultural taste to the masses. Plans for tours and aid from centralized
institutions were proposed, not with the idea of creating a monolithic
and centralizing national culture, but as supplements and encourage-
ments to local cultural activity. This conscientiousness was evident in
the brief of the National Gallery: 'Art in Canada, to be a living force
in education and in national life as a whole, must have its roots in
the people themselves, and not take the form of a pattern imposed
from above. Any policy which would encourage provincial centres to

look to the federal government for a major part of their exhibition programmes would hamper sound growth. Canada is rich in artistic resources and the policy of the National Gallery must be designed to encourage the spontaneous and progressive development of them.'[28] This respect for popular initiative did not mean, however, that federal cultural institutions could abdicate responsibility for national cultural development. Exposing a greater number of Canadians to a higher level of culture was necessary to stimulate cultural self-improvement. Federal cultural institutions could also provide services that were required to facilitate local cultural expression.

Dictating taste was out of the question, but some effective means of cultural development had to be pursued. As always, the answer to the question of how to bridge the gap between high culture and popular taste was found in education. Mr Harold Walker, president of the Art Gallery of Toronto, presented it as a gradual process that would not force anything upon those who did not want it: 'in giving them what they can absorb, you can give them something that they don't think they can absorb, make them reach. So that each exhibition would overlap and reach a little further so that you would carry them on up and educate them unconsciously.'[29] Here was an approach that the commissioners, with their aversion to dictating taste, found quite acceptable.

In simplest terms, the extension of federal cultural services appealed to the commissioners because it seemed most democratic to make the cultural resources of the nation available to as many citizens as possible. If this had been the extent of the justification for such a policy, if might easily have become a cloak for imposing elitist standards. But any such authoritarian tendencies were checked by other values. As always, nationalism offset elitism with the notion that a genuine Canadian culture identity could only emerge from the grass-roots. This led to a balancing of elitist standards with provisions for local expression. Moreover, the culture lobby believed high culture could instruct Canadians in the nature of liberal democratic civilization, and was not about to undermine this end by employing authoritarian means.

All of these concerns were reflected in the culture lobby's comments on the NFB. As one group put it, they wanted the NFB 'élever le niveau intellectuel de la masse.'[30] The desired result of such edification was summed up in the Canadian Citizenship Council's hope that NFB films would 'help Canadians have a better appreciation of Canada as a nation, a fuller understanding of democracy and the workings and the procedures of democracy.'[31] Finally, the cultivation of enlightened and democratic citizens was contrasted with 'le danger d'américanisation par le cinéma (dans le sens plus pejoratif) de notre vie et de notre culture canadienne.'[32] Here was the same amalgam of cultural elitism, liberal democratic values, and nationalism which guided the culture lobby on other cultural issues as well.

Although federal cultural institutions faded into the background as the Massey Commission dealt with contentious issues such as broadcasting, university funding, and the Canada Council, they still retained a significant role in the commission's strategy for cultural development. In the first place, the commission wanted to reverse the trend of government neglect that had crippled their ability to fulfil their existing roles as monuments to national taste and central cultural resources. More importantly, however, they saw federal cultural institutions as junior partners of the CBC in the quest to edify Canadians. The NFB was a special object of concern because, like the CBC, it had widespread appeal and established influence across the country. But the commission thought that even the more traditional cultural institutions could play important supplementary roles in cultural development by providing undiluted dollops of high culture to the masses and by strengthening outposts of the cultural elite. If people would not come to the National Gallery, then the National Gallery would go to the people. It was for their own good, whether they liked it or not.

PART FOUR

10

The Report

By the end of its public hearings the commission had received representations from 473 individuals and organizations. In twelve months
the commissioners had travelled over ten thousands miles, held 114
public sessions in sixteen cities in ten provinces, and heard from over
twelve hundred witnesses. They had mounds of briefs and transcripts
of hearings to show for their efforts. On top of this came the special
studies and countless other reports and evidence collected in the course
of their work. The Massey Commission was faced with a vast, indeed
an overwhelming, amount of information.

Fortunately the commission's avenues of inquiry into this thicket
of evidence were already well established. Before, during, and after
their public hearings the commissioners had been holding private
meetings to discuss the issues they faced. Over a hundred official
sessions were held between May 1949 and February 1951. Some were
convened in hotels when the commission was on the road, but most
took place in the commission's offices in the Laurentian Building in
Ottawa. As the public hearings progressed, concerns about the commission's public image became less important, and the commissioners
began to concentrate on formulating recommendations.

Massey and his colleagues knew that the success of their commission
would depend largely upon the reception of its report. It was critical
to come up with a convincing document that would capitalize on the
public interest generated by their hearings. In a sense the acceptability

of their report, which was bound to be something of a highbrow document, would be a test of whether their hopes for popularizing high culture were possible. In presenting their plan for promoting high culture, it had to be a promotional tool itself. Its authority would be bolstered by unanimity, and so Massey hoped that disagreements among the commissioners, especially Surveyer's dissent over broadcasting policy, could be ironed out as the report was put together.

But Surveyer consistently displayed a disturbing propensity to think for himself. He favoured publishing a series of interim reports on important issues that would maintain interest in the commission while staving off public pressure that might rush and compromise the final report. The other commissioners, fearful of the time and extra work involved, voted down his proposal. Since Massey had promised an interim report at the start of the commission's work, he sought and received the prime minister's approval for this decision.

Lévesque and Neatby began work on an outline of the final report in January 1950. Responsibilities for writing sections of the first part were assigned in late February in the hope that the second half, which would contain the commission's recommendations, could be started by June.[1] Final decisions on contentious issues remained to be made, but minor recommendations were drafted by commissioners or staff members, drawing upon the massive card index file compiled from briefs and hearings. Debates over constitutional, political, financial, class, and literary questions punctuated the writing process.[2]

Once the commissioners decided policy and delegated the writing of particular sections, the resulting drafts were read and edited by all. Letters shot back and forth between various commissioners and staff members; candid criticisms were exchanged behind the backs of authors, and gentle suggestions made to them directly. As Day described the process to MacKenzie's assistant, Geoffrey Andrew: 'We are ... trying to steer a devious course between the highly conflicting proposals of those who appeared before the Commission, the views of the several Commissioners, and the somewhat varying estimates of what is likely to be considered reasonable and practicable for the Government and Parliament.'[3] There were constant reminders that the ultimate fate of the commission's recommendations would depend upon politics. By the early summer of 1950 the government was having to field questions in the House of Commons about when the report would appear. St Laurent was impressed with the amount of interest it attracted. The commissioners assured the prime minister their report would be done by October, and to be safe St Laurent simply told the House that it would appear in the fall.

The pressure to produce a report quickly was a reflection of the commission's success in stirring up interest across the country. 'I don't know that even the Commission is aware of the intensity of the anticipation of their forthcoming report,' Geoffrey Andrew wrote to Day. 'On my recent trip across the country it was a matter of universal discussion and anticipation.'[4] But the promise of a report in the fall proved wildly optimistic. As the commissioners continued to wrestle with delicate issues, some chapters would have to be revised ten times. The first inklings that all would not proceed smoothly came in early July when some of the first draft chapters were circulated. Andrew thought their tone was too patronizingly highbrow.[5] MacKenzie added that laying out a clear course of action for the government to follow was more important than presenting every possible viewpoint. It was clear that it could take months to make everyone happy.

The commissioners had come to joint conclusions on numerous issues informally over the course of their public sessions, but there were still major questions outstanding that required serious discussion. A series of special meetings was scheduled to begin on 19 July in Ottawa to resolve these issues. They began without Massey in attendance, however, because he felt unable to leave his ailing wife. To accommodate the chairman, the meetings were moved to Batterwood the following week. There the commissioners tried to thrash out final positions on the controversial questions of university funding and broadcasting policy, but when the meetings finally ended there was still no unanimous agreement on these issues. Indeed, there was to be no stirring climax to their work together. Instead the commission would finish its task through months of fragmented long-distance discussion in conjunction with gradual revisions of the final report.

Delays continued to plague the process. Massey's concern for his wife's health had been justified. Alice Massey died in early August, and it took him some time to recover from the blow. It was September before Massey resumed his former workload. In the meantime the process of exchanging criticisms and revisions on a transcontinental basis continued to eat up weeks of time. It was Neatby who leaned into the harness as things bogged down and pulled the project towards completion. MacKenzie wrote to her in mid-September to thank her for her efforts: 'You need make no apologies whatever for the condition of the first draft of the sections of the report which you may have written and which I commented upon. I am far too grateful to you for the excellent work that you are doing to even venture a criticism, were it not that I know that you want as many suggestions as possible and that, without these suggestions, it would be more difficult to prepare subsequent drafts.'[6] No doubt the other commissioners felt much the same way; Neatby was the only one on the scene working full-time on the report. Lévesque would credit her with having had the greatest influence on the final result: 'Au moment de la réduction de notre rapport nous lui avons d'ailleurs confié la première écriture de plusieurs chapitres importants. [Massey a aimé son] esprit de synthèse comme aussi la qualité de son analyse des documents et des témoignages.'[7] The report would display Neatby's disproportionate influence in its keen concern for Canadian history and Canada's historical resources.

In early November the commissioners gathered in Ottawa to thrash out remaining problems, but after two weeks of meetings many rough spots remained. With the help of Day, Neatby revised and rewrote sections by various original authors until the final product had a logical and stylistic unity. It was Lévesque, however, who found in St Augustine's *The City of God* the perfect epigraph for the report: 'A nation is an association of reasonable beings united in a peaceful sharing of the things they cherish; therefore, to determine the quality of a nation, you must consider what those things are.'[8] He was delighted with his discovery. It struck just the right balance between individualism and nationalism, while suggesting that culture mediated between the two in a fashion that was critical to an understanding of any nation.

The final report was divided into two parts. The first reviewed issues and evidence; the second set out recommendations. The first section began with two introductory chapters which advanced the context and principles for further discussion. Then it went on to address different parts of the commission's mandate in chapters entitled 'Mass Media,' ' "Voluntary Bodies" and "Federal Agencies," ' 'Scholarship, Science and the Arts,' and 'Cultural Relations Abroad.'

Part 2 followed roughly the same order as part 1 but was organized around the specific agencies and institutions on which recommendations were made rather than around thematic groupings.

The introductory sections of the report tackled the major problems facing Canadian cultural development. In the process they clearly revealed the liberal humanist nationalism which guided the commissioners. The first chapter, 'The Nature of the Task,' justified federal involvement in culture with an argument written by Lévesque. While admitting the links between culture and education, it maintained that there was a difference between formal education and informal education. It was education outside the schools which concerned the commission. This distinction and a narrow reading of the BNA Act allowed for a federal role in culture.[9]

In a key passage the report went on to argue that cultural development was an absolute requirement – indeed, a duty – of the national state: 'All civilized societies strive for the common good, including not only material but intellectual and moral elements. If the Federal Government is to renounce its right to associate itself with other social groups, public and private, in the general education of Canadian citizens, it denies its intellectual and moral purpose, the complete conception of the common good is lost, and Canada, as such, becomes a materialistic society.'[10] Other 'civilized countries' assumed this responsibility, and the Canadian public was demanding the same from its government.[11] The reader was assured that such aid could be given 'without stifling efforts which must spring from the desires of the people themselves.'[12]

Canada's unique cultural predicament made state aid all the more necessary. Chapter 2, 'The Forces of Geography' (originally penned by Massey), recited the usual litany of Canada's national disadvantages. The country's modest population, linguistically divided and scattered along a five-thousand-mile front, made for regional differences and small markets that hindered cultural development. Canada had taken extraordinary measures to ensure its unity through transportation, finance, and communications in the past; now it was time to extend this tradition to the crucial realm of culture. By far the most important affliction for Canadian culture was the overpowering presence of a larger neighbour which shared the language of its anglophone majority. Canada was too dependent upon American media, education, ideas, and institutions, especially those responsible for mass culture.[13] While admitting that Canada was vastly indebted to the United States for some salutary cultural influences, the report declared that nevertheless American generosity was no substitute for self-sufficiency. Overt anti-Americanism was muffled, but the message that American cultural imperialism was a threat to Canadian nationhood still came through loud and clear.

The commissioners took pains to avoid the stigma of elitist paternalism. 'Nothing was further from our minds than the thought of dictating taste from some cultural stratosphere,' they insisted. Instead, cultural enlightenment had to be a matter of 'free choice.'[14] This was more than just public relations posturing. The commissioners trusted in education, 'primarily a personal responsibility,'[15] to bring about this edification: 'Education is the progressive development of the individual in all his faculties, physical and intellectual, aesthetic and moral. As a result of the disciplined growth of the entire personality, the educated man shows a balanced development of all his powers; he has fully realized his human possibilities.'[16] The report expressed the commissioners' confidence that the educational process could flow naturally from the individual's own curiosity and desire for self-improvement if the necessary cultural resources were available.[17] It was an expectation that reflected the commissioners' experience of their own intellectual development.

The introduction to part 2 of the report invoked the Cold War spectre of communist totalitarianism in contrast to the liberal democratic principles which the commissioners believed to be inherent in traditional high culture. Anticipating the criticism that the Cold War made defence spending a priority and culture a dispensable frill, the commissioners argued, 'If we as a nation are concerned with the problem of defence, what, we may ask ourselves, are we defending? We are defending civilization, our share of it, our contribution to it. The things with which our inquiry deals are the elements which give civilization its character and meaning. It would be paradoxical to defend something which we are unwilling to strengthen and enrich, and which we even allow to decline.'[18] To promote high culture was to defend the liberal democratic civilization of the West. It was only through the type of education provided by high culture that the individual could become an aware and responsible democratic citizen.

This point was made time and again.[19] It tied together all of the report's introductory themes, for American mass culture was a threat to liberal democracy that was similar in nature if not in degree to communist totalitarianism. The alternative proffered for Canada was high culture as national culture.

Although the commissioners believed that high culture and democracy were compatible, they remained sensitive to egalitarian suspicions. After Andrew criticized the early drafts of the report for being condescending, they made a conscious effort to eradicate any instances of a superior tone. Instead they cultivated a rhetorical style which led the reader, gently but relentlessly, from a reasoned acceptance of basic premises, through evidence presented dispassionately but with calculated effect, towards the conclusions they advocated. Irony and understatement were the report's stylistic hallmarks. It gave an appearance of being based on general public opinion rather than the views of interest groups in the cultural field, quoting freely from briefs and hearings to convey the impression that the commissioners were simply obedient servants of the popular will.

In order to sell its recommendations the report attempted to raise the cultural aspirations of many of its readers. Its very structure was designed to lead the reader from matters of general interest upward to more rarefied cultural heights. As Neatby later described it:

... we decided on a plan like a pyramid. We dealt first with what we called 'mass media,' radio, television, film, newspapers. These are means by which the largest possible number of people may enjoy arts, letters, and sciences ... On the second level of the pyramid we dealt with organizations and activities that touch a much smaller number of Canadians directly, although indirectly they exercise a very great influence over the lives of all – Our national libraries, museums, art galleries, archival collections, and our national universities ... the official repositories of the evidences and material of our civilization ... the great educational agencies through which this material is made really available to scientists, scholars, and lovers of the arts. They are, moreover, centres for the activities of the innumerable voluntary societies which alone can maintain a truly national culture and civilization in a democratic state ... The third level of our pyramid is represented by a few people whose names are unknown to the vast majority of their fellow Canadians; but it is these few who literally sustain and nourish us all. These are the painters, the sculptors and the architects; the musicians and the actors; the scholars and the scientists. They are the men and women who do the truly creative work which preserves, interprets and enriches our civilization.[20]

The way in which the commissioners intended the report to be read reflected their belief in a cultural hierarchy which could be ascended in stages through an educational process.

The recommendations made by the commissioners flowed naturally from the premises of liberal humanist nationalism. Their general goal was to promote high culture as national culture and make it more accessible to the average Canadian. At the apex of the report's pyramid was the Canada Council for the Encouragement of the Arts, Letters, Humanities and Social Sciences, designed to extend the federal government's support to refined levels of cultural activity that it had never before reached. The Council would handle grants and scholarships for artists and scholars, relations with national voluntary associations, aid for local arts activities, and information on Canadian cultural affairs. At the same time it would serve as a national commission for UNESCO and manage cultural relations abroad. In a democratic gesture, the report rejected the culture lobby's requests for special representation on the Council and instead recommended that its members be lay people.

In the middle of the pyramid the commissioners had placed the federal cultural institutions and universities which comprised the existing cultural infrastructure in Canada. Numerous recommendations were aimed at increasing the resources and prestige of federal cultural institutions, but a major goal was the extension of their exhibitions and services nationwide.[21] The universities already served as bastions of high culture across the country, and the report recommended not just enhanced scholarships and aid to research, but direct federal funding for universities. To avoid jurisdictional disputes with the provinces, the grants were to be apportioned on the basis of provincial populations and then split among the various provinces' universities in proportion to their student enrolments.

At the base of the pyramid lay the mass media. The Massey Report's majority recommendations in broadcasting came as no surprise; they rested on the commissioners' perception of the electronic media as the primary means of informing and educating Canadian citizens.[22] The commissioners believed that the existing system of public broadcasting accomplished these goals, making the CBC 'the single greatest agency for national unity, understanding and enlightenment.'[23] They dismissed the grievances of the private broadcasters as irrelevant in a system which by its very nature was not oriented towards commercial ends. In fact, while they judged that the CBC was fulfilling its programming responsibilities, they thought it was too lax in controlling the private stations.

The idea of a separate regulatory body was rejected outright on the grounds that it would 'divide and destroy, or merely duplicate the present system of national control.'[24] The commissioners echoed the culture lobby's belief that an independent regulatory board would lead to two distinct systems (one public and one private) and strip the CBC of its capacity to provide national coverage. Networks for private stations were expressly denied because 'any networks of private stations in Canada would inevitably become small parts of American systems' that would no longer serve as CBC outlets.[25] The status quo was to prevail in the new medium of television as well.[26] As a consolation prize, private broadcasters would be allowed to appeal CBC regulatory decisions to the CBC board of governors and thereafter to federal courts, and their licence tenure was extended from three to five years.

The commissioners rejected the CBC's proposal that radio licence fees be increased. They were no doubt aware of the unpopularity that both they and the CBC might suffer from such a move. They refused to abolish the fee outright, however, on the grounds that 'we think it is proper for the listener to make direct payment for the services received and we believe he appreciates these services the more for doing so.'[27] The same reasoning was applied to television.[28] They addressed the cultural elite's concern about commercialism and the private broadcasters' complaints about competition by instructing the CBC to refuse local commercial business except where no private radio outlets for advertising were available. On the national level, the CBC was too dependent on advertising revenue to forgo it entirely, but it was urged nonetheless to refuse 'inappropriate' commercials. Since this would only aggravate the CBC's financial problems, the government was advised to set the income of the CBC by statute for five-year periods and provide by parliamentary grant the funds not raised from licence fees and advertising revenue.

In short, the commissioners did all they could to reaffirm the goals of the existing system of public broadcasting and reinforce its means of fulfilling them. It was on this critical issue, however, that the authority of the report would be most seriously compromised. As the commissioners discussed fundamental questions during the summer of 1950, it became clear that Surveyer was unhappy with his colleagues' opposition to the demands of private broadcasters. In fact, he showed a disturbing willingness to credit the private broadcasters' argument that the CBC was both 'umpire and player.' On both broadcasting and film issues he also seemed to share the businessman's belief that government could never be as efficient as free enterprise.[29]

At first the other commissioners were hopeful that these differences could be bridged. At the end of the first week of September 1950, Guy Roberge went to Montreal to discuss the newly completed sections on broadcasting and the National Film Board with Surveyer, but the dissident only responded with a memorandum spelling out his objections in detail.[30] Massey did all he could to find a compromise, but by late September it seemed that Surveyer would insist on submitting a minority report on these critical questions. Surveyer knew that none of the other commissioners could be convinced he was right, yet he insisted on sticking to his opinions.

With the help of Roberge, Surveyer began to draw up a statement of his positions on broadcasting and the Film Board for inclusion in the report. His reasons for favouring an independent regulatory body were based in a recognition of the anomalous position private broadcasters occupied in a system that had originally been intended to expropriate them. It was 'a matter of elemental equity' for private broadcasters to be given rights commensurate with their indispensability to the system; recourse to the courts was in most cases too unwieldy a solution.[31] Surveyer thought that divorcing the system's regulatory and operational functions would be good for public broadcasting because each part would gain efficiency from being able to focus on one clear task. The CBC would be free to concentrate all its attention on fulfilling its mandate to provide quality Canadian programming, and an independent authority could ensure that it did so.

Surveyer wanted the CBC to delegate more production to private producers and restrict itself to producing only the types of shows which commercial enterprises would not provide. In a similar vein he agreed with private film producers' and photographers' complaints against the National Film Board, and rather than just vaguely recommending, like the majority report, that these private interests be assigned more work, he specified that they should be given at least half of the NFB's annual production of films and photographs.

Despite these policy differences with his colleagues, Surveyer's ultimate ends were in accord with theirs. He believed that an independent regulatory authority would 'raise the general standard of the programmes broadcast in Canada, for the purpose of fostering national unity, cultivating the artistic taste of the people, supplying well-balanced entertainment, and encouraging the study of the arts, letters, and sciences in general, and more particularly of the economic and social problems which face the nation.'[32] Surveyer based his recommendations on ruminations about the general effects of the mass media in modern society. He had been doing some reading on the subject and was very impressed by Gilbert Seldes's *The Great Audience* and H.A. Overstreet's *The Mature Mind*.[33] From Overstreet's book he derived the conviction that intellectual maturity was the problem at hand – most of the popular mass culture of the day was 'adolescent.' From Seldes he added the like notion that 'the policy adopted by advertisers in the various media aims at the glorification of youth and the prevention of maturity.'[34] Surveyer wove these insights into a pattern of thought that differed from that of his fellow commissioners only in its rhetoric:

> Nothing in the popular arts suggests to people of thirty or forty that they can safely read a book, discuss politics, bother about juvenile delinquency, serve on a jury, earn a living, or write a letter to the editor – all of these things and a thousand others are the stigmata of maturity and must be practised in secret, if at all ... The devices for delay in maturity are heavily capitalized; the enterprises that profit by our coming of age are relatively few.

> There is no vested interest in maturity, although the maturity of
> its citizens is the prime interest of the nation.[35]

The 'maturity' theme represented Surveyer's idiosyncratic way of
expressing the same liberal humanist point of view which guided the
other commissioners. As a practical man, he phrased his concern in
the familiar metaphor of growing up and emphasized economic and
political duties, yet his conviction that high culture held the key to
democratic citizenship was exactly the same as that of his colleagues.
One of the ironies of Surveyer's dissent was that in his enthusiasm
for his new insights he came across as being even more highbrow
than his peers. He was much less accomplished than the other commissioners at disguising his elitism.[36]

As soon as Massey received Surveyer's 'reservations and observations,' he turned them over to Neatby, asking for her comments.
Neatby was intolerant of such heresy. In a memorandum to Massey
dated 1 February 1951, she ripped apart Surveyer's arguments with
methodical hostility. Far from raising points that had been neglected,
Surveyer repeated material already covered in the report and introduced irrelevant information, she contended. Had he slept through
the commission's hearings and deliberations? 'Mr. Surveyer does not
indicate clearly how far he can go with his colleagues and at what
point or points he diverges,' she continued. 'Instead he marshals his
material and attacks the problem in complete independence.'[37]

Unfortunately, deriding Surveyer's dissenting opinions would not
make them disappear. That same month Lévesque wrote to Neatby,
having concluded that no amount of reasoning would change Surveyer's mind:

> Vous avez bien raison d'être indignée de la façon dont M. Sur-
> veyer présente son désaccord. Nous le sommes tous. J'ai fait un
> voyage spécial à Montréal pour essayer de rendre son interven-
> tion moins désagréable, mais sans résultat appréciable. Il est fixé
> dans ses opinions – depuis le début de notre travail peut-être.
> Une seule chose semble l'intéresser: la cause de l'entreprise
> privée. J'ai peine à trouver qu'il a été loyal envers l'idéal de la
> commission, envers nous, j'oserais peut-être dire plus particu-
> lièrement vers moi: Quoi qu'il en soit, nous ferons de notre

mieux pour diminuer l'effet de ses actes. Et je vous approuve en-
tièrement quand vous pensez que ses vues ne doivent être pre-
sentées qu'à la fin de notre rapport.[38]

Lévesque's final comment showed that, as it became clear that Surveyer would stick to his position, the other commissioners began to
concentrate on damage control. Neatby argued that Surveyer's arguments were so flimsy that they were embarrassing and should be
shunted to the back of the report rather than allowed to follow immediately after the recommendations of the majority. Massey agreed:
'I don't think that anything can or should be done to persuade him
to alter the text of his dissenting opinions, but I have already said to
Archie Day that they should most certainly be printed *at the end of
the Report* and not where he has asked to have them. There may be
quite a discussion at our meeting over this point and this is an additional reason why I very much hope you can be here.'[39] The meeting
referred to by Massey was scheduled for the second week of February
1951. He begged Neatby to attend this final session to back him up
on this and other issues.[40] Lévesque also wrote to urge her attendance,
telling her how much Massey relied on her and how indispensable
her moral and intellectual support would be in the confrontation with
Surveyer. Neatby was only human; she bowed to this onslaught of
cajolery and flattery and agreed to be there.

The majority commissioners were not above a little devious col-
lusion to assure that they got their way. 'I have arranged that we
should meet in Archie Day's apartment Monday morning,' Massey
informed Neatby.[41] There, without Surveyer's knowledge, they plotted how to deal with him at the official meeting of the commission
later in the day. When the fateful meeting convened on the afternoon
of 13 February, they manoeuvred the dissenter into accepting the
banishment of his reservations to the end of the report. A disgruntled
Surveyer left town that night even though another meeting was scheduled for the next day. He had paid the price for not sticking to the
party line.

The difficulties with Surveyer, however, were not quite over yet.
MacKenzie had been urging Massey all along not to forget the need
for a popular précis of the report. Eventually it was decided that a
press summary rather than a published digest would best serve im-

mediate needs, and journalist Wilfrid Eggleston was engaged to write one.[42] The question of how Surveyer's opinions should be presented in Eggleston's piece soon became a new source of contention. Surveyer was unhappy with Eggleston's initial draft, feeling that it underplayed his arguments and was biased in favour of the majority case. Although Massey was reluctant to make any concessions, Eggleston diplomatically made minor changes. Surveyer was not completely happy but did not push the matter further. In the meantime, Neatby had been thinking of other ways to minimize the impact of Surveyer's reservations and was busy revising certain sections of the majority recommendations on broadcasting in order to lessen the power of his argument.

The fuss stirred up by the Surveyer affair overshadowed the fact that the main body of the report was finally being whipped into shape. Throughout mid-January, Lévesque, Neatby, Massey, and the two secretaries thrashed out most of the outstanding details in a series of editorial meetings. On 27 January 1951 Day was able to report to MacKenzie that the process was almost over; Massey and Day had gone out for a drink the Wednesday before to celebrate.[43] The festivities were a trifle premature: MacKenzie was not quite through with his suggestions. Although he agreed with the other commissioners' concern for being scrupulously fair to French Canada, he feared that in the existing version of the report this conscientiousness had blossomed into reverse prejudice. He wrote to Day in late January to point this out: 'throughout there is a general acceptance of a view that most things in French Canada, culturally at least, are good, and many of the equivalent things in English Canada are bad ... I am ... always sceptical of such generalities and I would like more evidence before I were willing to accept the statements as being accurate. They grow in part out of a belief in and a worship of the French classical system of education, on the part of some of our people in the humanities, and out of a hankering after the good old days, without much real understanding of what the good old days were really like.'[44] Day brought the matter up with Massey, who acknowledged the validity of this criticism and asked MacKenzie to point out the worst cases so that they could try to get rid of them in the final draft.

In the meantime, problems with translating sections of the report from French into English and vice-versa were also holding up production. Parts of the English report originally written in French bore traces of their linguistic origins that had to be corrected.[45] The French version of the report was even more of a problem. Lévesque found the government translators' French versions of sections originally written in English to be totally unacceptable, and it took him, with Garneau's help, three months to rewrite them. Day estimated that this delay would hold up the final presentation of the report until about mid-April.

As the report crawled towards completion, the commissioners became more and more concerned with its presentation and public reception. The press was full of anticipation and speculation about their recommendations. They decided that to ensure maximum publicity they should release copies to the media forty-eight hours before it was tabled in the House of Commons. The dust cover and general appearance of the report were also a matter of great concern to Massey. He wanted an attractive jacket that would grab attention in bookshops and help to make the report more popular. Toronto artist Eric Aldwinckle was commissioned to design the cover, and Massey was pleased with the result, although he joked that, given the resurgent Red scare in the States, there was a risk that its lavish use of crimson would be taken as an indication of subversive intent.

In Parliament the opposition pressed the government about when the report would appear. Much to St Laurent's embarrassment, printing problems delayed its appearance throughout April and into May.[46] As the weeks slipped by, there was a danger that there would not be time to table the report during that parliamentary session. But finally everything was ready. On 1 June 1951, Massey, Lévesque, and Day filed into the public gallery overlooking the House of Commons to watch the prime minister table the Massey Report. St Laurent told the House that he was sure that the report would 'constitute a valuable guide to our future national development.'[47] At the same time he was careful to insulate himself from any negative repercussions that might come from controversial recommendations. 'The government has not yet had the opportunity to give consideration to the report, and, in fact, none of the members of the government has yet read it,' he declared.[48] St Laurent justified his government's ignorance of the report's contents with a populist pretext: 'I wished to lose no time in having the report made available to members of parliament and to the public, both because of the widespread interest in its subject matter and because the report itself will obviously call for careful study and discussion, not only by members of parliament but by the public at large.'[49] What this really meant was that the government would only act on recommendations which proved to be politically expedient.

After two years and two months, the Massey Commission's official existence came to an end. But the fate of its efforts was by no means certain. The cause that had been contested in endless hours of public hearings and private meetings now had to be fought again in the media, Parliament, and the back rooms of government. Though the commissioners' official duties were behind them and the culture lobby's moment in the public spotlight had passed, the supporters of the Massey Report were by no means helpless to pursue its implementation. In a sense the real battle had only just begun.

11

Response and Implementation

'Friday's Massey Report Looms as "Best-Seller"' ran the headline in the Windsor *Daily Star* on the Wednesday before the report's presentation to the House of Commons. 'The King's Printer, whose publications rarely cause excitement in the book stalls, thinks he's got one that may be as "hot" as the Royal Commission report on the spy trials of 1946,' the Canadian Press story reported.[1] This sort of hype was not entirely unfounded. All of the cultural interests directly affected by the report were, of course, eagerly awaiting its publication. But booksellers also reported enough interest from the general public that the King's Printer was expanding its first print run.

A day after the tabling of the report Day wrote to MacKenzie that 'it has been a great joy to us here to see how well the Report has been received by the press.'[2] The Massey Report made the front page in Canadian newspapers from coast to coast, surpassed in prominence only by the latest news of the Korean War. Most papers printed extensive Canadian Press reports from Ottawa and supplemented them over the following week with articles on local reaction. Almost every newspaper devoted at least one editorial to the report, and two were not uncommon. A few continued to run opinion pieces over the next month, but for the most part, newspaper coverage of the report died down within a week.

The CBC did its bit by scheduling a number of talks by Ottawa journalists to discuss the report, and interest was sustained over the next few months by the appearance of critical appraisals in Canadian magazines and journals. Although *Maclean's* printed only two editorials on the report, *Saturday Night* and *Canadian Forum* ran numerous pieces. Their coverage was followed by a second wave of articles in special-interest journals such as the CAAE's *Food for Thought, Canadian Art*, the *Canadian Geographical Journal*, and even such diverse publications as *Canadian Welfare* and *Canadian Banker*. In Quebec, practically every intellectual journal felt compelled to address an issue so crucial to *la survivance*. *L'Action nationale* was so anxious to repudiate the bicultural heresy purveyed by the commission that it kept up a relentless attack on the report and its authors for over a year.

Reaction to the Massey Report came from four sources within these media. The first three were predictable enough. One, of course, was the culture lobby, which exploited the cultural elite's connections and its own publications to get its endorsement of the report publicized. Another was the private broadcasters, who used every available forum to criticize the report's endorsement of the status quo in broadcasting. In addition, French-Canadian nationalist interests like *L'Action nationale* maintained a vociferous opposition from a limited base in Quebec. Aside from these antagonists there was a broad and relatively disinterested segment of opinion which included most daily newspapers. Much of the political success of the report would depend upon the response of these influential brokers of public opinion.

The majority of newspaper owners and journalists had no axe to grind on most of the issues raised by the report. But they all felt obligated to defend the interests of that mythical but omnipotent figure, the common man. Since the common man was, if nothing else, a taxpayer, newspapers first attacked the report for what they regarded as the extravagance of the expenditures it recommended. The New Westminster *British Columbia* noted that 'Canadians who are neither high brows, long hairs, nor rough necks may view with misgivings certain aspects of the Massey Commission's report' because of the tax dollars culture would cost them.[3] Newspapers thought of themselves as representatives of the common man's common sense, a role which equipped them to judge the report in 'realistic' and 'practical' terms. To this end they would conduct a pragmatic cost-benefit analysis of the commission's recommendations. Their initial outcry about costs struck an ominous note, but it was just a ritualistic opening protest prior to a more thoughtful consideration of the commission's proposals.

Most newspapers were not impressed by the cause of what some journalists sneeringly referred to as 'culchah.' In their early assessments of the report they reflected the popular image of culture as the indulgence of a self-styled social *crème de la crème*. In the *Financial Times*, E.C. Ertl ranted that 'to shepherd a lot of people to galleries so that they may see the outpourings of tortured minds who should never have left the psychoanalyst's couch is not to encourage culture. It only makes phoneys out of people and encourages others to make a living out of being phoneys.'[4] This disdain for dilettantism was supplemented by a conviction that the academics responsible for the report, being academics, were out of touch with reality. A damaging article by Douglas How of Canadian Press entitled 'Little Man Letting Down the Longhairs,' widely printed in dailies across the country, also exploited popular stereotypes by portraying the artist as misfit and freeloader: 'Little man, you've been letting down the long-hairs – the artists, writers, and painters. It's time you opened your heart, your soul, and your pocketbook and improved yourself. It says so in so many words in the Massey Report on the arts and sciences.'[5] Even papers that generally supported the report could not resist printing this kind of material as a gesture of solidarity with the common man.

No matter how adamantly they defended the interests of the common man, many journalists – who were themselves uncommon inasmuch as they made their living by writing – could not help admiring the polished style and intellectual content of the report. Admissions that it was well written invariably crept into even the most sceptical articles. Some incongruous comments could result from this covert esteem. One journalist, for instance, trying to show his respect for highbrow accomplishment without abandoning his lowbrow idiom, dubbed the report a 'massive hunk of intellectual meat.'[6]

Remarkably, the suspicions of culture evident in early news coverage were not reflected in editorials. Although editorial writers continued to make the requisite noises about practical concerns, most did not quibble with the fundamental premise that culture, and high culture at that, was an essential concern for contemporary Canada. An editorial in the Calgary *Herald* provided a good example of this acceptance of the importance of 'spiritual' concerns:

It is said that Canada, and for that matter North America as a whole, is deficient in culture in the historic sense. Our culture, it is alleged, is expressed rather in terms of refrigerators, garbage disposers, hydra-matic drives and automatic ditch diggers than in terms of symphonies, poetry, and great painting. We have been so busy – or so the critics say – arranging for the comfort of our bodies that we have neglected to arrange for the growth and development of our minds.

All this we must concede.[7]

The editors who made such comments were, of course, the highbrows of their profession. But even the Canadian Chamber of Commerce *News Letter* proclaimed that 'it is good, in this materialistic age, to see reference to the spiritual legacy of Canadians.'[8]

Newspapers accepted an otherwise suspicious cause because of the report's success in fusing culture with Canadian nationalism. Culture was one thing; but national pride, Canadian identity, and international prestige were something else again. As the Winnipeg *Tribune* sermonized, 'it is to be hoped that ... the rank and file of Canadians will increasingly realize that the subject under discussion is a vital and essential part of Canada's life and progress, of the happiness and well-being of her people.'[9] Similar sentiments were found in most editorials. The Lethbridge *Herald* even proclaimed that the Massey Commission would prove to be more historically significant than the Rowell-Sirois Commission because its cultural concerns were ultimately more important to national life.[10]

But the fact that editorials responded to the report's patriotic appeals did not mean they went along with its assumptions about the incompatibility of Canadian and American culture. Most played down this aspect of the report, preferring to be pro-Canadian without being anti-American. In general, English-Canadian newspapers considered Canada and the United States to be part of the same cultural stream, one in which Canada could and should have some marked differences, but no radical divergence. The *British Columbian*, for instance, argued that 'with ... minor modulations the culture of the North American continent is one culture and that state of affairs cannot be altered short of violence.'[11] The editorials' reluctance to adopt the elite point of view on this was understandable. To deny the American Dream would be to deny the way of life of the common man. Canadians could shift for themselves, but not without hydra-matic drive.

In this way newspapers responded to the emotional appeal of the report's cultural nationalism without subscribing to one of the logical premises upon which it was based. In the scholarly press the Massey Report's view of American mass culture found more support. Harold Innis, who was then engaged in studying the relationship between communications technologies and imperial power through the ages, attributed the erosion of English Canada's cultural identity to 'constant hammering from American commercialism.'[12] In his eyes Canada was justified in trying to control an invasion of foreign media; to do otherwise would be to allow virtual cultural annexation by the United States. But University of Toronto historian Frank Underhill challenged the assumption that Canada and the United States were two very different societies. Underhill ridiculed the cultural nationalists' assertion that mass culture was intrinsically American and representative of a way of life that was somehow foreign and a threat to Canadian culture. Canada, he maintained, was an American as the United States: 'These so-called "alien" American influences are not alien at all; they are just the natural forces that operate in the conditions of twentieth-century civilization. It is mass consumption and the North American environment which produce these phenomena, not some sinister influences in the United States.'[13] Underhill did not sympathize with the private broadcasters, but he echoed their comments in his assertion that Canada would find itself only through confident and unfettered interaction with the rest of the world.[14] He also suspected that Massey's anti-Americanism was rooted in anglophilia. Massey pooh-poohed the accusation. 'I have just read Frank Underhill's article on the Report,' he wrote to Neatby. 'He "suspects" that my "ultimate idea" is that "we can become another England!"'[15] Although each exaggerated the other's position, the basic divergence in views was clear.

In French Canada concerns about the Massey Report differed radically from those found in the English-Canadian press. Unlike their English-Canadian counterparts, French-Canadian newspapers needed little convincing that culture was an important concern for a nation or that American culture constituted a threat. The real question in French Canada was whether the Canadian culture promoted by the

Massey Report was not itself a menace to French-Canadian culture. In general, opinion in the French-language press was remarkably amenable to the type of biculturalism promoted by the commission. *La Presse* congratulated the commission for its work in 'la création d'un esprit patriotique plus conscient, plus agissant,' and *Le Soleil* called the report the 'fruit of an intimate collaboration between the worthy representatives of two great races and cultures' – a fine example of the bicultural ideal in action.[16] These reactions from newspapers with Liberal and federalist connections were to be expected, but favourable responses came from less sympathetic sources as well. Even wary nationalists were satisfied that the report respected provincial prerogatives and the French-Canadian way of life.[17] 'The commissioners seem to have overcome the difficulties inherent in a project of such magnitude,' remarked *L'Action catholique*, noting that a scrupulous regard for French-Canadian culture and provincial rights ran throughout the report.[18]

Of course, there were still some objections to the report. *Montréal Matin* argued that the preservation of two distinct cultures was Canada's best guarantee of maintaining its independence; 'to seek to mix these two together is to prepare for ourselves an unspeakable hashup of both.'[19] In *Le Devoir*, André Laurendeau warned that the Massey Commission's recommendations raised the spectre of an Ottawa-directed, pan-Canadian culture that would undermine French-Canadian culture.[20] Historian Michel Brunet also rejected the report's contention that a broad Canadianism would serve the interests of both cultural groups.[21] He saw the Massey Commission as an English-Canadian affair, a defensive reflex in response to an identity crisis that had followed the decline of Britain and the rise of American influence. To resist the American vortex, English Canadians had turned to central government initiatives that could only have negative implications for French-Canadian culture.

Despite such strong objections, on the whole French Canadians found the report quite acceptable. Many nationalists reacted positively because they thought that French-Canadian culture could benefit from federal dollars and that the funding mechanisms for culture recommended by the commissioners respected and even affirmed provincial jurisdiction in the field. Others simply wanted money for their cultural activities and did not look a gift horse in the mouth.

Clearly the report was winning over populist suspicions and French-Canadian nationalist hostility. There remained another major form of resistance: laissez-faire opposition to its insistence that the state should sponsor cultural development. All the standard arguments against state intervention were fervently expressed in the press, invigorated by Cold War fears of totalitarianism. More than a few newspapers pointed out that culture was one of the areas where state intervention was least necessary but most dangerous. 'We have been witnessing in recent years the methods by which Communism has been intervening by barbarous methods in this field,' warned the St John's *Telegraph*.[22]

Although the press was generally wary of state initiatives, moderate opinion was willing to consider each case on its merits. Once it had been accepted that cultural development was a necessary step in national life, the obvious need for some form of patronage for it outweighed fears of cultural despotism. The idea was accepted most easily in areas such as arts funding where government intervention did not restrict business profits. There were objections to the Canada Council based on the liberal notion that culture could not be artificially induced, but most journalists accepted the report's contention that the proposed council could encourage cultural development without controlling it. In general, rejecting arts subsidies was an ideological reflex, while defending them required some thoughtful exposition; therefore, more tended to be written in support of the proposal than against it. Ultimately the Canada Council met with lukewarm approval in the press.

The case for a state role in cultural development was also reinforced by the nationalist argument that intervention of this sort was distinctly Canadian. According to this interpretation, the Massey Report's recommendations represented an updating of the National Policy to deal with the new cultural realities of an electronic age.[23] This invocation of national tradition helped to blunt laissez-faire objections to the report. Nationalism deflected opposition to state intervention just as effectively as it curbed popular suspicions of high culture.

The recommendation for federal aid to universities was the only area where there were no objections raised to the report on practical or laissez-faire grounds in the English-Canadian press. The proposal was greeted with great enthusiasm and was the exclusive subject of

many editorials. Newspapers like the Calgary *Herald*, which opposed
state intervention in principle, nevertheless supported federal aid for
universities.[24] The fact that universities offered material as well as
spiritual advantages made aid for universities easier to accept than
arts subsidies. Education was a more familiar and practical concern
than culture, university graduates were needed by an expanding economy, and once again, there was no threat to free enterprise from
government aid in this area. And as Neatby observed, in Canadian
society it was possible to sneer at 'culchah,' but it was sacrilege to
denigrate education.[25]

Even though federal funding for universities seemed to intrude
upon provincial jurisdiction over education, the general consensus in
English Canada was that constitutional scruples were inconsequential
when such an emergency existed. In Quebec this was by no means
the case. *Le Devoir* concentrated its fire on this recommendation because it perceived it to be the single gravest threat to French-Canadian
culture presented by the report. It warned that grants to universities
were only the thin edge of the wedge of English-Canadian cultural
domination.[26] Even Pierre Elliott Trudeau of *Cité libre*, who usually
condemned Duplessis for using the provincial autonomy issue as a
red herring, saw federal funding for universities as a blatant case of
federal interference in provincial affairs. Supporters of the commission took pains to point out that the report had carefully differentiated
between federal funding and federal control.[27] Most opinion in the
French-Canadian press again agreed that the safeguards against federal control of education suggested by the report were sufficient to
protect provincial rights.

Yet for months to come Lévesque would have to contend with a
vocal and determined group of nationalists who accused him of selling
out French-Canadian interests. They launched a campaign against the
report in which the character assassination of Lévesque was a major
tactic. He was attacked so violently in the press, the Legislative As-
sembly, and the House of Commons that his colleagues at Laval felt
compelled to pass a motion in his support. But worse followed. In
L'Action nationale, François-Albert Angers portrayed Lévesque as an
anti-francophone and anti-Catholic traitor who was part of an anglophone conspiracy against French-Canadian culture. The Union Nationale reprinted part of this article as a pamphlet and distributed it

widely during the winter of 1952. Later these accusations were embroidered with the charge that Lévesque had literally been paid off by the federal government in return for his cooperation. The payments in question were actually compensation for the extra work he had taken on in translating the report and for expenses he had incurred overseas. Neatby had received similar amounts, but this was explained by 'insinuations malveillantes' that labelled them 'père et mère de la Commission Massey.'[28] Liberals rallied to defend Lévesque, and an acrimonious dispute that centred on his actions and character as much as on university funding raged for months before subsiding into the general ebb and flow of provincial autonomy issues in which Quebec was awash throughout the 1950s.

While federal funding for universities proved controversial in Quebec, elsewhere broadcasting was the most contentious issue. The proposal that the CBC. retain supervisory powers over broadcasting provoked more discussion and criticism than any other recommendation of the report. Entire editorials were devoted to this one subject in major newspapers across the country, eclipsing questions about CBC funding, programming, and television development. Unlike arts subsidies, cultural institutions, or university aid, broadcasting was an area which directly affected most Canadians. Suspicions of elitism were more rampant here than anywhere else. 'The Massey Commission's recommendations for Canadian radio will probably win wild applause from intellectuals and groups dedicated to uplift,' commented the Hodgeville (Saskatchewan) *Standard*, 'but there is little in them to cheer the average Canadian. Obviously the Commission is not interested in whether or not the man on the street gets the kind of radio listening he wants.'[29] Supporters of private broadcasting relentlessly exploited such sentiments in their attacks on the report's broadcasting recommendations.

It was on this vexed issue that most newspapers finally invoked their free enterprise principles. Most did not deny the need for public broadcasting but thought there was room for both public and private interests to coexist within the one system. An independent regulatory body, they argued, could continue to control broadcasting in the national interest. In short, they refused to accept the report's contention that only the CBC could regulate broadcasting in the proper manner. Many of the newspapers that took this stand were defending principal as much as principle. Numerous newspaper owners, including those of the Southam and Sifton chains, also owned radio stations. Their patriotic sentiments supported national cultural development only as long as private profits were not at stake.

There was plenty of ammunition available for proponents of an independent regulatory board. 'Our Montreal colleague,' Massey remarked to MacKenzie, 'has given the enemies of public service broadcasting, as we knew he would, a very powerful weapon and they are taking full advantage of it.'[30] Indeed, the president of the Canadian Association of Broadcasters (CAB) considered the Massey Report something of a breakthrough because Surveyer's minority report represented the first public endorsement of the CAB's demands from a source independent of the broadcasting lobby. Canadian newspapers assured their readers that it was to be expected that Surveyer would have better judgment on such an issue because he was, after all, the only businessman on the commission. All of the arguments made by the CAB and private stations before the commission resurfaced in their columns.

This sort of commentary was to be expected. The real shock came when Canada's premier magazines, *Maclean's* and *Saturday Night*, also endorsed the idea of a separate regulatory board. Both subscribed to Surveyer's suggestion that it would in fact be better for the CBC and public broadcasting. The only strong defence of the report's regulatory recommendations came from the left-leaning *Canadian Forum*, where, in contrast to the rest of the Canadian press, disrespect for free enterprise was the byword. Frank Underhill wrote that in their appearances before the commission the private stations had 'showed themselves up for the selfish cynical profit-making agencies that they are.'[31] In the same journal Allan Sangster argued that if anything the CBC should be encouraged to turn the screws a little tighter on the private stations.[32]

The press reaction to the report's recommendation on broadcasting regulation was generally critical and often nasty. But, on the whole, the Massey commissioners were pleasantly surprised by the extent of interest displayed in their report and the positive response it evoked. It was selling briskly enough that a second edition would have to be printed by the end of the year. Neatby admitted to MacKenzie in mid-June that 'the Report seems to be going over in a way that I find surprising as well as gratifying.'[33] She would later accurately summarize opposition to it as emanating from anti-elitist, laissez-faire, and French-Canadian nationalist opinion (she labelled these detractors 'barbarians,' 'nineteenth-century liberals,' and 'French-Canadian chauvinists').[34] The commissioners, however, had anticipated all of these objections in their report and were pleased to see that their arguments were holding their own in the public forum.

The prospect of action on the report was brightened by the fact that the opposition parties seemed to be favourably disposed to at least some of the commission's recommendations. Broadcasting was a sore point, of course, but there was unanimous support for federal funding for universities. While attacking the report's failure to recommend an independent regulatory board for broadcasting, both the Conservatives and Social Credit applauded the proposal for university aid. The CCF, on the other hand, enthusiastically embraced both proposals. With unanimous support in the Commons, there seemed to be a good possibility that something would be done for the universities in the immediate future. In fact, there had been pressure for action in this area for months, and although officially action was being delayed until the Massey Report was tabled, the government had been preparing to take immediate steps on the issue.

Despite these propitious omens, the National Conference of Canadian Universities (NCCU) was leaving nothing to chance. It launched a publicity campaign two weeks before the publication of the report to push for implementation of university funding. This was by no means an unnecessary measure, for St Laurent was still haunted by premonitions of constitutional controversy and conflict with Duplessis. At one point he considered skirting the issue by raising tax rental payments on the understanding that the provinces would use the money to increase their support for universities. Jack Pickersgill countered that there was no guarantee that such funds would reach their intended destinations and kept pressuring for direct funding for the universities.[35]

On 19 June St Laurent announced to the House of Commons that the government intended to take action on two of the report's recommendations by providing an interim grant for the CBC to cover its expenses for the rest of the fiscal year and grants to universities 'along lines recommended by the Massey commission.'[36] In the latter case, a sum of fifty cents for each Canadian citizen, or about $7 million, would be divided among the provinces in proportion to their populations. This announcement was welcomed by all of the opposition parties. In its initial form it was only a temporary emergency measure, but St Laurent proposed to work out a permanent scheme for distributing federal funds through talks with the NCCU and the provinces.

These negotiations proceeded over the next year, but not without running into snags. One problem was that opposition to distributing the grants on the basis of provincial populations emerged because it created a wide discrepancy in dollars per student from one province to another. Nova Scotia in particular was unhappy with the method of distribution. It had more universities and university students per capita than other provinces, so that it received less money for each of its students.

Although Premier Duplessis regarded the federal offer as another example of the central government's attempt to bribe Quebeckers with funds originally stolen from them by the federal hijacking of tax revenues, he delayed, quibbled, then finally accepted the grants on a provincial basis for one year in the winter of 1952.[37] Then, as nationalist protest against the grants mounted, he began to reconsider. When the federal government failed to address his concerns about provincial autonomy in the permanent funding arrangements it subsequently devised in 1953, Duplessis refused the grants outright. In retaliation for the Massey Commission and other federal centralizing plots, he created a royal commission of his own, the Tremblay Commission, on 12 February 1953 and instructed it to investigate 'constitutional problems.' It would delve into the historical and sociological foundations of Quebec society to justify the French-Canadian nationalist side of the federal-provincial quarrel on the basis of the compact theory of Confederation.[38]

In the meantime the commissioners were busy promoting their report. Although they had doubts about how active an advocacy role former commissioners should play, they did everything they could to promote the cause within reasonable limits. Massey was annoyed that the King's Printer had not marketed the report more aggressively and ensured that complimentary copies reached influential figures in Canada and abroad. Lévesque surpassed even the chairman in this department, giving away over 170 copies – including one to the Vatican – and causing bureaucratic consternation about who should pay for his largesse.[39] On the Prairies, Neatby gave talks in church halls and wrote articles explaining the report. MacKenzie arranged a cocktail party for local newspaper editors and radio commentators at the Hotel Vancouver and mobilized the UBC faculty to speak at clubs and schools, arranging invitations for them by pulling strings in the UBC Alumni Association.

Many of the commissioners' promotional activities intermeshed with the efforts of voluntary organizations. The Canadian Arts Council and its seventeen member organizations plotted ways and means of drawing public attention to the report.[40] Across the country meetings like that of the Community Arts Council of Vancouver, with its theme of 'Let's get action on the Massey Report,' were held to publicize the cause. As debate over the report intensified, the *Canadian Forum* sounded a call to arms for the culture lobby: 'The battle is joined. The energy and resources of the Friends of the Massey Report is [*sic*] pitted against the Enemies of the Massey Report. Take your side, select your weapons, and prepare for the fray.'[41] The CAAE's *Food for Thought*, observing that 'what we have in Canada is government by pressure,' urged its readers to 'press the government for a Canada Council.'[42] It would take more than public pressure, however, to ensure that action was taken on the commission's recommendations. Neatby encouraged Massey to use his influence to make sure the commissions' views were strongly represented to the government committee preparing permanent policy on federal funding for universities. Although she reproached herself for suggesting such deviousness – 'How I hate politics and (forgive me) diplomacy!' she exclaimed – she recognized that inside influence would have to be exercised if the report was to be implemented.[43]

Massey's influence with the government was temporarily limited because he was reluctant to stir up trouble at a time when his appointment as governor general hung in the balance. Nevertheless, Lévesque was a friend of St Laurent, and MacKenzie was intimately connected with many of the English Canadians of his generation in power. Within a year, in fact, the promise of a cabinet post would be dangled to entice MacKenzie to run in the next election. He would refuse the offer but remained well placed to monitor and lobby for the implementation of the commission's recommendations. With a future governor general, a friend of the prime minister, and a potential cabinet minister in their ranks, the former commissioners were capable of making their wishes heard where it counted.

'The climate in Ottawa seems receptive to some, at least, of our recommendations,' wrote Massey to MacKenzie in September. 'There is on the subject of broadcasting however going to be a bitter debate.'[44] Massey predicted that the CAB and its allies would make the most of the upcoming hearings of the parliamentary committee on radio and recommended that MacKenzie try to motivate defenders of public broadcasting to make representations there as well. In November the government presented a bill to amend the Broadcasting Act in accord with the recommendations of the Massey Report.[45] This touched off a spirited debate in the House of Commons in which the opposition parties continued to press their positions on the issue. After its second reading the bill went to the Select Committee on Radio Broadcasting for review, where the CAB appeared to argue its case. Although the CBC was under fire at the time for allowing 'antireligious' broadcasts, which critics interpreted as signs of godless communism on the air waves, the committee decided in favour of the legislative changes based on the report. A few months later Revenue Minister J.J. McCann informed the House that the CBC was also making progress in fulfilling the commission's directive to reduce its advertising.

In late March of 1952, MacKenzie wrote to Day (who was now head of the Information Division of the Department of External Affairs) asking for a 'low-down on our magnum opus' – who in cabinet was interested in it and the prospects for its further implementation – because he was planning to organize a private lobby 'to give it a little boost along.'[46] Day replied with an up-to-date score card:

(a) Radio and television – implemented pretty much as recommended.
(b) Film Board – some action including purchase of land for consolidated building in Montreal.
(c) National Gallery – the Director made a Deputy, the Board to be enlarged, and permission granted to carry over accumulated funds for purchases into next fiscal year; new building shelved.
(d) Museums – no visible action.

(e) National Library – this to come into legal being in two or three months, but the Commission has had little to do with this matter.

(f) Archives – no action, though I understand there has been some slight stirring in the organization.

(g) Historic sites and monuments – no action apart from $125,000 provided for Halifax Citadel.

(h) Aid to universities – $7,100,000 granted.

(i) National scholarships – no action likely this session.

(j) Information abroad – no action except that External Affairs will have a very few additional officers this year and next, and some of them may be assigned to information work.

(k) Canada Council – this has been given definitely a hoist for this year.[47]

Besides the provision of funding for universities and the CBC legislation, gains had been relatively minor. In general, the culture lobby was disappointed that so little had been done.

As time passed things did not get any better. Only 12 of the report's 146 recommendations were implemented two years after its release.[48] The National Library Act received royal assent on 18 June 1952, and plans for a new building were in the works. The National Film Board was promised a $5-million new building in Montreal to consolidate its operations, and a sum of $1 million was set aside in 1953–4 to provide for a public records storage building for the Archives. But these modest gains were offset by some significant losses. There was no sign of action on a national scholarships plan. Ignoring the warnings of the report, the government bowed to pressure from private sector demands for television licences. By the summer of 1953 seven private licences had been granted and eight more applications were in the works, contrary to the commissioners' recommendation that they be denied until the public system was well under way. In the same year the government contravened another recommendation of the report by dropping the unpopular licence fees for radio and television sets. It seemed that the commission's impact had been minuscule and fleeting. 'After all the polite speeches,' Neatby wrote sadly in 1956, 'the public voice has pronounced against the recommendations of the report.'[49]

Neatby's glum conclusion reflected a disappointment that pervaded the culture lobby. The lack of action on the Canada Council proposal was particularly disillusioning. It was an initiative that had lain at the heart of the report's strategy for national cultural development. But the very qualities which made the proposal so dear to its supporters made the government shy away from it. It was too novel an idea – its purposes too exclusively cultural – to warrant the prompt action accorded broadcasting and university funding. Throughout the early 1950s the Liberal government tossed the Council proposal around like a hot potato, but could never bring itself to serve it up to the public.

The culture lobby fought hard to get action on the Council, sending letters and telegrams to the prime minister and lobbying individual MPs to apply pressure in the House.[50] The government was considering introducing legislation on the Canada Council in the fall of 1951 but ended up deferring any action until the following year. Day speculated that there had been second thought at this stage because of concern about Massey's name being dragged into a contentious debate on the eve of his appointment as governor general.[51] In the winter of 1952 MacKenzie wrote to Pickersgill for an update. Pickersgill replied that ministers like Claxton, Pearson, and Walter Harris were interested in the project but had yet to introduce any concrete plans.[52] As expectations that something would happen that year gradually dissipated, the culture lobby despaired. The original impetus provided by the Massey Report was petering out, and the odds of anything being done grew longer each time action was deferred.

Then, in a debate in the House of Commons in April 1953, St Laurent attributed the lack of progress on the Council to a seemingly trivial obstacle: problems in recruiting suitable members for its board of directors. The best candidates, he explained, were too busy with other concerns to take up such an appointment. The prime minister assured the House that action would come soon: 'I think I have planted seeds that will germinate, and that it will be possible for the Canadian government, whoever may be at the head of it then, within a reasonable time to get the kind of men who would honour themselves and honour the position by undertaking the responsibilities of that kind of council ... It is something which should not be delayed, something which should be done reasonably soon.'[53] But once again months went by with no sign of any action. In September 1953 MacKenzie again wrote to Pickersgill, who had recently joined the cabinet as secretary of state, to urge him to give the government a prod.[54] He outlined how he felt the Council should be set up and offered to send along a more detailed plan if it would help.

Pickersgill replied with a report of his latest discussion with St Laurent on the Council. The prime minister professed to be still very much interested in the idea, but his visit to the Far East was distracting him from any immediate action. He had told Pickersgill, however, that 'he would be most grateful if you and Geoff could quietly do some detailed work on it, as and when you could find the time, so that we could really get something worked out next year.'[55] MacKenzie seized upon the prime minister's suggestion, and Andrew drew up a draft act for the Canada Council, using the National Research Council as a model. A delegation from the Canadian Arts Council was told by government ministers the following March that the Canada Council was still very much on their agenda.[56] But progress came at a glacial pace. It was the fall of 1954 before Pickersgill had some good news for MacKenzie: 'Your letter with the draft bill on the Canada Council arrived most opportunely. An Interdepartmental Committee is, at the moment, preparing a scheme for consideration by Mike Pearson, Walter Harris, Jean Lesage and me, with a view to submitting something to Cabinet at an early date.'[57] The committee was being kept secret in order to avoid arousing concern in Quebec about another federal violation of its jurisdiction.[58] But nothing came of the committee's efforts because the government became distracted by the fallout of the truce over taxes negotiated between St Laurent and Duplessis at the Windsor Hotel in Montreal on 5 October 1954. St Laurent became noncommittal when questioned about the fate of the Council in the House. Once again hope dissolved into frustration. Lobbying for the Council had become a painful ritual, and continuing frustration made it difficult to maintain enthusiasm for the cause.

But the Council's supporters refused to give up. The university community, which had an obvious interest in the scholarship functions of the Council, kept pressing the government. Voluntary associations and artists' groups held meetings to publicize the cause and push the government for action. Early in 1955 J.R. Kidd, Ned Corbett's successor as director of the Canadian Association for Adult Education, wrote to H.H. Hannam, head of the Canadian Federation of Agriculture, about his 'growing concern about the fate of the recommendations of the Massey Report.' He attributed the lack of action to opposition within the Liberal party and the government: 'Most of the Liberal party, believing that "there isn't a single vote in a stack of Reports" may let it die quickly, if they can ... Some powerful people, one of whom is Howe, have joined with other opponents in an effort to sneer away the Report ... Others have said that only "funny little minorities" presented their views.'[59] Kidd was trying to breathe life back into the culture lobby to reassert pressure on the government. He wanted the Canadian Federation of Agriculture to pass a resolution calling for implementation of the Massey Report's recommendations.

While MacKenzie was pestering Pickersgill and the culture lobby was pressing for action, Massey and Lévesque were using their connections in the capital to press towards the same goal. Massey had constitutional scruples about openly campaigning for the Council from his vice-regal post, but he actively encouraged Lévesque to do so. Lévesque often sought audiences with his friend St Laurent to urge him to act:

> Il m'arrivait donc de faire souvent la navette entre le 24 Sussex et Rideau Hall, parfois accompagné gentiment par mon ami et ancien étudiant Maurice Lamontagne, alors membre du Conseil privé. J'avais beau plaider de mon mieux, M. Saint-Laurent semblait toujours atermoyer et devenait de plus en plus embarrassé devant mon insistance. Un jour il crut bon de se délivrer d'un secret qui lui pesait: 'Ce que vous demandez n'est pas facile à réaliser. Du reste, je dois affronter passablement d'opposition au sein même de mon cabinet. Particulièrement, le ministre C.D. Howe n'est guère intéressé à consacrer des fonds à la promotion de nos valeurs culturelles.'[60]

When Lévesque reported this encounter to Massey, the governor general arranged to have Lévesque sit next to Howe at an upcoming state dinner at Rideau Hall, telling his Dominican accomplice to 'please do your job.'[61] After exchanging small talk and establishing a rapport with the formidable 'Minister of Everything,' Lévesque pried open a chink in his opponent's armour:

'Monsieur le ministre, lui dis-je, j'ai lu récemment dans les journaux que l'on vient de dessiner pour votre ministère de la Défense nationale un prototype d'avion de chasse qui, paraît-il, est assez impressionnant. – Ah! oui, répond-il fièrement. Sans doute réussirons-nous à le vendre également à d'autres pays.' Je reprends: 'Si j'ai bien compris, ce prototype coûtera environ cent millions de dollars. – Oui, exactement.' J'enchaîne: 'Et si éclate une nouvelle guerre mondiale – ce qu'à Dieu ne plaise! – probablement que nous vous servirez de ces avions, selon la formule publicitaire bien connue lors de la dernière guerre, pour défendre la civilisation chrétienne, les valeurs de l'humanisme, etc. – En effect, pourquoi pas? dit-il.' Une fois lancé, je continue de plus belle: 'C'était là un de vos grands thèmes publicitaires contre le nazisme, n'est-ce pas? Avec raison, du reste. Mais ce qui m'étonne, c'est qu'on soit prêt à dépenser cent millions de dollars pour un prototype d'avion destiné à sauver nos valeurs morales et culturelles, alors qu'on refuse de payer le même montant pour les conserver et les défendre en temps de paix. Cette attitude est difficile à comprendre, je vous l'avoue bien honnêtement.' On devine que M. Howe saisit vite la balle au bond et que je n'ai pas à lui faire un dessin, come on dit. Il se tourne vivement vers M. Massey en lui disant d'un air entendu et légèrement malicieux: 'Le père Lévesque vous aurait fait un bon avocat, vous ne pensez pas?' Connsaissant bien l'intérêt que le gouverneur général porte au Conseil des arts à créer, il a facilement percé notre complot.[62]

Nevertheless, Howe seemed impressed by this encounter. One of the major obstructions in the way of the Canada Council had been battered if not breached.

There followed a conjunction of circumstances which gave the Council proposal a final push forward. Pickersgill was in the habit of walking to work from his home in Rockcliffe, and one summer morning in 1956 he fell in with John Deutsch, secretary of the Treasury Board, who made the same daily trek. Deutsch mentioned that the estates of two fabled Canadian millionaires who had died the year before, Izaak Walton Killam and Sir James Hamet Dunn, promised to yield succession duties of over $100 million. He thought it would be nice if this windfall could be put to some special use instead of simply being absorbed into general revenues. It was natural that Pickersgill, given his interest in getting the Canada Council idea off the ground over the previous five years, would put two and two together: ' "John," he said, "how would it be if we persuaded the government to provide 50 million of this 100 million to meet these capital needs – or some of them – of the universities. And another 50 million to provide an endowment for the Canada Council." '63 Deutsch passed the suggestion on to Maurice Lamontagne, St Laurent's economic adviser and Lévesque's friend and former pupil.

Lamontagne had already been pushing St Laurent to set up the Council. At the time he had to write a speech for St Laurent for a special conference of the NCCU that was to meet in Ottawa that fall to consider ways of meeting the demand for university education that was anticipated in the decade ahead. St Laurent was at a loss about what to say on this occasion, so Lamontagne, taking long odds but with nothing to lose, suggested that he announce the doubling of federal grants to universities and the creation of the Canada Council. 'St Laurent looked at him as if he had "devenu fou." But when Lamontagne explained about the succession windfalls, "le visage du prime minister commenca alors à s'éclairer." '64 St Laurent, impressed by the logical conspiracy of coincidence, could think of no good reason not to pursue this suggestion. 'I will speak to Howe,' he replied, and later phoned Lamontagne to tell him to go ahead with preparing both the speech and the necessary legislation.65

On 12 November 1956 St Laurent announced at the NCCU conference that legislation establishing the Canada Council would be presented to the next session of Parliament. In his speech he pledged a doubling of existing university grants, plus $50 million in capital grants for university expansion over the next decade, and $50 million to endow the Canada Council. The Canada Council had piggy-backed into existence behind the government's efforts to deal with the more politically significant issue of funding the expansion of post-secondary education. Legislation establishing the Council was passed on 28 March 1957; its first head would be none other than Brooke Claxton, now retired from politics. It was last-minute timing. Less than a month later St Laurent called the election that would banish the Liberal friends of the cultural elite from the corridors of power until the middle of the next decade.

While these intrigues surrounding the Canada Council were unfolding, only piecemeal action had been taken on recommendations for existing federal cultural institutions. Improvements were made to the Historic Sites and Monuments Board in 1952; various scholarship schemes and means of promoting Canada's image abroad were adopted; and the NFB moved into its new headquarters in Montreal in 1956. Looking back on the report ten years after its publication, John Robbins would summarize progress in this area as follows: 'Recommendations concerning the National Gallery included a new building; this has been erected and is now occupied. A similar request for a new building for the National Museum has not been met, but more space has been allocated in the old building. A National Library "without delay" was demanded. While there has been some delay in the provision of a building, certain services have been established and building plans completed. Various recommendations concerning the Public Archives have been implemented.'[66] The National Gallery's 'new building,' however, was just a temporary home in the Lorne Building on Elgin Street in Ottawa. At least this move gave the National Museum some of the room it needed. The Geological Survey moved out of the Victoria Building in 1959, and when the National Gallery left in 1960 the National Museum was finally able to take over the entire building originally constructed for it fifty years earlier. Meanwhile the Public Archives and the National Library had to wait for their new home. It was planned during the 1950s, but a series of delays kept it from being completed until 1967.

The attention accorded the Massey Report and the government's quick action in the areas of broadcasting and universities certainly made a splash in the summer of 1951. But the commotion subsided quickly, and thereafter it became very difficult to get the government to take decisive steps on any of the commission's other recommendations. The government's indifferent response to the report was not surprising when its original reasons for establishing the commission are taken into account. The areas which got attention were those which had prompted the creation of the commission; both were political quagmires into which the commission had been dispatched to chart a path that the government could safely follow. The other issues had originally provided camouflage for this venture and were forgotten when they were no longer useful. The ruse had been taken seriously by the commissioners and the culture lobby, however, and they kept these cultural interests alive, hoping that the government would fulfil all the expectations it had unwittingly created. After disgorging its cargo, the Trojan Horse had taken on a life of its own.

Conclusion

The Massey Commission is often proclaimed to have been one of the most effective of Canadian royal commissions. Invariably this judgment is based on the claim that it had far more of its recommendations implemented than most royal commissions. This leads to assertions that its influence changed the course of Canadian cultural development for generations to come. Massey's biographer presented a typical assessment of this sort: 'By 1957, all of the major recommendations of the report had been implemented ... No other Canadian commission, before or since, has had such an immediate and transforming effect.'[1] It is romantic to think that the Massey Commission had a revolutionary impact, but both of these assertions are debatable and require some examination and qualification.

A cynic might divide the major recommendations of the commission into three general categories: those that were about to be fulfilled in any case; those that were never acted upon or were reversed; and those that eventually came into being, but not necessarily because of the commission. Federal funding for universities falls into the first category. It was not part of the commission's original mandate, and the government had decided to go ahead with it before the commission's report was tabled. Likewise, television policy was established before the commission was created, and the new Film Act based on the Woods-Gordon Report on the National Film Board was introduced while the Massey Commission was still in the middle of its work.

The founding of the National Library was yet another example: before the commission was created, the government had already committed itself to the bibliographical project that was expected to lead to the establishment of the Library.

In the second category – omissions and reversals – fall numerous lesser recommendations and one of the commissioners' major policy concerns. As we have seen, less than 10 per cent of the commission's recommendations had been followed two years after the report was tabled. The administrative arrangements suggested for the National Museum and the National Library, for example, were ignored by the government. There was no action on a national scholarships plan. Perhaps these can be dismissed as relatively minor matters. But even on major issues the commissioners' vision was less than triumphant. The Massey Commission's great defensive victory, the rejection of the private broadcasters' demand for a separate regulatory body for broadcasting, was destined to be short-lived. The Fowler Commission, established in 1955 in response to both the continuing financial problems of the CBC (another indication of the commission's failure) and the Massey Commission's own recommendation for a further study of television, came out in favour of an independent regulatory body for broadcasting. The Diefenbaker government established the Board of Broadcast Governors with the Broadcasting Act of 1958.

Finally, there were those recommendations which eventually were acted upon but after a time-lag that renders the real impact of the commission somewhat questionable. The enhancement of federal cultural institutions falls into this category. Were improvements that came ten or twenty years later the result of the commission's influence? Is it realistic to suggest, as Lévesque did in his memoirs, that the government was still implementing the Massey Report when it build a new National Museum and National Gallery in the 1980s?[2] Questions such as these could be asked at tedious length, but the Canada Council is the most obvious and important case in point. The Council idea was around well before the Massey Commission came into being – the Arts Council of Great Britain was known and admired in cultural circles across the country. Moreover, it was six years following the Massey report and only after a conjunction of happy coincidences that the Canada Council was created. This was hardly a case of the Massey Commission having an 'immediate and transforming effect.' Most of the Massey Commission's reputation rests on a recommendation that almost never saw the light of day.

In each of these cases the commission enjoyed a less than complete victory over the different types of opposition that its report aroused. French-Canadian nationalist intransigence prevented a universal acceptance of federal funding for universities until a compromise was reached between Ottawa and Quebec at the end of the decade. The private broadcasters, with their free enterprise arguments, eventually got their way in broadcasting regulation. And the prejudices of certain government insiders, coupled with a political fear of the popular suspicion of 'culchah,' almost prevented the creation of the Canada Council. Even then, Brooke Claxton suspected that a popular backlash against the Council's creation helped defeat the Liberals in the 1957 election.

An argument could be made, then, that the Massey Commission had a limited or negligible effect in many of the areas where it supposedly succeeded. But if counting the number of recommendations implemented suggests that claims made for the commission on this level have been exaggerated, it is nevertheless an inadequate means for fully gauging its impact. In a less restrictive sense it is undeniable that the Massey Commission did have a significant influence in each of the four major areas of its work. The role that the commission's public hearings played in publicizing the universities' cause and generating the pressure that moved the government to act in this area cannot be discounted. Similarly, the commission put the Canada Council proposal squarely on the public agenda and determined the form in which it would eventually be realized. Its efforts on behalf of federal cultural institutions raised their profiles and, at the very least, made them harder for the government to ignore. Even its attempts to shore up the hegemony of the CBC can be seen as a successful holding action against forces that would ultimately prove to be overwhelming.

Still, the real significance of the Massey Commission lies less in the fate of its major initiatives than in the general impact it had upon the attitudes of the public and the policies of the government. It helped usher in a new age in which a conscious and coordinated government cultural policy came to be expected.[3] One has to ask, however, how much of this change was due to the commission and how much was attributable to changing times of which the commission itself was simply a reflection. In the postwar era, Canadians were becoming increasingly affluent, educated, and leisured. Under these conditions it is not surprising that their cultural activities increased. Nationalistic feelings spurred by a sense of independence, accomplishment, and international status also made them eager to embrace the cultural trappings of nationhood that were associated with other more mature nations. Since the state was becoming increasingly interventionist in the same period, it is hardly surprising that it assumed greater responsibility in cultural affairs.

The Massey Commission was itself a product of these changing postwar conditions. But, as Neatby would later observe, it 'was, in a sense, a symptom which in turn became, no doubt, in part a contributory cause.'4 The scattered ranks of the cultural community rallied around the commission and were forged into a purposeful lobby. The commission translated their ideas and energy into a public crusade in which the main focus was on generating enough publicity to sway public opinion and impress the government so that new policies could be initiated by sympathetic insiders. By associating high culture with national development, the culture lobby identified its vested interests with the contemporary aspirations of the Canadian nation. This process hastened the arrival of a new era in which culture was recognized as a legitimate concern of government, and as such, one that required serious attention, coordinated management, and a comprehensive strategy. Through its public hearings and its report, the Massey Commission expedited an incipient change of attitude within Canadian political culture. This is hardly the dramatic stuff of revolutionary progress, but it is often the way in which history is made.

The culture lobby learned from the experience and would continue trying to influence government cultural policy in the future. The lessons gleaned by the Radio League, ignored during years of depression and war, had been revived and would pay off in the postwar years of prosperity and peace. The humanist intellectuals of the cultural elite benefited most from this new activism, since they staffed the universities and cultural institutions and did the research which received new government support. Although they had not vanquished their rival elites in business and science, they had been raised to a similar status as clients of the expanding service state. They had finally achieved access to government support which other interest groups had enjoyed for generations.[5]

But the culture lobby was motivated by ideological conviction as well as self-interest. The political implications of culture were very pronounced in the thinking of the commissioners, the cultural elite, and much of the culture lobby they led. The Cold War made intellectuals and the general public alike acutely concerned about the meaning of liberal democracy and the need to defend it against rival political ideologies. At the same time, peacetime prosperity was reviving a consumer economy driven by advertising that in turn accelerated the growth of mass culture through the media. The culture lobby found the materialistic and acquisitive values promoted by the consumer economy distasteful, but it thought that the potential of the media for mass persuasion was truly frightening. Mass culture was to be feared because it seemed so closely related to the propaganda employed by both communist and fascist totalitarian regimes.

By opposing mass culture the culture lobby pitted itself against business and technology, two dominant forces in modern Western society. It believed that society should instead be guided by the humanistic values implicit in high culture. This conviction reflected the 'moral imperative' that ran through the thought of many of Canada's earlier educational, religious, and cultural leaders. The fact that the Massey Commission displayed this traditional concern has led more than one observer to characterize its outlook as conservative. Some see the commissioners' philosophy as just one link in a tory intellectual tradition which connects the dreams of turn-of-the-century imperialists with George Grant's despair about the possibility of fulfilling that vision in the 1960s.

Whether one characterizes the ideology of the Massey Commission as conservative or not is largely a question of semantics, but the label can be misleading. If liberalism is defined by a commitment to unfettered capitalistic and technological growth, the commission's outlook certainly was not liberal. But the commissioners resisted mass culture precisely because they saw it as a threat to liberty. They defined liberal freedom in human terms, while capitalism defined it in terms of free enterprise and science, in terms of freedom of inquiry. The humanistic principles with which they would infuse society were, admittedly, a form of moral authority, but it was a minimal authority derived from a high culture that the citizen would imbibe voluntarily and impose individually. In their eyes the only alternative was an increasing subjection of liberal democracy to technological and capitalist imperatives that presented far greater menaces to liberty. The traditional high culture they promoted might seem reactionary or elitist, but they embraced it because they believed that a liberal humanist ethic essential to modern society lay at its core.

The commissioners may have echoed the concerns of earlier generations of Canadian intellectuals, but their outlook was conditioned most profoundly by their determination to apply their own convictions to the problems of their times. Canada's wartime accomplishments and new international status encouraged a feeling among Canadians that their nation was coming of age and defining its character in the process. The commissioners responded, not by applying a stale set of prejudices, but by drawing on basic principles to chart a course for a nation whose future seemed to be full of promise and amenable to guidance. In the past, when Canadian cultural nationalists identified the difference between their liberal democratic tradition and that of the American republic, their emphasis had been on social order. Whether it was imperialists invoking British tradition or idealists stressing Christian faith, the accent was on sources of authority that would prevent the liberal society from degenerating into chaos. In the Cold War context, however, despotism seemed more of an immediate danger than anarchy. The cultural elite fused this concern with Canadian nationalism by associating the United States not with freedom but with the illiberal menace of mass culture. The moral was obvious: Canada alone represented the last best hope for liberal democratic values in an uncertain world. In retrospect this may be dismissed as a naïve notion arising out of optimistic extrapolations upon a fleeting nationalist moment, but at the time it infused Canadian cultural nationalism with hope for the future rather than with bitterness about a lost past.

The culture lobby's combination of high culture and nationalism was not without its internal tensions. Cultural elitism emphasized high standards and a cosmopolitan frame of reference; cultural nationalism sought popularity and particularity. But the potential differences between elitism and nationalism were overshadowed by the fact that they shared a common enemy. American mass culture was a threat to Canadian nationalism because it was foreign; to high culture because it was unedifying. In the ideology of the Canadian culture lobby, nationalism and elitism merged in an alliance aimed at developing a Canadian culture opposed to the invasion of 'American' mass culture. The commissioners exploited contemporary nationalist aspirations by offering a coherent vision of a superior national identity. By brandishing the flag, they made the cause of high culture both less recognizable and more attractive to the average Canadian.

The culture lobby's outlook on cultural issues was framed by certain habitual points of reference. The most obvious was its tendency to view all cultural questions in terms of a conflict between high culture and mass culture. Perhaps certain cultural activities could be rated as 'high' or 'low' according to set criteria, but this simple dichotomy distorted the complex reality of cultural consumption. How did one categorize a household that tuned into the 'Metropolitan Opera' on Saturday afternoon and 'Hockey Night in Canada' that same evening? Was the university president who patronized burlesque shows a highbrow or a lowbrow? Indeed, the occasional voices which the commission heard from the general public suggested that most Canadians were neither aspiring aesthetes nor zombies programmed by media brainwashing. No doubt both irredeemable lowbrows and thoroughly enlightened highbrows existed in Canadian society, but most people had unique cultural preferences that placed them somewhere in between. Belief in a cultural hierarchy was not, however, exclusive to the culture lobby: widespread public suspicions of high culture demonstrated that it was a convention accepted throughout Canadian society. In the postwar world, more Canadians were patronizing or participating in activities that could be considered 'high' culture. Yet they seemed to be able to retain a suspicion of culture in the abstract even when it was an enriching part of their lives.

The culture lobby interpreted what it saw of Canadians' cultural activities in a way that reinforced its own ideology and displayed the fundamental tension between liberalism and democracy. On the one hand, it wanted to show that high culture was something demanded by the democratic will of the people. To this end it cited examples of how the liberal faith in self-improvement was confirmed through Canadians' growing interest in painting, theatre, literature, music – indeed, in all the arts thriving in the newly prosperous and leisured postwar world. The problem was that if mass culture were similarly construed as an expression of democratic will, quite different conclusions would necessarily follow. So mass culture was portrayed, not as a popular choice, but as a repressive force which stifled the individual's free progress towards cultural edification. The abstract conception of high culture versus mass culture was overlaid with a good versus evil, humanism versus technology, liberal versus authoritarian dichotomy. It was an attractive analysis because it implied a simple solution. Since high culture was the free choice of the educated and mass culture the oppressor of the ignorant, cultural and political salvation became a relatively straightforward matter of edifying the unenlightened.

This demonization of mass culture absolved Canadians of their cultural sins by denying that they were a matter of conscious choice. If the culture lobby had instead seen Canadians as worldly consumers who consciously exercised certain preferences within a diverse cultural scene, mass culture could not have been portrayed as a monolithic, manipulative, and mind-numbing threat. But in classic liberal fashion, it preferred to assume that individuals were inherently good (according to its definition of human goodness) and needed only to be freed from the bonds of mass culture to fulfil their innate capabilities. Equality of opportunity was the only prerequisite, and the culture lobby was unduly optimistic about its attainment. Factors such as economic status, social conditioning, ethnic origins, and simple predilections in taste were discounted in the expectation that every individual would naturally seek self-improvement by emulating the culture lobby and embracing traditional high culture.

This assumption clearly displayed the peculiar mixture of liberalism and elitism that distinguished the ideology of the commissioners as well. Their desire to popularize high culture was a generous impulse in that they wished to confer upon others the benefits that they enjoyed, but their idea of what was good for others was entirely defined by the cultural limitations of their elitist point of view. Their enterprise continually bumped up against the fact that high culture was not very amenable to popularization. Patriotic Canadians would support the idea of state-sponsored high culture, but that did not mean they were interested in personally sampling the goods. The commissioners were unwilling to debase high culture in order to popularize it, but neither would they force it down people's throats. In the end their liberal democratic consciences ensured that their elitist dream of edifying the masses would never be realized.

Their cause would, in any case, lose much of its urgency in ensuing decades. As their worst fears about mass culture failed to materialize, a wide variety of cultural activities won greater acceptance as vibrant expressions of modern life. The rise of television, rock and roll, and the 1960s counter-culture would expand this new tolerance far past previously established boundaries and alter the cultural scene beyond recognition. In the process the critics of mass culture would have some of their favourite arguments turned against them. Mass culture, rehabilitated as popular culture, would be celebrated for its ability to accept and legitimize a variety of regional and ethnic traditions in a tolerant and pluralistic fashion. High culture would be portrayed as inflexible and authoritarian in comparison.

At the same time high culture was itself being transformed in ways that the commissioners would neither recognize nor sanction. The political and social ends for which they valued culture were predicated on a generally accepted classical canon that provided a rational and integrated sense of civilization. But modern art was being transformed by abstract painting, stream-of-consciousness writing, improvisational jazz, and myriad other novel cultural expressions which constituted an overwhelming assault on established conventions and the rule of reason. A variety of marginal and discordant voices were drowning out the harmonious ideal of a wholistic Western culture. These trends were clear enough even during the Massey Commission's existence. Its indifference to them again reflected the relative insignificance of artists, and especially avant-garde artists, among its supporters. But it was also a wilful resistance to an unpleasant reality. Cultural modernism could not serve the political and social ends that the commissioners demanded of high culture. Instead of fostering, as Matthew Arnold had hoped, a free yet cohesive society, modern high culture was itself degenerating into chaos, undermining their vision of a coherent social order based on liberal humanist values derived from traditional high culture.

The commissioners would probably have been appalled at some of the artistic activities that would be sponsored by the government cultural apparatus they helped to create. But they would have been pleased by the dynamism of the Canadian cultural scene in decades to come, especially inasmuch as it reflected critical assessments of a society moulded by materialism, technology, and mass media. The irony was that so many in the next generation would see the traditional high culture championed by the Massey Commission as part of the problem rather than part of the solution. No doubt the commissioners would have regarded this attitude as an ignorant rejection of the lessons of the past and a sad failure of critical intelligence.

Nevertheless, in the diversity of the modern Canadian cultural scene there would still be room for their brand of cultural nationalism. In years to come a wide assortment of Canadian intellectuals would expound views that were variations on the Massey Commission's basic themes.[6] The liberal humanist formulation of cultural nationalism also continued to appeal to the Canadian state because it proffered a national identity that justified the existence of Canada as an independent nation. Sustained by an appropriate myth and guarded by an honour corps of influential intellectuals, government-sponsored culture would enjoy an increasingly affluent future. Ironically, this denouement suggests one way in which Canada actually was different from the United States. American intellectuals railing against mass culture could not equate high culture with their national identity in the same way. Through the Massey Commission, the Canadian cultural elite proved to be closer to power and more successful in getting a political response to its concerns. Its conception of Canadian culture was true insofar as it became a self-fulfilling prophecy.

Appendix A

SUBMISSIONS TO THE COMMISSION

The submissions to the Massey Commission, in briefs and hearings, can be broken down into the following categories:

1. Voluntary Associations/Institutions (Arts, Letters, Sciences)
2. Voluntary Associations/Institutions (General)
3. Professional Organizations (Arts, Letters, Sciences)
4. Universities
5. Government Institutions/Departments
6. Business Organizations
7. Private Broadcasters
8. Individuals

Some of these categories, such as universities, business organizations, and private broadcasters, are self-explanatory and clearly delimited. In categories 1, 2, 3, and 5, however, some entries could fit into two or more categories. The final choice was made on the basis of what was deemed to be the primary motivation in submitting a brief or making an appearance before the commission.

The first three groups were distinguishable from one another by the different relationship between their central purposes and the commission's mandate. Category 1 includes voluntary organizations and institutions whose primary interest was some form or another of the arts, letters, and sciences within the commission's purview. They were distinct from category 2, which comprises bodies with purposes not directly related to the commission's mandate that nevertheless believed that culture could make a significant contribution to their work.

A distinction was also made between the cultural groups of category 1 and those placed in category 3, where professional interests were judged to be among the principal motivations behind the organization's interest in culture. On the other hand, government organizations were considered worthy of a category of their own (5), even though many could have fit into category 1.

1. Voluntary Associations/Institutions
(Arts, Letters, Sciences)

National

1 Academie canadienne-française
2 Arctic Institute of North America
3 Association canadienne-française pour l'avancement des sciences
4 Canada Foundation
5 Canadian Arts Council
6 Canadian Association for Reconstruction through UNESCO
7 Canadian Ballet Festival Association
8 Canadian Handicrafts Guild – General Committee
9 Canadian Music Council
10 Canadian Social Science Research Council
11 Canadian Writers' Foundation
12 Conservatoire populaire et le chouer de France
13 *Contemporary Verse: A Canadian Quarterly*
14 *Culture: Revue trimestrielle*
15 Dominion Drama Festival
16 Federation of Canadian Music Festivals
17 Fiddlehead Poetry Society
18 First Statement Press
19 *Here and Now*
20 Humanities Research Council of Canada
21 International Student Service of Canada – Administrative Council
22 Maisons des étudiants canadiens (Paris) – Canadian Committee
23 National Farm Radio Forum
24 National Film Society of Canada
25 Royal Architectural Institute of Canada
26 Royal Astronomical Society of Canada
27 Royal Canadian Academy of the Arts
28 Royal Canadian Institute
29 Royal Society of Canada
30 Société canadienne d'histoire naturelle et ses filiales
31 Société de bienfaisance des artistes

Provincial / Regional

32 British Columbia Drama Association

33 British Columbia Historical Association
34 British Columbia Indian Arts and Welfare Society
35 Canadian Handicrafts Guild – Alberta Provincial Branch
36 Canadian Handicrafts Guild – Manitoba Provincial Branch
37 Canadian Handicrafts Guild – Ontario Provincial Branch
38 Competitive Festival of Music, New Brunswick
39 Conservatoire national de musique de Québec
40 Federation of British Columbia Film Councils
41 Federation of Film Councils of Eastern Ontario
42 Historical and Scientific Society of Manitoba
43 International Student Service of Canada – University of Saskatchewan Committee
44 Maritime Art Association
45 New Brunswick Museum
46 Newfoundland Museum
47 Newfoundland Public Libraries Board
48 Nova Scotia College of Art
49 Nova Scotia Drama League
50 Nova Scotia Museum of Science
51 Ontario Association of Film Councils
52 Ontario Historical Society
53 Orchestre symphonique de Québec
54 Orchestre symphonique des jeunes de Montréal
55 *Revue canadienne de biologie*
56 Royal Ontario Museum
57 Saskatchewan Drama League
58 Saskatchewan Musical Association
59 Société pro musica
60 Société Richelieu
61 Upper Canada Genealogical Society
62 Vancouver Island Film Councils
63 Western Canada Art Circuit
64 Western Stage Society

Local

65 Les Amis de l'art
66 Antiquarian and Numismatic Society of Montreal
67 Archives de folklore
68 Art Gallery of Hamilton
69 Art Gallery of Toronto
70 Art, Historical, and Scientific Association, Controllers of the Vancouver City Museum
71 Arts Centre of Greater Victoria
72 Ballet Appreciation Club of Ottawa

73 Banff School of Fine Arts
74 Bellman Male Chorus
75 Bibliothèque des enfants de Montréal
76 Boag Foundation Limited
77 Calgary Allied Arts Centre
78 Calgary Civic Centre Committee – Calgary Women's Musical Club, Calgary Branch of the Alberta Registered Music Teachers' Association, Calgary Symphony Orchestra, Central Alberta Music Festival
79 Canadian Handicrafts Guild – Edmonton
80 Centre d'études amérindiennes de l'Université de Montréal
81 Community Arts Councils of Vancouver
82 Community Arts Councils of Vancouver – Drama Section
83 Community Children's Theatre
84 Concerts symphoniques de Montréal
85 Conseil du film de St-Jérome
86 Conseils du film de St-Lambert, St-Jean, St-Rémi, Salaberry de Valleyfield et Rigaud
87 de Rimanoczy String Players' Society
88 Disciplines de Massenet
89 Discussion Group of Hamilton
90 Don Valley School of Arts
91 Drama Playhouse
92 Edmonton Museum of Arts
93 Fraser Canyon Indian Arts and Crafts Society
94 Fredericton Art Club
95 ad hoc Group of Fredericton
96 Group of Representative Citizens of Greater Victoria
97 Halifax Conservatory of Music
98 Harris Memorial Gallery
99 Historical Society of Ottawa
100 Institut botanique de l'Université de Montréal
101 Institut canadien de Québec
102 Institut d'études médiévales
103 Institut de biologie générale et de zoologie de l'Université de Montréal, Faculté des sciences
104 Institut de géographie de l'Université de Montréal
105 Institut de microbiologie et d'hygiène de l'Université de Montréal
106 Institut de traduction de l'Université de Montréal
107 Jardin botanique de Montréal
108 Jeunesses musicales de Canada (St-Hyacinthe)
109 John O'London Society
110 Ladies Morning Musical Club of Montreal
111 Little Symphony of Montreal
112 Little Theatre Guild of Charlottetown
113 London Public Library and Art Museum

114 McGill University Museum
115 Montreal Museum of Fine Arts
116 Montreal Museum of Fine Arts – School of Art and Design
117 Montreal Special Libraries Association
118 Montreal Women's Symphony Orchestra
119 National Film Society of Canada – Toronto Branch
120 New Westminster Arts Committee
121 Northern Ontario Art Association
122 Ottawa Coin Club
123 Pontifical Institute of Mediaeval Studies
124 Regina Art Centre Association
125 Regina Library Association
126 Regina Orchestral Society
127 Royal Conservatory of Music, Toronto
128 Saint John Art Club
129 St John's Art Club, Inc.
130 St John's Players
131 Saskatoon Archaeological Society
132 School of Theatrical Arts, Victoria
133 Sir Ernest MacMillan Fine Arts Club
134 Société de géographie de Montréal
135 Société des festivals de Montréal
136 Société historique de Montréal
137 Société historique de Québec
138 Theatre Guild of Saint John
139 Theatre under the Stars
140 University of Toronto Press
141 Vancouver Art Gallery Council
142 Vancouver Children's Theatre Limited
143 Vancouver Film Council
144 Vancouver Little Theatre Association
145 Vancouver Symphony Society
146 West Vancouver Sketch Club
147 Winnipeg Symphony Society
148 Women's Musical Club of Winnipeg
149 York-Sunbury Historical Society Limited

2. Voluntary Associations/Institutions
(General)

National

150 Agricultural Institute of Canada – Victoria Natural History Society
151 Alliance Française
152 *Amérique française*

153 Association of Canadian Clubs
154 Association of United Ukrainian Canadians – National Executive Committee
155 Canadian and Catholic Confederation of Labour
156 Canadian Association for Adult Education
157 Canadian Association of Consumers
158 Canadian Catholic Conference
159 Canadian Citizenship Council
160 Canadian Committee on Youth Services
161 Canadian Congress of Labour
162 Canadian Education Association
163 Canadian Federation of Agriculture
164 Canadian Federation of Home and School
165 Canadian Federation of University Women
166 Canadian Home Economics Association
167 Canadian Institute of International Affairs
168 Canadian Inter-American Association
169 Canadian Jewish Congress
170 Canadian Legion of the British Empire Service League
171 Canadian Welfare Council – Recreation Division
172 Chess Federation of Canada
173 Church of England in Canada
174 Clubs 4-H Inc.
175 Comité permanent de la survivance française en Amérique
176 Compagnons de Saint-Laurent
177 Conseil canadien de la coopération
178 Co-operative Commonwealth University Federation
179 Co-operative Union of Canada
180 Co-ordinating Committee of Canadian Youth Groups
181 Federated Women's Institutes of Canada
182 Frontier College
183 Imperial Order, Daughters of the Empire
184 Ligue d'action nationale
185 National Advisory Council on School Broadcasting
186 National Council of Women of Canada
187 Public Affairs Institute
188 Société canadienne d'enseignement postscolaire
189 Société d'étude et de conférence
190 Société des visites interprovinciales
191 Sports College Association
192 Trades and Labour Congress of Canada
193 Ukrainian Canadian Committee
194 Ukrainian Catholic Brotherhood of Canada
195 Unions des Latins d'Amérique
196 United Church of Canada – Commission on Culture

197 United Farmers of Canada
198 United Nations Association in Canada
199 Young Women's Christian Association – National Council
200 World Calendar Association International – Canadian Affiliate

Provincial / Regional

201 Alberta Federation of Agriculture
202 Alberta Federation of Home and School Associations
203 Alberta Tuberculosis Association
204 Association canadienne-française d'éducation d'Ontario
205 Association of United Ukrainian Canadians – Manitoba Section
206 Association of United Ukrainian Canadians – Provincial Committee for Quebec and the Maritimes
207 British Columbia Parent-Teacher Federation
208 Cercles des fermières de la province de Québec
209 Corporation des agronomes de la province de Québec
210 Federated Women's Institutes of Ontario
211 Fédération des mouvements de jeunesse du Québec
212 Fédération des sociétés Saint-Jean-Baptiste du Québec
213 Group of Citizens of Manitoba Interested in Adult Education
214 Manitoba Association for Adult Education – French Section
215 Manitoba Federation of Agriculture and Co-operation
216 Maritime Federation of Agriculture
217 Maritime Federation of Agriculture and Co-operation
218 Ontario Federation of Home and School Associations
219 Prince Edward Island Adult Education Council
220 Provincial Council of Women of New Brunswick
221 Société d'éducation des adultes du Québec
222 Women's Institute of Manitoba

Local

223 Les Apprentis
224 Calgary Business and Professional Women's Club
225 Centre d'études orientales de la faculté des lettres de l'Université de Montréal
226 General Ministerial Association of Greater Winnipeg
227 Halifax District Trades and Labour Council
228 Imperial Order, Daughters of the Empire – Agnes Hudson Chapter, Vancouver
229 Inter-Ethnic Citizens' Council of Toronto
230 Junior League of Toronto
231 Junior League of Vancouver
232 Junior League of Winnipeg

233 Kinsmen Club of Saskatoon
234 Saint John's High School Memorial Centre Council
235 Saskatoon Council of Home and School Associations
236 Saskatoon Council of Women
237 Union catholique des cultivateurs d'Ottawa
238 University Women's Club of Regina
239 Vancouver Business and Professional Women's Club
240 Victoria and District Trades and Labour Council
241 West Vancouver Community Association
242 Winnipeg Council of Women
243 Women's Canadian Club of Winnipeg

3. Professional Organizations
(Arts, Letters, Sciences)

National

244 American Federation of Musicians of United States and Canada
245 Association canadienne des bibliocaires de langue française
246 Association canadienne des éducateurs de langue française
247 Association des médecins de langue française du Canada
248 Association of Canadian Radio Artists
249 Canadian Authors Association
250 Canadian Group of Painters
251 Canadian Historical Association
252 Canadian Library Association
253 Canadian Mathematical Congress
254 Canadian Museums Association
255 Canadian Schools of Social Work – National Committee
256 Canadian Society of Landscape Architects and Town Planners
257 Canadian Teachers' Federation
258 Canadian Writers' Committee
259 Community Planning Association of Canada
260 Federation of Canadian Artists
261 Institute of Professional Town Planners
262 National Federation of Canadian University Students
263 Professional Institute of the Civil Service of Canada
264 Radio Programme Producers
265 Sculptors' Society of Canada
266 Société des écrivains canadiens
267 Société des editeurs canadiens du livre français
268 Union fédérale des employés des postes radiophoniques

Provincial / Regional

269 Alberta Library Association

270 Alberta Society of Artists
271 Alberta Teachers' Association
272 Association des musiciens de Québec
273 British Columbia Library Association
274 British Columbia Registered Music Teachers' Association
275 British Columbia Teachers' Federation
276 Collège des médecins vétérinaires de la province de Québec
277 Federation of Canadian Artists – Alberta Region
278 Federation of Canadian Artists – British Columbia Region
279 Fiction Writers of Saskatchewan
280 Maritime Library Association
281 Metal Arts Guild
282 New Brunswick Teachers' Association
283 Nova Scotia Music Teachers' Association
284 Nova Scotia Society of Artists
285 Nova Scotia Teachers' Union
286 Ontario Library Association
287 Ontario Registered Music Teachers' Association
288 Ontario Teachers' Federation
289 Prince Edward Island Teachers' Federation
290 Provincial Association of Protestant Teachers of Quebec
291 Saskatchewan Library Association
292 Saskatchewan Teachers' Federation
293 Union des artistes lyriques et dramatiques de Québec

Local

294 Association of Canadian Radio Artists – Vancouver Branch
295 Association technologique de langue française d'Ottawa
296 Canadian Authors Association – Vancouver and Mainland Branch
297 Canadian Authors Association – Victoria and Islands Branch
298 Federation of Canadian Artists – Edmonton Branch
299 Federation of Canadian Artists – Prince Albert Branch
300 Groupe de peintres de Montréal
301 Société des traducteurs de Montréal
302 Student Veterans at the University of British Columbia
303 Superintendent and Supervisors of Winnipeg Schools
304 Vancouver Poets
305 Winnipeg Musicians' Association
306 Writers and Players Club of Ottawa

4. Universities

National

307 Fédération canadienne des universitaires catholiques
308 National Conference of Canadian Universities

Local

309 Acadia University
310 University of Alberta (Dr Robert Newton, president)
311 University of British Columbia
312 Carleton College (Senate)
313 Dalhousie University
314 University of King's College, Halifax
315 Université Laval
316 Memorial University of Newfoundland
317 Mount Allison University
318 Mount Saint Vincent College
319 University of New Brunswick
320 Nova Scotia Technical College
321 Prince of Wales College
322 Université du sacré-coeur de Bathurst
323 St Dunstan's College
324 St Francis Xavier University
325 Université Saint-Joseph
326 University of Saint Mary's College
327 St Thomas College
328 University of Saskatchewan (Dr W.P. Thompson)

5. Government Institutions/Departments

National

329 CBC
330 CBC Alberta
331 CBC British Columbia Region
332 CBC French Network
333 CBC Maritimes
334 CBC Newfoundland
335 CBC Prairie Region
336 Canadian War Museum Board
337 Central Mortgage and Housing Corporation
338 Department of Transport (Radio Division) and Co-ordinator of Civil
    Defence
339 Library of Parliament
340 National Film Board of Canada
341 National Film Board of Canada – Alberta Region
342 National Gallery of Canada
343 National Museum of Canada

344 National Scholarships – Department of Veterans Affairs and the Dominion Bureau of Statistics
345 Public Archives of Canada

Provincial / Regional

346 Alberta Cultural Development Boards
347 Alberta Drama Board
348 Alberta Music Board
349 Alberta Visual Arts Board
350 Arts Council of Manitoba
351 Manitoba Legislative Library
352 National Film Board of Canada (Alberta Region) and University of Alberta (Department of Extension)
353 New Brunswick Department of Education
354 New Brunswick Department of Industry and Reconstruction, Handicrafts Division
355 Newfoundland Department of Education
356 Nova Scotia Department of Education, Division of Adult Education – Mr Donald Wetmore
357 Ontario Department of Education
358 Ontario Research Foundation
359 Prince Edward Island Government
360 Research Council of Ontario
361 Saskatchewan Archives Board
362 Saskatchewan Arts Board
363 Saskatchewan Department of Education

Local

364 Cobourg, Town of

6. Business Organizations

National

365 American Stockholders Union
366 Association of Canadian Advertisers Inc.
367 Association of Motion Picture Producers and Laboratories of Canada
368 Broadcast Music Incorporated Canada Limited
369 Canadian Chamber of Commerce
370 Canadian Daily Newspapers Association
371 Canadian Marconi Company
372 Chambre de commerce de Québec
373 Chambre de commerce des jeunes de Chicoutimi

374 Chambre de commerce du district de Montréal
375 Commercial and Press Photographers'Association of Canada
376 Composers, Authors, and Publishers Association of Canada, Ltd
377 Mr Walter E. Elliott (president, Elliott and Haynes Audience Polling)
378 Periodical Press Association
379 Radio Manufacturers Association of Canada
380 Town Meeting Limited

Provincial / Regional

381 Associated Boards of Trade of Central British Columbia
382 Fédération des chambres de commerce des jeunes de la province de Québec
383 Innkeepers of Prince Edward Island
384 Maritime Professional Photographers' Association
385 Ontario Society of Photographers

Local

386 Board of Trade of the City of Toronto, Book Publishers' Branch
387 Calgary Board of Trade
388 Montreal Board of Trade
389 Privately Published Publications and Leaf and Quill Publications
390 Vancouver Board of Trade
391 Victoria Chamber of Commerce

7. Private Broadcasters

National

392 All-Canada Mutually Operated Radio Stations
393 All-Canada Radio Facilities Limited
394 Canadian Association of Broadcasters

Provincial / Regional

395 British Columbia Association of Broadcasters
396 Colonial Broadcasting System Limited
397 Mr J.J. Gourd
398 Maritime Association of Broadcasters

Local

399 CFAC Calgary
400 CFAR Flin-Flon

401 CFCY Charlottetown
402 CFNB Fredericton
403 CFQC Saskatoon
404 CFRB Toronto
405 CFRN Edmonton
406 CHAB Moose Jaw
407 CHFA Edmonton
408 CHLO St Thomas
409 CHLP Montreal
410 CHML Hamilton
411 CHNS Halifax
412 CHUM Toronto
413 CJCA Edmonton
414 CJCH Halifax
415 CJGX Yorkton
416 CJIB Vernon
417 CJOB Winnipeg
418 CJOR Vancouver
419 CJVI Victoria
420 CKAC Montreal
421 CKBI Prince Albert
422 CKCK Regina
423 CKCL Truro
424 CKCW Moncton
425 CKEY Toronto
426 CKNW New Westminster
427 CKOC Hamilton
428 CKRC Winnipeg
429 CKRD Red Deer
430 CKRM Regina
431 CKTB St Catharines
432 CKVL Verdun

8. Individuals

433 Mr Joseph Banigan
434 Mr William Bendickson, MP
435 Mr H.G. Bowley
436 Mr David Brock
437 Mrs Gisele Commanda
438 Mr David C. Corbett
439 Mrs Douglas Adams (Jean Coulthard)
440 Mr Walter d'Hondt
441 Mr André Forget
442 Mr Charles F. Fraser and Mr Garnet T. Page

443 Mr John Wesley Gibson
444 Mr A.H.S. Gillson
445 Mr K.W. Gordon
446 Miss Margaret K. Hall
447 Mr J.M. Inglis
448 Miss Frances James
449 Miss Lucy Jarvis
450 Mr Douglas Kerr
451 Miss Ethel Kinley
452 Dr. S.R. Leacock
453 Mr Albert Edward Leary
454 Mr E. Lindner
455 Mr W.J. McBain, Mr James A. Murray, Mr John C. Parkin, Mr-
    George A. Robb (joint brief)
456 Mr J.S. McMahon
457 Mr John McNaughton
458 Mr Walter B. Mann
459 Miss Louise Manny
460 Mr Georges Morisset
461 Mr Ben Nobleman
462 Prof. Robert Orchard
463 Mr John Parton
464 Mr Allan Phillips
465 Mr Howard A. Prentice and Mr John Pollock
466 Mr Hugh Savage
467 Mr David Smith
468 Miss Madge Smith
469 Miss Dorothy Somerset
470 Mr Gordon V. Thompson
471 Dr C.P. Wright
472 Mr François Zalloni
473 Rev. Dr Morris Zeidman (Scott Mission Inc.)

Appendix B

PUBLIC AND PRIVATE MEETINGS

OF THE COMMISSION

PUBLIC MEETINGS

The schedule of the first series of Ottawa hearings is presented in some detail below in order to demonstrate the important role played by national voluntary associations. Subsequent hearings are only outlined to provide a rough itinerary of the commission. If the session was oriented towards a particular subject, that subject heads the listing and the organizations which appeared at the session are indented. Otherwise only the organizations appearing are listed.

Initial Ottawa Hearings

DATE   SUBJECT/ORGANIZATION

Aug. 3–4   National Museum
  – National Museum of Canada
  – Perth Museum
Aug. 5   National Gallery
  – National Gallery of Canada
Aug. 9   National War Museum
  – National War Museum Board
Aug. 10   Public Archives and Administration of Public Records
  – Public Archives
Aug. 11   Royal Architectural Institute of Canada
  Canadian Writers' Foundation

Aug. 12   Dominion Drama Festival
           Canadian Citizenship Council
Aug. 16   National Scholarships
           – Government Officials
           – Humanities Research Council of Canada
Aug. 17   – Canadian Social Science Research Council
Aug. 18   Library of Parliament
           – Library of Parliament
           National Library
           – Canadian Library Association
Aug. 19   – Canadian Historical Society
Aug. 23   Community Planning Association of Canada
           National Conference of Canadian Universities
Aug. 24   National Film Board
           – National Film Board
           – National Film Society of Canada
Aug. 26   Royal Society of Canada
Aug. 30   UNESCO
           – Canadian Teachers' Federation
           – Canadian Education Association
Aug. 31   – Canadian Council for Reconstruction through UNESCO
           – United Nations Association in Canada
Sept. 1   – C.F. Fraser and Garnet T. Page
           Canadian Association for Adult Education
Sept. 2   Central Mortgage and Housing Corporation
Sept. 6   Broadcasting
           – Canadian Broadcasting Corporation
Sept. 8   – Canadian Association of Broadcasters
           – Canadian Federation of Agriculture
           – National Farm Radio Forum

Itinerant Hearings

DATE	LOCATION	ABSENTEES
Western Canada		
October 1949		
11, 12, 13	Winnipeg	Surveyer (for
17, 18	Saskatoon	the entire
19, 20, 21	Edmonton	Western tour)
24, 25, 26	Vancouver	
28, 29	Victoria	
November 1949		
1, 2	Calgary	MacKenzie (for

DATE	LOCATION	ABSENTEES
November 1949		the rest of the
3, 4	Regina	Western tour)
Central Canada		
15–19	Toronto	
23–6	Montreal	
January 1950		
10–12	Quebec City	
Eastern Canada		
16–17	Fredericton	Surveyer (for
18–19	Saint John	the entire
20–4	Halifax	Eastern tour)
26	Charlottetown	MacKenzie
Ottawa (Second Series of Hearings)		
April 1950		
8–20	Ottawa	
Newfoundland		
July 1950		
7–8	St John's	Surveyer

PRIVATE MEETINGS

MEETING NO.	DATE	LOCATION	ABSENTEES
1–2	May 2–3 (1949)	Ottawa	
3	June 20	Ottawa	Lévesque Surveyer
4–11	Aug. 1–10	Ottawa	
12–14	Aug. 17–18	Ottawa	
15–17	Aug. 23–4	Ottawa	
18–21	Aug. 31–Sept. 2	Ottawa	Surveyer
22	Sept. 7	Ottawa	
23	Sept. 9	Ottawa	MacKenzie Surveyer
24	Oct. 15	Winnipeg Saskatoon (en route)	Surveyer
25	Oct. 15	Saskatoon	Surveyer
26	Nov. 7	Ottawa	MacKenzie

27	Nov. 16	Toronto	
28	Nov. 24	Montreal	MacKenzie
29–34	Jan. 7–13 (1950)	Quebec City	
35	Jan. 15	Fredericton	Surveyer
36–8	Feb. 24–5	Ottawa	MacKenzie Surveyer
39	April 10	Ottawa	
40	April 18	Ottawa	
41	April 19	Ottawa	
42–3	June 5	Ottawa	
44–7	June 19–20	Ottawa	
48–54	July 12–17	Ottawa	Massey Surveyer
55–64	July 18–25	Batterwood	Lévesque (63–4)
65	July 26	Ottawa	
66–8	Sept. 5–6	Ottawa	MacKenzie Surveyer
69–82	Nov. 7–15	Ottawa	Surveyer (77–82)
83	Nov. 16	Ottawa	MacKenzie Surveyer
84	Nov. 22	Ottawa	MacKenzie
85–6	Dec. 2	Ottawa	MacKenzie Surveyer
87–8	Dec. 27–8	Ottawa	MacKenzie Surveyer
89–92	Jan. 3–4 (1951)	Ottawa	MacKenzie Surveyer
93–105	Jan. 11–19	Ottawa	MacKenzie Surveyer
106–10	Feb. 12–14	Ottawa	Surveyer (108–10)

Appendix C

PARODY OF A COMMISSION MEETING*

ROYAL COMMISSION ON NATIONAL DEVELOPMENT
IN THE ARTS, LETTERS AND SCIENCES
One Hundred and Thirty-first Meeting – November 13, 1950.

Minutes

The one hundred and thirty-first meeting was held in the offices of the
Royal Commission in the Laurentian Building, Ottawa, at 10 a.m. on Friday, November 13, 1950, the Chairman presiding.

THOSE PRESENT WERE:
    Dr. Hilda Neatby
    Father Georges-Henri Levesque [*sic*]
    Dr. Norman MacKenzie
    Dr. Arthur Surveyer
    Mr. Peter Wright
    Mr. Guy Roberge
    The Secretary
    The Associate Secretary

1. The Chairman read under the section *Canadian Letters*, Part II, the following:

---

* Neatby Papers, Saskatchewan Archives Board, University of Saskatchewan, Saskatoon, A139 36, Minutes of the One Hundred and Thirty-
  first Meeting–13 November 1950. (See chapter 10, note 2.)

We recommend:
THAT A SPADE BE CALLED A SPADE.

2. This important recommendation led to prolonged and learned discussion which occasionally proceeded in scattered formation. The Secretaries, after some searchings of memory, heart, and conscience, were able to agree that the following questions were raised, and the accompanying directions given:

(i) Is this permitted by the British North America Art? (Check Section 94)

(ii) Does it trespass on education? Or could it pass as vocational training?

(iii) Is the spade a truly bilingual tool, fully adapted to each of our two cultures, acceptable to our ethnic groups, giving no offence to the Roman Catholic Church (check views of Dominicans and Jesuits on this matter), the Church of England, the United Church of Canada, or any of the lesser sects? (Check views of Presbyterians and Doukhobors.)

(iv) Can the spade be considered a truly Canadian instrument with no Americanizing tendencies?

(v) Is the spade really suitable to a sparse and scattered population?

(vi) Can the spade promote the cause of national unity and the flowering and cross-pollination of Canadian culture?

(vii) Can the spade develop local talent? (Check with private stations and the C.B.C.)

(viii) Can the spade help solve the economic problems of the Canadian artist, musician, writer? (Secretary requested to address inquiry on this matter to the President, Canadian Federation of Artists, and comparable bodies in other fields. Also instructed to procure for the Commission life of Bronson Alcock.)

(ix) What is the attitude of free enterprise groups towards the spade? (Check Mr. Norris and the Montreal Board of Trade.)

(x) Had the F.C.C. pronounced on the different systems of nomenclature?

(xi) What will be the expenditure involved? Can we make this sound less elaborate? How many members have been able to ascertain the probable views of the government or near-government on such a recommendation? (Check recent speeches of the Prime Minister.)

(xii) Is there a possibility of government action on the spade before completion of the Report? (Suggested that the Secretary communicate with Mr. Gardiner. Discussion. Chairman undertook to sound out the Minister of Agriculture in informal telephone conversation.)

(xiii) Does not the word spade imply a certain class distinction? Would it be better to say 'an instrument chiefly devoted to horticultural purposes'? Objection raised that a hostile critic would insist on other possible interpretations. Further objection that expression is highbrow, giving just offence to many worthy citizens.

(xiv) Should not the word 'should' be inserted in the recommendation? Objection raised that should implies moral obligation; morality cannot be separated from education, and education outside terms of reference.

(xv) Is not 'called' ambiguous? Lends itself to the interpretations of shouting telephone communications, words used in certain card games. Various suggestions – designated, styled, described, stigmatized, dubbed, referred to as, regarded as, deemed, considered to be in the order of. Discussion animated and frank.

3. The Chairman closed the meeting requiring the Secretaries to revise the recommendation in such a way that it should convey the meaning of the Commissioners without ambiguity while expressing it in words accept-able to all parties, provinces, religious [sic], ethnic groups, lawyers, free enterprisers, Americans – and Commissioners.

The meeting adjourned at 12:45 p.m.

Picture Credits

National Archives of Canada: The Royal Commission on National Development in the Arts, Letters and Sciences (PA C16986); St Laurent receiving a copy, 1951 (PA 116801); National Liberal Convention, 1948 (C 20619); NFB offices, 1947 (PA 169549, NFB Collection, photograph by E. Scott); Victoria Building (PA 12912, W.J. Topley Collection); a string quartet, 1945 (PA 144972, NFB Collection, photograph by Fred Warrander); artists at the National Gallery, 1941 (PA 157301); foyer of the Odeon Theatre, 1948 (PA 145104, photograph by Frank Royal); Public Archives, 1953 (C 10228); Public Archives and National Library, 1967 (C 23726); contemporary radio production, 1950 (C 64056, Station CKAC Collection); Lloyd Saunders with Maurice Richard and Elmer Lack (PA 148351, photograph from the Regina *Leader Post* by L.H. Shaw); rural circuit film audience, 1942 (PA 130019, NFB Collection); art class in Yellowknife, 1953 (PA 166275, photograph by G. Hunter); demonstration of television at CBC building (PA 77940, Montreal *Gazette*); Lévesque, Massey, and Claxton arriving at inaugural Canada Council meeting, 1957 (PA 149996, Duncan Cameron Collection)
Saskatchewan Archives Board: The commission in Saskatchewan (S-B1185)

Notes

INTRODUCTION

1 Canada, Royal Commission on National Development in the Arts, Letters and Sciences, *Report* (Ottawa 1951), 3
2 Ibid., 271
3 This view of the Massey Commission as a watershed has been criticized in Maria Tippett, 'The Writing of English-Canadian Cultural History,' *Canadian Historical Review* 67, no. 4 (Dec. 1986), 558; subsequently Tippett described the active cultural life of Canadians before the commission in *Making Culture: English-Canadian Institutions and the Arts before the Massey Commission* (Toronto 1990).
4 See Robert Ayre, 'The Press Debates the Massey Report,' *Canadian Art* 9 (Oct. 1951), 38. A classic statement of this view can be found in Arthur Lower, 'The Massey Report,' *Canadian Banker* 59, no. 1 (Winter 1952), 22–32.
5 See Wilfred Eggleston, 'Canadian Geography and Canadian Culture,' *Canadian Geographic* 43 (Dec. 1951), 254–73; Donald Creighton, review of the Massey Report, *Canadian Historical Review* 32 (Dec. 1951), 378; Donald Creighton, *The Forked Road: Canada 1939–1957* (Toronto 1976), 185–7; Bernard Ostry, *The Cultural Connection* (Toronto 1978), 77; Dominique Clift, *The Secret Kingdom: Interpretations of the Canadian Character* (Toronto 1989), 149; Erna Buffie, 'The Massey Report and the Intellectuals: Tory Cultural Nationalism in Ontario in the 1950s' (MA thesis, University of Manitoba, 1979), 10.
6 Mason Wade, ed., *Canadian Dualism: Studies of French-English Relations* (Toronto 1960), 416. The Massey-Lévesque label has been especially popular in government circles where there exists a desire to rewrite

history according to bicultural principles. See, for example, Canada, *Report of the Federal Cultural Policy Review Committee* (Ottawa 1982), 5; or note the title of a Library of Parliament report: Brooke Jeffrey, *Cultural Policy in Canada: From Massey-Lévesque to Applebaum-Hébert* (Ottawa 1982).

7 See George Woodcock, *Strange Bedfellows: The State and the Arts in Canada* (Vancouver 1985), 51; J.M. Bumsted, 'Canada and American Culture in the 1950s,' in J.M. Bumsted, ed., *Interpreting Canada's Past* (Toronto 1986), 2:401–2 [reprinted from *Bulletin of Canadian Studies* 4, no. 1 (April 1980)]; Paul Rutherford, *When Television Was Young: Primetime Canada 1952–1967* (Toronto 1990), 14–15; Susan Crean, *Who's Afraid of Canadian Culture* (Toronto 1976), 128–9.

CHAPTER 1 The Origins of the Commission

1 Apparently 'Babbitt Rex' was Loring Christie's nickname for King. See J.L. Granatstein, *The Ottawa Men: The Civil Service Mandarins, 1935–1957* (Don Mills 1982), 65.

2 Claxton Papers, National Archives of Canada (NAC), MG 32, B 5, vol. 126, Memorandum for the Prime Minister: re Commission on National Gallery, etc., 23 November 1948. Claxton noted that some of the original resolutions that the committee had to deal with were in an accompanying appendix, but this document is not attached to the memorandum in his papers.

3 Claxton Papers, vol. 50, 'Liberal Record,' National Liberal Convention – Draft Resolutions, 27 July 1948

4 The national parks and national capital initiatives did not fit neatly into any of these categories, but they would soon be dropped from the list. Some other ideas, such as a proposal for establishing a Canadian government travel bureau, were dropped much earlier.

5 Claxton Papers, vol. 126, Memorandum, 23 Nov. 1948

6 Ibid.

7 Ibid.

8 See, for example, Arthur Phelps, 'Action for the Arts,' *Canadian Review of Music and Art* 3, nos. 9–10 (Oct.–Nov. 1944), 7–8. This journal broached many different proposals for arts subsidies throughout the 1940s. See also R.B. Tolbridge, 'Does Radio Need a Royal Commission?' *Canadian Forum*, Oct. 1947, 156–7.

Guy Roberge, who would become the associate counsel for the Massey Commission, recalled that in the late 1940s artists pestered Claxton with the refrain 'we've got to have a commission' (Guy Roberge, interview, Ottawa, 7 June 1988).

9 J.W. Pickersgill, *My Years with Louis St Laurent: A Political Memoir* (Toronto 1975), 139
10 Bernard Ostry, *The Cultural Connection: An Essay on Culture and Government Policy in Canada* (Toronto 1978), 59
11 Pearson Papers, NAC, MG 26, N 1, vol. 10, Pearson to Pickersgill, 5 Nov. 1948
12 Claxton Papers, vol. 126, Memorandum, 23 Nov. 1948
13 Ibid.
14 Donald Creighton, *Dominion of the North* (Toronto 1957), 577
15 Vincent Massey, *On Being Canadian* (Toronto 1948), 46
16 Creighton, *Dominion of the North*, 581
17 Phelps, 'Action for the Arts,' 8
18 Claxton Papers, vol. 220, Memoirs, 287
19 For a good description of the growth of the cultural elite in the 1920s, see Mary Vipond, 'The Nationalist Network: English Canada's Intellectuals and Artists in the 1920s,' *Canadian Review of Studies in Nationalism* 5, no. 1 (Spring 1980), 32–52. In William R. Young, 'Making the Truth Graphic: The Canadian Government's Home Front Information Structure and Programmes during World War II' (PHD diss., University of British Columbia, 1978), 23–7, this group is shown to be still active and effective in the early 1940s.
20 Claxton Papers, vol. 220, Memoirs, 254–5
21 In Ron Faris, *The Passionate Educators: Voluntary Associations and the Struggle for Control of Adult Educational Broadcasting in Canada, 1919–1952* (Toronto 1986), 121, it is claimed that Lévesque was also a member of the CIIA, but Lévesque does not list any such association in his curriculum vitae.
22 Faris, *The Passionate Educators*, xiv
23 E.A. Corbett as quoted in Young, 'Making the Truth Graphic,' 24.
24 Claxton Papers, vol. 220, Memoirs, 302–3
25 The development of these societies and their links to voluntary associations are discussed in Douglas Owram, *The Government Generation: Canadian Intellectuals and the State, 1900–1945* (Toronto 1986), 148–59. Their growth reflected the expansion of universities, the evolution of the social sciences, and the accompanying conceit of intellectuals that they had the expertise needed to solve social problems.
26 André Biéler, 'The Kingston Conference – Ten Years Afterwards,' *Canadian Art* 8 (Summer 1951), 151. Edward Rowan, assistant to the director of fine arts projects under the Works Progress Administration, came from the United States to speak to the conference. See Frances K. Smith, *André Biéler: An Artist's Life and Times* (Toronto 1980), 91.
27 Smith, *André Biéler*, 93
28 Pickersgill, *My Years with Louis St Laurent*, 139

29 Frank Peers, *The Politics of Canadian Broadcasting* (Toronto 1969), 393–4
30 Gary Evans, *John Grierson and the National Film Board: The Politics of Wartime Propaganda* (Toronto 1984), 262–3
31 Claxton Papers, vol. 126, Memorandum, 23 Nov. 1948
32 Ibid.
33 Claxton did add historic sites and monuments and the national battlefield commission as possible subjects for investigation. See Claxton Papers, vol. 123, Memorandum to the Prime Minister: Re: Commission on National Gallery, etc., 29 November 1948.
34 Claude Bissell, *The Imperial Canadian: Vincent Massey in Office* (Toronto 1986), 197
35 J.W. Pickersgill, interview, Ottawa, 27 March 1987
36 Robert M. Hamilton and Dorothy Shields, *The Dictionary of Canadian Quotations and Phrases* (Toronto 1979), 570
37 Georges-Henri Lévesque, interview, Montreal, 26 Mar. 1987
38 Massey Diary, 6 Jan. 1949, as quoted in Bissell, *The Imperial Canadian*, 195. The Massey Papers, formerly in Massey College, University of Toronto, were not opened to this researcher despite repeated requests. Therefore all subsequent references to Massey's diary and his correspondence are drawn from this and other secondary sources written by authors who were given access to the collection before it was permanently loaned to the University of Toronto Archives.
39 Lévesque, interview, 26 Mar. 1987
40 Canada, *Official Report of Debates* (House of Commons), Fifth Session, Twentieth Parliament, 1 (26 Jan. 1949), 46
41 Ibid., 31 Jan. 1949, 77
42 Ibid., 78
43 Lévesque, interview, 26 Mar. 1987
44 Roberge, interview, 7 June 1988
45 MacKenzie Papers, University of British Columbia Library, Special Collections, 194 1–1, Massey to MacKenzie, 22 Feb. 1949. Massey had known MacKenzie since the early 1920s, when they had taught at the University of Toronto and had also been involved in the Institute of Pacific Relations. In 1927 Massey had considered MacKenzie as a possible first secretary to accompany him as minister to the United States. At that time MacKenzie decided that 'temperamentally Vincent and I were not too compatible' because he was 'something of a rough diamond and Vincent "the perfect gentleman"' (Norman MacKenzie to Claude Bissell, 12 July 1976, quoted in Bissell, *The Imperial Canadian*, 206). In the case of the Massey Commission, however, this combination would give the commission an invaluable catholicity.
46 MacKenzie Papers, 194 1–1, MacKenzie to the Hon. E.W. Hamber, 24 Feb. 1949
47 P.B. Waite, *Lord of Point Grey: Larry MacKenzie of UBC* (Vancouver

1987), 146. Waite bases his treatment of this phase of MacKenzie's career partly on Vincent Massey's papers, which he was given access to in his research.

48 Georges-Henri Lévesque, *Souvenances II: Remous et éclatements* (Ottawa 1988), 227–8

49 Canada, Royal Commission on National Development in the Arts, Letters and Sciences, *Report* (Ottawa 1951), xvii

CHAPTER 2 The Cultural Elite and the Cultural Lobby

1 Doug Owram, *The Government Generation: Canadian Intellectuals and the State* (Toronto 1986), 158

2 Ibid, 140. This point must be made in passing here but is dealt with at length in chapter 4.

3 Georges-Henri Lévesque, o.p., 'Humanisme et sciences sociales,' *Canadian Journal of Economics and Political Science* 18, no. 3 (Aug. 1952), 263

4 F. Dolores Donnelly, *The National Library of Canada* (Ottawa 1973), 65. Massey was addressing Freda Waldon, president of the Canadian Library Association, in this 3 May 1947 letter.

5 William R. Young, 'Making the Truth Graphic: The Canadian Government's Home Front Information Structure and Programmes during World War II (PHD diss., University of British Columbia, 1978), 298

6 MacKenzie Papers, University of British Columbia Library, Special Collections, 196 3–14, Minutes of the Royal Commission on National Development in the Arts, Letters and Sciences, first meeting, 2 May 1949. Copies of these minutes can also be found in the National Archives of Canada's holdings (NAC, RG 33 28, vol. 1a). Further references to the commission's minutes will refer simply to the number and date of the meeting in question.

7 Ibid.

8 Ibid.

9 *Globe and Mail*, 4 May 1949

10 Vancouver *Sun*, 4 May 1949

11 Winnipeg *Free Press*, 4 May 1949

12 *Globe and Mail*, 4 May 1949

13 Ibid.

14 MacKenzie Papers, 197 4–3, Massey to MacKenzie, 6 May 1949

15 Sandwell and Eggleston wrote special studies for the commission and promoted it in their work. Ferguson, a friend of MacKenzie, gave the commission active support in his paper and was not above writing an editorial to help alleviate the commission's publicity concerns (MacKenzie Papers, 194 1–3, Ferguson to MacKenzie, 28 Nov. 1949).

16 Claude Bissell, *The Imperial Canadian: Vincent Massey in Office* (Toronto 1986), 201

17 MacKenzie Papers, 194 1–1, Massey to MacKenzie, 4 Mar. 1949

18 Ibid., MacKenzie to Massey, 7 Mar. 1949. The men suggested by Andrew were journalist Wilfrid Eggleston, Blair Fraser, the well-connected editor of *Maclean's*; Roby Kidd, assistant head of the Canadian Association for Adult Education, and Walter Herbert, a former federal Liberal party organizer and head of the Canada Foundation, a private arts funding body. See MacKenzie Papers, 194 1–1, Andrew to MacKenzie, n.d. Hugh MacLennan's name was also under consideration by Massey. Massey was unlikely to take up MacKenzie's suggestion of Herbert, whom he disliked (see John A.B. McLeish, *A Canadian for All Seasons* [Toronto 1978], 120–3).

19 Young, 'Making the Truth Graphic, 5. The WIB had been one of Claxton's responsibilities in wartime. Its general manager was first John Grierson, head of the NFB, and later Davidson Dunton. René Garneau, who would become assistant secretary of the commission, worked for the WIB as well; E.A. Corbett, director of the CAAE, had collaborated in its work, and Lester Pearson had sat on its board.

20 Massey Papers (see ch. 1, note 38), Royal Commission files, T.W.L. MacDermott to Massey, 18 Mar. 1949, personal and confidential, as quoted in P.B. Waite, *Lord of Point Grey* (Vancouver 1987), 147

21 Letter from Kate Neatby, sister of Hilda Neatby, to the author, 24 Feb. 1988

22 Minutes, second meeting, 3 May 1949

23 Massey Commission Papers, NAC, RG 33 28, vol. 1a, Duplessis to Massey, 21 Sept. 1949

24 Georges-Henri Lévesque, *Souvenances II* (Ottawa 1988), 246

25 While in New York Neatby talked informally with television viewers and an actor from Canada who worked in television, who watched fifteen hours of television herself, an experience she described as generally 'an unrewarding occupation' (Neatby Papers, Saskatchewan Archives Board, University of Saskatchewan, Saskatoon, A139 37, Memorandum to the Chairman on an Informal Investigation of Television Programmes Made in and near New York, May 1949, by Dr. Hilda Neatby, Commissioner).

26 Peter Wright Papers, Government Publications Section, Robarts Library, University of Toronto, CA1 Z1 49A22, Briefs Submitted to the Royal Commission on National Development in the Arts, Letters and Sciences, Brief of the Canadian Association for Adult Education, 7. The commission's legal counsel, Peter Wright, donated his copies of the briefs submitted to the commission to the Robarts Library. Further references to these papers will be abbreviated, under the title 'Briefs,' to the name of the organization submitting the brief, followed by a cross-reference to the volume and number assigned the briefs in the commission's papers in the National Archives of Canada, and a page number. For example, in this case the citation would be: Briefs, Canadian Association for Adult Education (vol. 8, no. 101), 7.

The CAAE was referring specifically to the Wartime Information Board's activities, which had provided support for adult educators in pursuit of its public information programs that ceased at the end of the war. See Young, 'Making the Truth Graphic,' 298. Young also comments perceptively: 'The investigations of the Royal Commission on National Development in the Arts, Letters and Sciences provided an opportunity for many of "the boys" to get together again in 1949 to rehash the problems of national cultural development. This reunion gives a clue to the most lasting contribution of the men associated with wartime information. Their work in the WIB constituted just one episode in their continuing efforts to build up Canadian national feeling and cultural institutions, a job which they began in the voluntary associations of the 1920's and 1930's and continued through to their support for the operations of the Canada Council' (Ibid., 299).

27 'Brief Summer,' *Food for Thought* 14, no. 2 (Nov. 1949), 2–3, as cited in Ron Faris, *The Passionate Educators* (Toronto 1986), 123

28 Frank Peers, *The Politics of Canadian Broadcasting* (Toronto 1969), 402–3

29 Doris Shadbolt, 'The Federation Meets the Royal Commission,' *Canadian Art* 8 (Summer 1951), 152

30 Minutes, twenty-second meeting, 7 Sept. 1949; Neatby Papers, A139 36, Neatby to K.W. Gordon, 2 Sept. 1949; Neatby to W.P. Thompson, 2 Sept. 1949, MacKenzie Papers, 194 2–1, MacKenzie to R. Gushie, 3 Feb. 1950; 194 2–2, MacKenzie to A.G. Hatcher, 3 Feb. 1950

31 Neatby Papers, A139 12, draft, Canadian Club speech, 6

32 Canada, Royal Commission on National Development in the Arts, Letters and Sciences, *Report* (Ottawa 1951), 74

33 Royal Commission on National Development in the Arts, Letters and Sciences, NAC, RG 33 28 (Toronto: Micromedia, C-1998—C-2021, 1972), vol. 29, no. 368, transcript of the hearing of the Saskatoon Archaeological Society, 84. Hereafter the transcripts of the commission's hearings from this source will be cited under 'Hearings' by the name of the organization in question, volume, number, and page number.

34 Hearings, Mr Howard A. Prentice and Mr John J. Pollock, vol. 28, no. 331, 1. One might suspect that this duo was encouraged by private broadcasting interests, but even so their complaints about representation would still apply.

35 *Report*, 9, 268

36 Neatby Papers, A139 202 3, 'Notes on John L. McDougall'

37 Ibid.

38 *Report*, 71

CHAPTER 3 The Promotional Tour

1 Matthew Halton, 'Will the Atlantic Pact Work?' *Maclean's*, 15 Jan. 1949

2 The above description of contemporary Canadian periodicals is based on an examination of the *National Home Monthly*, Mar. 1949–Nov. 1950; *Maclean's*, 1 Jan. 1949–15 April 1949; and *Saturday Night*, 1 Jan. 1949–19 April 1949.

3 Hearings (see ch. 2, note 33), Association of Canadian Clubs, vol. 3, no. 34b, 416

4 Vancouver *Sun*, 25 Oct. 1949

5 Briefs (see ch. 2, note 26), Canadian Welfare Council (vol. 15, no. 153), 2–3

6 Hearings, Miss Ethel Kinley, vol. 21, no. 250, 46

7 Neatby Papers, Saskatchewan Archives Board, University of Saskatchewan, Saskatoon, A139 36, Eric Arthur to Neatby, 17 Aug. 1949

8 Ottawa *Journal*, 27 Aug. 1949

9 Pierre Berton, 'There'll always Be a Massey,' *Maclean's*, 14 Oct. 1951

10 Claude Bissell, *The Imperial Canadian: Vincent Massey in Office* (Toronto 1986), 204

11 Ibid. The quotation is from Blair Fraser, 'The Fight over Father Lévesque,' *Maclean's*, 1 July 1950.

12 Massey Papers (see ch. 1, note 38), Surveyer to Massey, 26 June 1950, as quoted in Bissell, *The Imperial Canadian*, 203

13 Briefs, Arts Council of Manitoba (vol. 3, no. 28), 19

14 Vancouver *Sun*, 24 Oct. 1949

15 Neatby Papers, A139 39. This is from a newspaper clipping in Neatby's papers that is undated with no masthead.

16 Ibid. This is a separate clipping from the one cited above, but it too lacks a date and masthead.

17 Hearings, University Women's Club of Regina, vol. 32, no. 412, 207–8

18 Neatby Papers, A139 36, René Garneau to Neatby, 28 Dec. 1949. It is interesting that Day chose Surveyer as a target; the fact that he could be made an object of ridicule suggests that he was already considered something of an outsider.

19 Canada, Royal Commission on National Development in the Arts, Letters and Sciences, *Report* (Ottawa 1951), 8–9

20 MacKenzie Papers, University of British Columbia Library, Special Collections, 194 1–5, MacKenzie to Mrs Harry Jackman, 9 Dec. 1949

21 Vancouver *News-Herald*, 27 Oct. 1949

22 Hearings, Vancouver Board of Trade, vol. 32, no. 414, 470–1

23 Ibid., 471

24 Hearings, Calgary Allied Arts Centre, vol. 7, 95, 5–6

25 Briefs, CKEY (vol. 7, no. 86), 28–9

26 Berton, 'There'll Always Be a Massey'

27 Hearings, Sports College Association, vol. 31, no. 392, 207

28 Ibid., 208

29 Briefs, Central Mortgage and Housing Corporation (vol. 15, no. 147), 3

30 Frank Peers, *The Politics of Canadian Broadcasting* (Toronto 1969), 428
31 MacKenzie Papers, 128 2, Memoirs, 17
32 Peers, *The Politics of Canadian Broadcasting*, 428
33 Briefs, Fédération des sociétés Saint-Jean-Baptiste (vol. 18, no. 197), 1
34 Ibid., 2
35 Georges-Henri Lévesque, *Souvenances II* (Ottawa 1988), 255
36 Canada, *Official Report of Debates* (House of Commons), Second Session, Twenty-first Parliament (9 Mar. 1950), 617
37 Suzanne Myette, 'La Nation, l'état et la culture: Quelques réactions québecoises à la Commission Massey, 1949–1951' (MA thesis, Université de Montréal, 1984), 69–86
38 Briefs, Innkeepers of Prince Edward Island (vol. 20, no. 232), 1
39 Ibid.
40 Massey Diary, 21 Jan. 1950, as quoted in P.B. Waite, *Lord of Point Grey* (Vancouver 1986), 151–2
41 Briefs, Writers and Players Club (vol. 32, no. 432a), attachment, 'Report on Thunderbird,' 1
42 Hearings, Writers and Players Club, vol. 32, no. 432a, 854
43 Ibid., 852–5
44 Hearings, Newfoundland Department of Education, vol. 26, no. 304a, 2. This was not the first time this had happened. In Vancouver, Mrs Marjorie Agnew, representing the Sir Ernest MacMillan Fine Arts Club, put Massey in his place by commenting that 'I don't know whether you like being introduced in this way, but these young people first knew of you through your brother Raymond, because they go to the movies.' Massey was equal to this introduction. 'Thank you very much,' he replied, 'I am sure they do' (Hearings, Sir Ernest MacMillan Fine Arts Club, vol. 30, no. 375, 509).
45 Hearings, Newfoundland Department of Education, vol. 26, no. 304a, 2
46 George Woodcock, *Strange Bedfellows: The State and the Arts in Canada* (Vancouver 1985), 50

CHAPTER 4 Liberal Humanism

1 Vincent Massey, *On Being Canadian* (Toronto 1948), 48. See also Arthur Lower, *This Most Famous Stream* (Toronto 1954) for an elaboration of this same theme from later in the decade. Carl Berger's description of Arthur Lower's ideas shows how close they were to those of the commission. See Carl Berger, *The Writing of Canadian History* (Toronto 1986), 203.
2 Hearings (see ch. 2, note 33), Pontifical Institute of Mediaeval Studies, vol. 27, no. 330b, 804
3 Briefs (see ch. 2, note 26), National Council of Women of Canada (vol. 23, no. 288), 3

4 Briefs, Competitive Festival of Music, New Brunswick (vol. 17, no. 166), 7–8
5 Briefs, Canadian Federation of Home and School (vol. 13, no. 121), 3
6 Briefs, Discussion Group of Hamilton (Vol. 18, no. 187), 2
7 La Société des écrivains wrote that 'broadcasting and television are to-day in the first rank of the instruments which are apt to raise or lower the intellectual culture of a people' (Briefs, Société des écrivains [vol. 30, no. 383], 10). The Boag Foundation rued the fact that commercial interests had a head start in winning a popular following: 'In the past we have accepted the fact that knowledge and good taste were the privileges of the few. With the growth of our scientific resources, we now admit that culture could be more widespread and therefore richer and more vital. But instead, we are finding a danger that modern industrialism and commercialism are creating a mass of cultural illiterates and even destroying the grass-roots cultures of the simpler patterns of folk-life' (Briefs, Boag Foundation Ltd. [vol. 3, no. 48], 3). This sentiment was widespread. When a new mass medium had appeared in earlier decades, the initial elite response had also been to hope that it could be used to edify the masses. It is significant that the Massey Commission was operating at a time when yet another new media technology – television – was in the early stages of development, raising such an expectation again. See also Daniel Czitrom, *Media and the American Mind* (Chapel Hill, NC, 1982), 183, 187.
8 Hearings, W.J. McBain et al., vol. 21, no. 1
9 Briefs, Fiddlehead Poetry Society (vol. 19, no. 207), 2
10 Bernard Iddings Bell as quoted in Hilda Neatby, *So Little for the Mind* (Toronto 1953), 245
11 Briefs, Canadian Association for Adult Education (vol. 8, no. 101), 7–8
12 Hearings, Church of England in Canada, vol. 16, no. 155, 1
13 Briefs, Saskatoon Council of Home and School Associations (vol. 29, no. 367)
14 Georges-Henri Lévesque, *Souvenances II* (Ottawa 1988), 258; Georges-Henri Lévesque, interview, Montreal, 26 Mar. 1987
15 For a parallel discussion of this point, see A.B. McKillop, *Contours of Canadian Thought* (Toronto 1987), 42
16 Neatby Papers, Saskatchewan Archives Board, University of Saskatchewan, Saskatoon, A139 202 5, 'The European Problem,' n.d.
17 A.B. McKillop, *A Disciplined Intelligence: Critical Inquiry and Canadian Thought in the Victorian Era* (Montreal 1979), 230–1
18 Ibid., 229
19 S.E.D. Shortt, *The Search for an Ideal* (Toronto 1976), 144–7; McKillop, *Contours*, 119
20 Douglas Owram, *The Government Generation* (Toronto 1987), 140
21 George P. Grant, 'Philosophy,' in Canada, *Royal Commission Studies: A Selection of Essays Prepared for the Royal Commission on National Development in the Arts, Letters and Sciences* (Ottawa 1948), 121

22 Briefs, United Church of Canada (vol. 19, no. 406), 3
23 Neatby, *So Little for the Mind*, 11–12, 14–17, 235, 240. For an earlier statement of Neatby's educational ideas, see Neatby Papers, A139 202 1, 'Education for Democracy.'
24 A representative compilation of this writing can be found in Bernard Rosenburg and David Manning White, *Mass Culture: The Popular Arts in America* (New York 1957).
25 Czitrom, *Media and the American Mind*, 143–4
26 Douglas T. Miller and Marion Nowak, *The Fifties: The Way We Really Were* (Garden City, NY, 1977), 228
27 Czitrom, 102, 121–2
28 Ibid., 119
29 See George K. Kneller, *Higher Learning in Britain* (Berkeley 2955).
30 Czitrom, 167. Marshall McLuhan was an early disciple of Leavis and the New Criticism.
31 Between 1938 and 1951 *Scrutiny* included many articles on planning, education, and culture. Discussions of Eliot and Arnold were particularly prominent, and these and other articles provided evidence of a transatlantic awareness.

   Many of Leavis's writings expressed concerns similar to those heard by the Massey Commission. See, for example, F.R. Leavis, *Education and the University: A Sketch for an English School* (London 1943), 10, 16; and F.R. Leavis and Denys Thompson, *Culture and Environment: The Training of Critical Awareness* (London 1962 [1933]), 3.
32 Both Massey and Neatby displayed an uncommonly close acquaintance with the writings of Matthew Arnold. See Massey, *On Being Canadian*, 33; and Hilda Neatby, 'The Massey Report: A Retrospect,' *Tamarack Review* 1, no. 1 (Autumn 1956), 45–6. In his special study on philosophy, George Grant began with a distinction between the active and the contemplative life that paralleled Arnold's definitions of Hebraism and Hellenism. See Grant, 'Philosophy,' 119.
33 Frank Underhill, 'So Little for the Mind: Comments and Queries,' *Transactions of the Royal Society of Canada* 48 (June 1954), 23–3
34 Hilda Neatby, *A Temperate Dispute* (Toronto 1954), 39
35 Patricia Jasen, 'The English Canadian Liberal Arts Curriculum: An Intellectual History' (PHD diss., University of Manitoba, 1987), 151–3, 184
36 See, for example, Briefs, Student Veterans of the University of British Columbia (vol. 31, no. 393), 11; Saskatchewan Teachers' Federation (Vol. 29, no. 367), 5; Trades and Labour Congress of Canada (vol. 31, no. 400), 2.
37 Matthew Arnold, *Culture and Anarchy* (1869); reprinted in A. Dwight Culler, ed., *Poetry and Criticism of Matthew Arnold* (Boston 1961), 426. Arnold linked culture and religion: 'culture in like manner, places human perfection in an *internal* condition, in the growth and predomi-

nance of our humanity proper, as distinguished from our animality'
(ibid., 411). Neatby agreed; in the absence of a common religious
faith, culture cultivated the shared values which could hold society together while preserving the dignity and freedom of each individual.
38 Ibid., 408
39 Carl Berger, *The Sense of Power: Studies in the Ideas of Canadian Imperialism, 1878–1914* (Toronto 1971), 261–2
40 Erna Buffie, 'The Massey Report and the Intellectuals: Tory Cultural
Nationalism in Ontario in the 1950s' (MA thesis, University of Manitoba, 1982), 7. Buffie emphasizes Massey's membership in the Round
Table Movement and his personal connections with leading imperialists when a young man, including his wife's father, George Parkin, and
his brother-in-law's family, the Grants.
41 Berger, *Sense of Power*, 265
42 For an early example of this characteristic in British Canadian
thought, see Terry Cook, 'John Beverley Robinson and the Conservative Blueprint for the Upper Canadian Community,' *Ontario History* 64,
no. 2 (June 1972), 79–94. S.F. Wise developed this aspect of early to
mid-nineteenth-century Canadian political thought more fully. See, for
example, S.F. Wise, 'God's Peculiar Peoples,' in W.L. Morton, ed., *The
Shield of Achilles* (Toronto 1968), 36–61; 'Sermon Literature and Canadian Intellectual History,' in J.M. Bumsted, ed., *Canadian History before
Confederation* (Georgetown 1972), 253–69; and 'The Conservative Tradition in Upper Canada,' in *Profiles of a Province* (Toronto 1967), 20–33.

CHAPTER 5 Liberal Humanist Nationalism

1 Briefs (see ch. 2, note 26), University of Saint Mary's College (vol. 29,
no. 359), 1
2 Hearings (see ch. 2, note 33), Canadian Association of Broadcasters,
vol. 8, no. 101a, 1221
3 Briefs, Canadian Writers' Committee (vol. 15, no. 144), 5
4 Ibid., 5
5 Vincent Massey, *On Being Canadian* (Toronto 1948), 124. One of the
many flaws in this association of the United States with mass culture
was that many of the highbrow cultural projects that existed in Canada owed their beginnings to the financing of American foundations
like the Carnegie Corporation or the Rockefeller Foundation. The
elite did not consider this cultural imperialism, however, arguing that
foundation grants and similar forms of American involvement were al-
truistic and left Canadians free to be themselves.
6 Briefs, Canadian Authors Association (vol. 9, no. 103), 4
7 Hearings, Co-ordinating Committee of Canadian Youth Groups, vol.
17, no. 179, 628
8 Briefs, Comité permanent de la survivance française (vol. 16, 157), 4

9 Briefs, National Conference of Canadian Universities (vol. 23, no. 287), 50. Arthur Irwin, appearing for *Maclean's* magazine (and soon to be the new head of the NFB), told the commission that 'quite frequently, the readers of Canadian magazines take exception to the theme in a fiction story ... on the grounds that it might be all right, or they would accept it, in a United States magazine, but the fact that it is published in a Canadian magazine annoys them. They distinguish between the two' (Hearings, Periodical Press Association of Canada, vol. 27, no. 330, 296). A conviction of moral superiority is generally an important part of nationalist ideologies, and the Canadian cultural elite was able to fill this criterion by defining Canada in opposition to American mass culture. It is worth noting that doubts about U.S. power at the time were deepened by the moral fallout of Hiroshima.

10 Minutes (see ch. 2, note 6), third meeting, 20 June 1949

11 Ibid.

12 Hearings, Canadian Federation of Agriculture, vol. 13, no. 120, 1337

13 Briefs, Western Stage Society (vol. 32, no. 427), 3

14 Briefs, Saskatoon Council of Home and School Associations (vol. 29, no. 369), 10

15 Hearings, Canadian Group of Painters, vol. 13, no. 123, 211. Massey handled all of the questioning in this session on painting except for one ill-fated sortie by Surveyer. Puzzled by all the arty talk, he suddenly blurted:

> SURVEYER: How does modern painting fit into this idea of using the Canadian spirit?
> LISMER: Could I have half an hour to answer that question? (laughter)
> SURVEYER: I take it back.
> (laughter) (Ibid., 213)

Laughter there must have been, for rarely did the sober court reporters serving the commission take note of the audience's responses.

16 Hearings, Canadian Writers' Committee, vol. 15, no. 144, 592

17 As the Canadian Handicrafts Guild put it: 'The folk arts of a community are the roots from which the fine arts grow. If these are allowed to die, the main source of national inspiration dies with them'' (Briefs, Canadian Handicrafts Guild, General Committee [vol. 13, no. 126], 1). Significantly, the Massey Commission would not give folk arts a high priority; its special study on handicrafts was one of the last to be commissioned and came as an afterthought.

18 Briefs, Western Stage Society (vol. 32, no. 427), 2

19 Hearings, University of Toronto Press, vol. 32, no. 411, 10

20 Briefs, Mrs. Elsie Graham, Vancouver (unlisted), 3

21 Briefs, Ligue d'action nationale (vol. 21, no. 257), 23

22 Hearings, Université Laval, vol. 21, no. 253, 180
23 Briefs, Comité permanent de la survivance française (vol. 16, no. 157), 4
24 The report included a few pages on 'Indian Arts and Crafts,' but no direct recommendations emerged from this discussion. The commissioners would also write that 'we were impressed by what they [ethnic groups] are doing to enrich our national heritage by preserving their distinctive and vigorous cultural activities' (Canada, Royal Commission on National Development in the Arts, Letters and Sciences, *Report* [Ottawa 1951], 72), but this was one of the briefest points made in the entire document and no action followed from it. See also Briefs, Ukrainian Canadian Committee (vol. 31, no. 401); Ukrainian Catholic Brotherhood of Canada (vol. 31, no. 402); Inter-Ethnic Citizen's Council of Toronto (vol. 20, no. 239; Canadian Jewish Congress (vol. 14, no. 132); and Hearings, Bellman Male Chorus, vol. 4, no. 43.
25 MacKenzie Papers, University of British Columbia Library, Special Collections, 128–2, Memoirs, 18
26 In pushing this thesis commentators can also point to Massey's family connections. His nephew, George Grant, grandson of leading imperialists G.R. Parkin (Massey's father-in-law) and G.M. Grant, was the author of a special study on philosophy for the commission. Grant would become famous in Canadian nationalist circles for his attack on materialism, technology, and Americanization in *Lament for a Nation* (Toronto 1965).
27 Massey's thoughts on the importance of British to Canada were in fact quite typical of the general attitude of the political elite of the day. See J.L. Granatstein, 'The Anglocentrism of Canadian Diplomacy,' in A.F. Cooper, ed., *Canadian Culture: International Dimensions* (Waterloo 1983). See also Claude Bissell, *The Imperial Canadian: Vincent Massey in Office* (Toronto 1986), 234.
28 Neatby Papers, Saskatchewan Archives Board, University of Saskatchewan, Saskatoon, A139 36, Lévesque to Neatby, 6 Feb. 1951
29 Georges-Henri Lévesque, *Souvenances II* (Ottawa 1988), 239–40
30 Lévesque as quoted in Bernard Ostry, *The Cultural Connection* (Toronto 1978), 83
31 Neatby Papers, A139 36, Lévesque to Neatby, 6 Feb. 1951
32 Michael Hayden, *So Much to Do, So Little Time* (Vancouver 1983), 32
33 P.B. Waite, *Lord of Point Grey* (Vancouver 1987), 151
34 Neatby Papers, A139 36, MacKenzie to Neatby, 10 Feb. 1950

CHAPTER 6 The Battle for the Air Waves

1 Frank Peers, *The Politics of Canadian Broadcasting* (Toronto 1969), 394
2 E. Austin Weir, *The Struggle for National Broadcasting in Canada* (Toronto 1965), 251

3 Peers, *The Politics of Canadian Broadcasting*, 396
4 Ibid., 392
5 Ibid., 399
6 Hearings (see ch. 2, note 33), Canadian Broadcasting Corporation, vol. 10, no. 107, 6
7 Briefs (see ch. 2, note 26), Canadian Association of Broadcasters (vol. 8, no. 101), 9. The above paragraphs are based on this brief and Guild's testimony. See Hearings, Canadian Association of Broadcasters, vol. 8, no. 101.
8 Private stations also had a host of petty complaints against CBC regulations which included their resentment of 'excessive' charges for transmission lines, insecurity of tenure of licences, and restrictions on the use of transcriptions.
9 Briefs, Canadian Broadcasting Corporation (vol. 10, no. 107), 16
10 Briefs, M. André Forget (vol. 19, no. 209), 2
11 Briefs, Association of Canadian Radio Artists, National Council (vol. 3, no. 35), 8
12 Hearings, Prince Edward Island Adult Education Council, vol. 28, no. 332, 74
13 Hearings, CKRD Red Deer, vol. 7, no. 90, 108
14 Hearings,Federated Women's Institutes of Canada, vol. 18, no. 192a, 3
15 Hearings, Calgary Business and Professional Women's Club, vol. 8, no. 97, 236. See also Hearings, Canadian Catholic Conference, vol. 12, no. 113, 666.
16 Hearings, Dr Robert Newton, vol. 26, no. 305, 1
17 Briefs, Public Affairs Institute (vol. 28, no. 340), 3. In a similar vein Neatby asked Provost Seeley of Trinity College in Toronto, who was appearing on behalf of the Church of England, if there was hope of broadening the 'cultured' audience:

> NEATBY: Do you think they [the CBC] should continue to look after them as a minority, or that there should be an effort to increase the group?
> SEELEY: No, I think it is part of the task of education to build up gradually a larger audience, but it is a slow process building up that larger audience and the commercial broadcasting people cannot afford the long time investment to build it up. Therefore, a national broadcasting system should undertake that task as an educational project. (Hearings, Church of England in Canada, vol. 16, no. 155, 977)

This was one of Neatby's favourite topics. She had another interesting exchange on the subject with Mrs. Dorothy Steeves, a representative of the Boag Foundation (Hearings, Boag Foundation, vol. 4, no. 48, 115).

18 Briefs, Canadian Broadcasting Corporation (vol. 10, no. 107), 'Programming,' 4

19 Briefs, Canadian Broadcasting Corporation (vol. 10, no. 107), enclosures

20 Briefs, CFAR Flin Flon (vol. 5, no. 61), 5–6

21 Ibid. See also Hearings, CKVL Verdun, vol. 7, no. 93, 362; and CKRD Red Deer, vol. 7, no. 90, 106, for other warnings that realism precluded excessive cultural programming.

22 Briefs, Canadian Association of Broadcasters (vol. 8, no. 101a), 20

23 Briefs, Canadian Writers' Committee (vol. 15, no. 144), 2

24 Briefs, Canadian Broadcasting Corporation (vol. 10, no. 107), enclosure, 'Good Listening,' a talk by Arthur L. Phelps, of the Department of English, McGill University, on the first CBC 'Wednesday Night,' 3 Dec. 1947, 2, 6. This is the same Phelps who called for a royal commission in 1944 (see ch. 1, pp. 18–19). In the interim he had worked for the CBC International Service.

25 Hearings, Mr Walter E. Elliott, vol. 18, no. 192, 433

26 Ibid.

27 Wright Papers, Government Publications Section, Robarts Library, University of Toronto, Canadian Association of Broadcasters file items, 'Control of Radio: An Urgent Canadian Problem: A Brief with Analysis, Constructive Criticism, and Specific Proposals Submitted to the Parliamentary Committee on Radio Broadcasting by The Canadian Association of Broadcasters, June, 1947.' This submission had also called for a 'Radio Bill of Rights' to match the existing principle of freedom of the press. Without it, the CAB had claimed, 'democracy cannot survive' (ibid., 2). It maintained that 'on each occasion (as in Nazi Germany or Fascist Italy) that a Dictator overthrew and eliminated a Democratic Government, both "The Right" as well as "The Practice" of free speech were ended' (ibid., 3).

28 Letter Review, no. 131 (13 Dec. 1943), as quoted in Ron Faris, The Passionate Educators (Toronto 1975), 127. Faris provides a number of other examples of this sort of publicity. See also Briefs, American Stockholders' Union (vol. 2, no. 18a), 6.

29 Wright Papers, Canadian Association of Broadcasters file items, Memo, Dan E. Cameron to Prairie Regional Representative of the CBC, 29 April 1948

30 Briefs, CKRD Red Deer (vol. 7, no. 90), 1–3

31 Hearings, CKVL Verdun, vol. 7, no. 93, 376

32 Briefs, Mr J.J. Gourd (vol. 19, no. 217), 5

33 Briefs, Association of Canadian Advertisers (vol. 3, no. 34a), 5

34 Briefs, CKCW Moncton (vol. 7, no. 85), 1–2

35 Hearings, American Federation of Musicians of the United States and Canada, vol. 2, no. 18, 536

36 Hearings, CFQC Saskatoon, vol. 5, no. 64, 151. CJOR Vancouver agreed,

telling the commission that it was reluctant to broadcast bad talent, and that good talent left just as soon as it became good (Hearings, CJOR Vancouver, vol. 6, no. 79, 4).

37 Briefs, Canadian Congress of Labour (vol. 13, no. 116), 3

38 This reality had to be taken into account no matter how patriotic a programmer's intentions: 'CKOC has no desire to fill up its schedule with American programs. We do require, however, a number of them to form the back-bone of our schedule to meet the competition from Buffalo and other American stations' (Briefs, CKOC Hamilton [vol. 7, no. 88], 17). The same was true for the CBC, for even if it had not needed commercial revenue, it would have had to run American programming in order to prevent its audience from switching to the more popular fare on American border stations (Briefs, Canadian Broadcasting Corporation [vol. 10, no. 107], 'Programming,' 3).

39 Briefs, Arts Centre of Greater Victoria (vol. 3, no. 27), 1

40 Vancouver *Sun*, 14 April 1950

41 Robert Owen, 'Canada in Range of Television Now!' *National Home Monthly*, May 1949

42 Ibid.

43 Briefs, Canadian Broadcasting Corporation (vol. 10, no. 107), 55, 57

44 Peers, *The Politics of Canadian Broadcasting*, 413

45 Minutes (see ch. 2, note 6), thirty-first meeting, 9 Jan. 1950

46 Minutes, fifty-eighth meeting, 19 July 1950

47 Minutes, fifty-ninth meeting, 20 July 1950

CHAPTER 7 From Scholarships to University Funding

1 Canada, Royal Commission on National Development in the Arts, Letters and Sciences, *Report* (Ottawa 1951), xi

2 See John Bartlet Brebner, *Scholarship for Canada* (Ottawa 1945).

3 Minutes (see ch. 2, note 6), first meeting, 2 May 1949

4 Briefs, (see ch. 2, note 26), St Dunstan's College (vol. 29, no. 355), 2

5 MacKenzie Papers, University of British Columbia Library, Special Collections, 196 3–26, minutes, First Meeting of the Scholarships Committee of the Royal Commission on National Development in the Arts, Letters, and Sciences, 22 Aug. 1949

6 Ibid.

7 Minutes, first meeting, 2 May 1949

8 In 1947 the Humanities Research Council had published a book that captured contemporary opinion on the subject. See Watson Kirkconnell and A.S.P. Woodhouse, *The Humanities in Canada* (Ottawa 1947).

9 Briefs, Humanities Research Council of Canada (vol. 20, no. 228), 6

10 Hearings (see ch. 2, note 33), Mount Allison University, vol. 22, no. 283, 73

11 Hearings, National Conference of Canadian Universities, vol. 23, no. 287, 699
12 Minutes, first meeting, 2 May 1949
13 Hearings, Humanities Research Council of Canada, vol. 20, no. 228, 439
14 Minutes, twenty-third meeting, 9 Sept. 1949
15 Hearings, National Scholarships, vol. 26, no. 298, 388
16 Four-year undergraduate scholarships, it was proposed, could be divided as follows: 25 Canada Scholarships at $1,000 per year; 250 National Scholarships, at $250 per year; and 1,200 to 1,500 bursaries and loans at a maximum of $500 per year (MacKenzie Papers, 197 4–2, Meeting of the Scholarships Committee, 17 Mar. 1950).
17 MacKenzie Papers, 197 4–2, Robbins to MacKenzie, 1 April 1950
18 Ibid., Garneau to MacKenzie, 22 Mar. 1950
19 Ibid., Robbins to MacKenzie, 1 April 1950. Brown also blamed Neatby for all of this trouble (ibid., Brown to MacKenzie, 14 April 1950).
20 Ibid., Robbins to MacKenzie, 1 Mar. 1950
21 Ibid., MacKenzie to Garneau, 24 Mar. 1950
22 Ibid., Meeting of the Scholarships Committee, 17 Mar. 1950
23 Ibid., MacKenzie to Robbins, 4 April 1950
24 Ibid., 196 3–26, minutes, Committee on Scholarships and Research, 10 April 1950 .
25 Ibid.
26 Hearings, Association canadienne-française pour l'avancement des sciences, vol. 3, no. 33, 26
27 The roots of this problem extended back to the 1930s, when the Depression had impoverished the universities along with the rest of the country. The Rowell-Sirois Commission had made a recommendation in favour of federal funding for universities, but this proposal was overshadowed at the time by the immediate need to provide for the education of veterans. See David A.A. Stager, 'Federal Government Grants to Canadian Universities, 1951–66,' *Canadian Historical Review* 54, no. 4 (Sept. 1973), 288–9
28 Hearings, National Conference of Canadian Universities, vol. 23, no. 287, 656
29 Briefs, National Conference of Canadian Universities (vol. 23, no. 287), 8
30 *Globe and Mail*, 24 Aug. 1949
31 Alain Stanké, *Georges-Henri Lévesque: Père de la renaissance québécoise* (Montreal 1976), 63; Georges-Henri Lévesque, interview, 26 Mar. 1987
32 Briefs, Chambre de commerce de Québec (vol. 15, no. 151), 107. See also Hearings, Fédération des sociétés Saint-Jean-Baptiste du Québec, vol. 18, no. 197; Chambre de commerce du district de Montréal, vol. 15, no. 153.
33 Briefs, Association canadienne des éducateurs de langue française (vol. 3, no. 31), 7–8

34 Hearings, Saskatchewan Department of Education, vol. 29, no. 363, 181. See also Hearings, New Brunswick Department of Education, vol. 26, no. 304a, 1–4.
35 Briefs, Saskatchewan Department of Education (vol. 29, no. 363), 1
36 Hearings, Alberta Federation of Home and School Associations, vol. 1, no. 8, 41
37 Briefs, Canadian Teachers' Federation (vol. 15, no. 141), 4
38 Briefs, Saskatchewan Department of Education (vol. 29, no. 363), 4. See also Briefs, Alberta Teachers' Association (vol. 1, no. 12), 1–2; Newfoundland Department of Education (vol. 26, no. 304a), 11.
39 Minutes, forty-sixth meeting, 20 June 1950
40 Ibid. Besides James, this delegation included Principal R.C. Wallace of Queen's, President A.W. Trueman of the University of New Brunswick, and Dean J.S. Thomson of McGill Divinity College.
41 Ibid.
42 Stager, 'Federal Government Grants to Canadian Universities,' 290–1
43 See Canada, *Official Report of Debates*, First Session, Twenty-first Parliament, vol. 1 (19 Oct. 1949), 932–6; Second Session, Twenty-first Parliament, vol. 3 (22 May 1950) 2697–742.
44 Minutes, forty-eighth meeting, 12 July 1950
45 MacKenzie Papers, 194 1–3, Massey to MacKenzie, 15 Sept. 1950. Massey added that 'I was very much impressed by the arguments on this subject presented by Cyril James when he met us a few weeks ago.' Massey and Neatby preferred grants directly to the humanities and social sciences rather than the NCCU's plan for funding professional schools. MacKenzie's reply, not surprisingly, was supportive (MacKenzie Papers, 194 1–3, MacKenzie to Massey, 19 Sept. 1950). MacKenzie had been working to convince Surveyer of the need for action in aid of the universities as well. Surveyer reported to MacKenzie on 23 October that the two papers MacKenzie had sent (probably 'Federal Aid to Universities' and 'General Problems of Education,' for which Day also thanked MacKenzie) had influenced his opinions on the subject. 'The percentage of the population which goes to universities is much smaller than I expected, so that my views have changed since reading these data,' he noted (Mackenzie Papers, 194 1–3, Surveyer to MacKenzie, 23 Oct. 1950).
46 Louis St Laurent, 'Address to the Autumn Convocation,' University of Toronto, 20 Oct. 1950 (mimeograph) as quoted in Stager, 'Federal Government Grants to Canadian Universities,' 292. An editorial in the *Globe and Mail* indicated that this was not the first time the prime minister was on record to this effect. See *Globe and Mail*, 31 Oct. 1950.
47 Lévesque to Bissell, 15 April 1977, as quoted in Claude Bissell, *The Imperial Canadian: Vincent Massey in Office* (Toronto 1986), 205–6
48 Ibid., 206
49 MacKenzie Papers, nu 194 1–5, Lévesque to MacKenzie, 31 May 1950
50 Hearings, University of New Brunswick, vol. 26, no. 303, 49

51 Pickersgill to Bissell, 10 Mar. 1979, as quoted in Bissell, *The Imperial Canadian*, 339. The same proposal had been made by the Rowell-Sirois Commission in its recommendation on the subject. MacKenzie mentioned Pickersgill's idea in a letter he wrote to Massey in September 1950: 'The only suggestion I have to offer of any consequence, and this grows out of a suggestion of Jack Pickersgill, has to do with the method of measuring Federal aid to the universities. It was his view that, if it were made on a per capita basis for the population of each Province, it might be easier to have it accepted. However, this is by way of suggestion only' (MacKenzie Papers, 194 1–3, MacKenzie to Massey, 21 Sept. 1950). In his memoirs MacKenzie recalled things somewhat differently: 'The other recommendation which was important ... was that the Federal Government should make direct grants of money ... to the universities of Canada. My colleagues understandably ... were most reluctant to include anything about education in our final reports. However, I kept on badgering them and insisting upon some recommendations, so finally in the last meeting that we held on the last day of our sessions Mr. Massey, a little tired of all this ... turned to me and said, "Well if we were to propose anything what would you suggest?" Off the top of my head I said it would be very simple. I would recommend that ... fifty cents per head of population should be made available by the Federal Government, to assist higher education in Canada. This would be distributed between the provinces on the basis of the population of those provinces and on the basis of the certified enrollment of full-time students in each of the universities in the province ... As they were getting exhausted and wanted to wind up the discussion, my colleagues agreed that this should go in and it did' (MacKenzie Papers, 128 2, Memoirs, 20).

CHAPTER 8 Hand-Outs for Longhairs

1 Briefs (see ch. 2, note 26), Vancouver Little Theatre Association (vol. 32, no. 419), 1
2 Fredericton Art Club (vol. 19, no. 211), 2
3 Hearings (see ch. 2 note 33), Miss Margaret Hall, vol. 19, no. 224, 125–6
4 Hearings, Canadian Music Council, vol. 14, no. 137, 390
5 Briefs, Discussion Group of Hamilton (vol. 18, no. 187), 2
6 Hearings, Canadian Welfare Council, Recreation Division, vol. 15, no. 143, 946
7 Hearings, Northern Ontario Art Association, vol. 26, no. 307, 308
8 Hearings, Miss Dorothy Somerset, vol. 31, no. 391, 412
9 Briefs, Board of Trade of the City of Toronto, Book Publishers Branch (vol. 4, no. 49), 2

10 Briefs, Canadian Authors Association, Vancouver and Mainland Branch (vol. 9, no. 104), 1
11 Briefs, Theatre under the Stars (vol. 31, no. 396), 2
12 Briefs, Canadian Authors Association, Vancouver and Mainland Branch (vol. 9, no. 103), 1
13 Hearings, Canadian Ballet Festival Association, vol. 9, no. 106, 605
14 Hearings, Canadian Teachers' Federation, vol. 15, no. 141, 847, 849–50
15 Hearings, Nova Scotia Teachers' Union, vol. 26, no. 314, 219. This was another point on which MacKenzie and Neatby differed. Mac-Kenzie would later criticize the sort of intellectual contempt for UNESCO that Neatby expressed, and urge that the commission excise any such cynicism from its report: 'I know too well the vagueness and the woolly-mindedness, the generalities and the weaknesses of organizations like UNESCO and of work done or intended in this field. On the other hand, I haven't seen much evidence that their critics are doing much of a practical kind about the problems of the world we live in and of the relations of the groups of people within it. In other words, unless they show the same keenness and more intelligence, I am inclined to be suspicious of cynicism and sarcasm, which the psychologists explain in terms of a defence complex. However, again, it may not be wise or feasible to raise this at this date, but I wanted to have it on file somewhere' (MacKenzie Papers, University of British Columbia Library, Special Collections, 197 4-3, MacKenzie to Day, 29 Jan. 1951). Massey agreed and promised to go through the UNESCO section to alleviate its smugness.
16 MacKenzie Papers, 194 1-1, Day to Andrew, 16 May 1949
17 Briefs, Arts Council of Manitoba (vol. 3, no. 28), 14
18 Briefs, Mr J.S. McMahon (vol. 21, no. 264), 1–2
19 Letter Review, no. 431 (7 Feb. 1949) as quoted in Ron Faris, The Passionate Educators (Toronto 1975), 127
20 Hearings, Mr David Smith, vol. 30, no. 375a, 1–2
21 Briefs, Calgary Allied Arts Centre (vol. 7, no. 95), 1
22 Briefs, Mr. David Brock (vol. 7, no. 94), 9
23 Ibid., 3, 8–9
24 Briefs, Orchestre symphonique de Québec (vol. 27, no. 326), 1
25 Vincent Massey, On Being Canadian (Toronto 1948), 48
26 MacKenzie Papers, 196 3-15, Memorandum to the Chairman, 'Evidence on the "National Arts Board,"' Ottawa, 13 June 1950. The same sort of question dominated discussions about the national commission for UNESCO which Canada, as a signatory to the UNESCO treaty, was expected to establish. The problem here was how to coordinate the activities of a UNESCO commission, voluntary organizations, and the Department of External Affairs in a manner that would represent the interests of each without inducing bureaucratic paralysis.

27 Minutes (see ch. 2, note 6), forty-fifth meeting, 19 June 1950
28 Minutes, first meeting, 2 May 1949
29 MacKenzie Papers, 194 1–1, Day to Andrew, 16 May 1949
30 Minutes, fifty-second meeting, 14 July 1950
31 Georges-Henri Lévesque, *Souvenances II* (Ottawa 1988), 287

CHAPTER 9 Cultivating the Hinterland

1 The National Gallery, the Public Archives, the proposal National Library, the National Museum, the National War Museum, the Historic Sites and Monuments Board, the National Film Board, and even the consideration of a system of honours and awards are all included as 'federal cultural institutions' in this chapter, although there is insufficient room to discuss each in detail.

2 Briefs (see ch. 2, note 26), National Museum of Canada (vol. 26, no. 297), 2

3 MacKenzie Papers, University of British Columbia Library, Special Collections, 196 3–15, Memorandum to the Chairman, Analysis of the Evidence for Agenda Item 2(e) National Museum, 16 June 1950. In their report the commissioners would make a similar comparison of the staff, annual purchase fund, and annual budget of the National Gallery with prominent regional galleries in the United States:

	Staff	*Purchase Fund*	*Budget*
Philadelphia Museum of Art	46	–	$798,094
Cleveland Museum of Art	45	$157,305	$493,754
Museum of Fine Arts, Boston	43	$317,498	$955,963
National Gallery of Canada	4	$ 32,000*	$ 90,000*

* These figures represented an average of expenditures over the previous ten years. For 1950–1 the Gallery had been granted substantially more: $75,000 for purchases and a total budget of $260,770 (Canada, Royal Commission on National Development in the Arts, Letters and Sciences, *Report* [Ottawa 1951], 80).

4 For discussions on the number and types of new museums that should be created, see MacKenzie Papers, 196 3–15, Memorandum to the Chairman, Analysis of the Evidence for Agenda Item 2(e) National Museum, 16 June 1950; and Minutes (see ch. 2, note 6), forty-fourth meeting, 19 June 1950.

5 Massey was chairman and Lévesque vice-chairman of this committee;

and its other members were Dr Kaye Lamb, Dominion archivist, Col. C.P. Stacey of the Department of National Defence, Dr F.J. Alcock, chief curator of the National Museum, Mr H.O. McCurry, director of the National Gallery, and Professor Gerard Brett, director of the Royal Ontario Museum.

6 Lamb and Stacey were members of this committee as well, along with G. de T. Glazebrook of the Department of External Affairs, Abbé A. Maheux, archivist at Université Laval, Mr. F. Desrochers, general librarian of the Library of Parliament, and Mr F.A. Hardy, parliamentary librarian. Stacey, a Department of National Defence historian, was quite popular with the commissioners. He served on the Historic Sites and Monuments Subcommittee, as well, and was regularly called on for advice on historical issues. Lamb was equally ubiquitous. He was well connected with the Liberal cabinet and was a friend of Pickersgill and MacKenzie. Lamb was later surprised to discover, however, that Massey disliked him for some reason and had been trying to have him removed from his post in 1950 (see P.B. Waite, *Lord of Point Grey* [Vancouver 1987], 148).

7 MacKenzie Papers, Minutes of the Second Meeting of the Committee on Libraries and Public Records of the Royal Commission on National Development in the Arts, Letters, and Sciences, 26 Aug. 1949

8 Briefs, Saskatoon Archaeological Society (vol. 29, no. 368), 1

9 MacKenzie Papers, 196 3–15, Memorandum to the Chairman, Analysis of the Evidence for Agenda Item 2(e) National Museum, 16 June 1950

10 Hearings (see ch. 2, note 33), National Museum of Canada, vol. 26, no. 297, 39–40

11 See *Report*, xxi. To make this subterfuge officially correct, Day had the prime minister's office send the commission two new back-dated letters which separated honours and awards from the other two requests. See Massey Commission Papers, National Archives of Canada, RG 33 28, vol. 1a, Day to Pickersgill, 29 Sept. 1950.

12 Hearings, National Film Board of Canada, vol. 23, no. 291, 757

13 Ibid., 723

14 See, for example, Briefs, Conseils du film de Saint-Lambert, Saint-Jean, Saint-Rémi, Salaberry de Valleyfield et Rigaud (vol. 17, no. 173), 8.

15 Hearings, National Film Board of Canada, vol. 23, no. 291, 745

16 Briefs, Association of Motion Picture Producers and Laboratories of Canada (vol. 3, no. 36a), 17

17 Hearings, Association of Motion Picture Producers and Laboratories of Canada, vol. 3, no. 36a, 17–18

18 Minutes, seventh meeting, 4 Aug. 1949

19 *Financial Post*, 19 Nov. 1949

20 Montreal *Daily Star*, 24 Nov. 1949; Canada, *Official Report of Debates*, First Session, Twenty-first Parliament, vol. 3 (7 Dec. 1949), 2850–4

21 Irwin's memo provided an excellent example of the Cold War mind-set which had made the cultural elite so preoccupied with the importance of emphasizing democratic values:

> If we can win this war of ideas, we may never have to fight the war of bodies ... Canada is in a position to make a unique contribution to the winning of this battle of ideas ... There are many ways in which Canada can speak to the world, but probably the most powerful of any is the motion picture. In the National Film Board, Canada has one of the most effective government operated motion picture agencies in the western world ... Here is a powerful instrument ready for use in the war of ideas.
>
> It is, therefore, recommended that the National Film Board initiate a film program designed to counter Communist propaganda with a positive re-emphasis of the advantages of the Democratic system. (MacKenzie Papers, 'Summary of Preliminary Proposals for the Use of Film in Psychological Warfare,' Ottawa, 16 Nov. 1950)

Irwin's appeal was nicely timed to capitalize on the escalation of Cold War tensions that followed China's intervention in the Korean War that month. It was a handy justification for increasing the NFB's budget.

22 Minutes, fifty-seventh meeting, 19 July 1950. Surveyer was not totally in accord with this point of view. His opinions on the NFB will discussed in chapter 10.

23 Hearings, Canadian Chamber of Commerce, vol. 12, no. 114, 258

24 Guy Roberge, interview, Ottawa, 7 June 1988. It is interesting to note that John Grierson, the former head of the National Film Board, was inspired in his work by a concern about how to make the complex problems of modern life understandable for the average citizen (see D.B. Jones, *Movies and Memoranda: An Interpretive History of the National Film Board of Canada* [Ottawa 1981], 6–7). Grierson's concerns reflected how the problem of making democracy work in a mass society preoccupied the cultural elite in this period. Grierson wanted to make documentary film a vehicle by which social and political problems could be rendered comprehensible to the average person. The cultural elite heard by the Massey Commission took the opposite tack, preferring to improve individuals' critical faculties rather than simplifying problems for them.

25 Hearings, Group of Representative Citizens of Greater Victoria, vol. 19, no. 219, 6

26 Hearings, Royal Architectural Institute of Canada, vol. 28, no. 348, 260

27 An example of this sort of critique can be found in Susan Crean, *Who's Afraid of Canadian Culture* (Toronto 1976), 2–4.

28 Briefs, National Gallery of Canada (vol. 25, no. 296), 5

29 Hearings, Art Gallery of Toronto, vol. 2, no. 25, 39–40
30 Briefs, Chambre de commerce des jeunes de Chicoutimi (vol. 15, no. 152), 8
31 Hearings, Canadian Citizenship Council, vol. 12, no. 115, 345–6
32 Briefs, Association canadienne d'éducateurs de la langue française (vol. 3, no. 31), 5

CHAPTER 10 The Report

1 MacKenzie Papers, University of British Columbia Library, Special Collections, 194 1–3, Massey to MacKenzie, 28April 1950
2 Archibald Day wrote a satirical profile of the average commission meeting which conveyed the essence of the commission's discussions. See Appendix C.
3 MacKenzie Papers, 194 1–2, Day to Andrew, 21 June 1950
4 Ibid., Andrew to Day, 26 June 1950
5 Ibid., Andrew to MacKenzie, 5 July 1950. At the same time Mac-Kenzie sent a copy to his friend George Ferguson at the Montreal *Star* for comment. Ferguson replied: '[W]hoever wrote that memo for you has his head screwed on and seems to have some perception of what a lofty, snotty tone could do public-relations wise. I think it would be important, if you feel it necessary to discuss the press, to couch your critical comments in such a way that the taking of offence will not follow. Otherwise the reception of the report as a whole will be damaged' (ibid., 194 1–3, Ferguson to MacKenzie, 1 Sept. 1950). Ferguson added that some sympathetic and knowledgeable person like himself should go over the chapter, and perhaps the entire report, with an editing pencil.
6 Neatby Papers, Saskatchewan Archives Board, University of Saskatchewan, Saskatoon, A139 36, MacKenzie to Neatby, 16 Sept. 1950
7 Lévesque to Hayden, 25 Jan. 1981, as quoted in Michael Hayden, *So Much to Do, So Little Time* (Vancouver 1983), 27
8 Canada, Royal Commission on National Development in the Arts, Letters and Sciences, *Report* (Ottawa 1951), frontispiece
9 This distinction was a standard argument of the Canadian Association for Adult Education. MacKenzie had made the same point a decade earlier when he had presented the CAAE brief to the Rowell-Sirois Commission.
10 *Report*, 8
11 Ibid., 5–6
12 Ibid., 5
13 Ibid., 18
14 Ibid., 5. Later the report would admit, however, that some guidance was necessary in this educational process: 'Culture, it is true, cannot be forced on us from above, and nothing is more distasteful than pre-

scribed and regimented amusement. But in an age when we call on the expert to advise us on everything ... there is surely no harm in accepting helpful suggestions ... And it is the function of national radio in a democratic state to offer helpful suggestions' (ibid., 300).

15 Ibid., 7
16 Ibid., 6
17 Ibid., 5
18 Ibid., 274
19 The commissioners invariably presented the role of culture as that of cultivating the informed and responsible democratic citizen. This was, for instance, why broadcasting issues were so important: 'Radio in any democratic country has three main functions: to inform, to educate, and to entertain ... We fully believe in the educational importance of radio in a democratic state, where everything depends on the intelligent and well-informed cooperation of the ordinary citizen' (ibid., 299). The same held true for film: 'In a democratic state, national effort in war and national unity in peace are maintained only by the informed conviction of its citizens. No democratic government can afford to neglect at any time a means of public information so far-reaching and persuasive as the film' (ibid., 310). But such concerns were not restricted to the mass media. Even the historians' professional interest in a liberal policy of access to public records was justified in terms of the common good of a democracy: '[T]he public interest is best served by a liberal policy in the matter of access by historians to public records. The free pursuit of truth by scholars is a most important feature of our democratic system and one meriting every consideration from the Government ... In this manner he will be able to make his full contribution to the unending task of public education and to the constant play of free public discussion, which are such essential parts of the democratic process' (ibid., 338–9). The commission's recommendations on scholarships would emphasize the importance of democratic access to higher education (ibid., 145, 356).
20 Neatby Papers, A139, 202 5, Hilda Neatby, 'The Massey Report and National Defence,' Current Affairs Course for Officers of the Canadian Forces at the University of Saskatchewan, 1953
21 *Report*, 321. Even the CBC was encouraged to produce more shows in locations other than Toronto and Montreal to encourage local talent in other regions.
22 Ibid., 276–7
23 Ibid., 279
24 Ibid., 285
25 Ibid., 288
26 The report proclaimed a greater need for public control in television than in radio. Fewer broadcasting channels made monopoly more of a

problem in television; and 'it promises to be a more popular as well as a more persuasive medium,' the report contended (ibid., 301). The greater capital investment and operating costs of TV would make its operators even more dependent on advertising revenue and commercialization (ibid., 301–2). The commissioners would have preferred to see a slow and cautious development of television, but the United States had set the pace and a Canadian system had to be established soon. They recommended that the CBC retain control of television just as it did in radio and that no private licences be granted until the CBC had national programs for private stations to carry. The commissioners also felt that a thorough review of the television system would be wise in about three years, once the nature of television development was more apparent.

27 Ibid., 294

28 To pay for the high cost of television development, they recommended that the government provide loans to finance start-up costs. The finances of the two media were to be kept separate, although television would derive its income in exactly the same manner – from a combination of licence fees, advertising revenue, and statutory grants.

29 Ibid., 399

30 MacKenzie Papers, 194 1–2, Day to MacKenzie, 15 Sept. 1950. MacKenzie wrote to Massey that he thought parts of Surveyer's memorandum made sense, but his desire for an independent regulatory body was misguided: 'Quite frankly, I don't see that it would make much change in the nature or the method of control exercised over broadcasting in Canada. You and I know that the present Board of Governors of the C.B.C. really act in very much the kind of way that Mr. Surveyer's Board of Control would presumably act. At the present time, the technical operation and administration of C.B.C. is in the hands of the officials of C.B.C. For this and other reasons, I see no particular justification for recommending any substantial change in the existing organization, other than those that we discussed and agreed to in Port Hope' (MacKenzie Papers, 194 1–3, MacKenzie to Massey, 19 Sept. 1950).

31 *Report*, 391

32 Ibid., 392

33 As Surveyer himself put it: 'I found in them the expression of views which I shared and which were expressed better than I could have done ... they have shown facets of the broadcasting problem which were not raised at our hearings but which are vitally important and basic to Canada's broadcasting and telecasting problems, in which the question of our matureness is at stake' (ibid., 398).

34 Ibid., 397.

35 Ibid.

36 Ibid., 403
37 Neatby Papers, A139 37, Memorandum, Neatby to Massey, 'On the Dissenting Views of Mr. Surveyer on BROADCASTING, ' 1 Feb. 1950
38 Ibid., A139 36, Lévesque to Neatby, 6 Feb. 1951
39 Neatby Papers, A139 36, Massey to Neatby, 1 Feb. 1951
40 Massey was quite willing to acknowledge how much he depended on Neatby. His letter included the following: '[T]he meeting on the 12th and 13th will be quite important, and I would be most grateful if you could manage to be here. I hope I have not exaggerated the importance of the meeting. I know I have not exaggerated the importance of the contribution you could make to it' (ibid.). In a later letter Massey would append the following handwritten message before signing: 'Let me tell you again how very deeply I appreciate all you have done to bring our onerous task to a successful conclusion. You have been a pillar of strength throughout and I can't begin to say how grateful I am' (Neatby Papers, A139 36, Massey to Neatby, 1 Mar. 1951).
41 Ibid., A139 36, Massey to Neatby, 5 Feb. 1951
42 There would nevertheless be other attempts to publish a summary of the report. The publication of a one-dollar digest of the Massey Report by Thomas Nelson and Sons was later blocked by the King's Printer on copyright grounds (Massey Commission Papers, National Archives of Canada, RG 33 28, vol. 1a, Edmond Cloutier to B.F. Neary, managing director of Thomas Nelson and Sons, 12 June 1951). Eventually a summary of the report was written by Albert Shea, a political scientist at Université de Montréal who had also worked at the Wartime Information Board with MacKenzie and Andrew. See Albert Shea, *Culture in Canada* (Toronto 1952). Not surprisingly, the CAAE was involved in its publication.
43 MacKenzie Papers, 197 4–3, Day to MacKenzie, 27 Jan. 1951
44 Ibid., MacKenzie to Day, 29 Jan. 1951
45 Ibid.
46 *Canada, Official Report of Debates*, Fourth Session, Twenty-first Parliament, vol. 4 (16 May 1951), 3077
47 Ibid. (1 June 1951), 3613
48 Ibid.
49 Ibid. Pickersgill recalls that this approach had been Massey's idea and that St Laurent had gone along with it because of its obvious political advantages. See Jack Pickersgill, *My Years with Louis St Laurent* (Toronto 1969), 139–40. See also *Debates*, Fourth Session, Twenty-first Parliament, vol. 4 (16 May 1951), 3077.

CHAPTER 11 Response and Implementation

1 Windsor *Daily Star*, 30 May 1951

2 MacKenzie Papers, University of British Columbia Library, Special Collections, 194 1–4, Day to MacKenzie, 2 June 1951
3 Robert Ayre, 'The Press Debates the Massey Report,' *Canadian Art* 9 (Oct. 1951), 25
4 Ibid., 38
5 Vancouver *Sun*, 1 June 1951
6 Harold Weir in the Vancouver *Sun*, as quoted in Ayre, 27
7 Calgary *Herald*, 2 June 1951
8 Ayre, 'The Press Debates the Massey Report,' 38
9 Winnipeg *Tribune*, 2 June 1951
10 Ayre, 28
11 Ibid.
12 Harold Innis, *The Strategy of Culture* (Toronto 1952), 18–19
13 Frank Underhill, 'Notes on the Massey Report,' *Canadian Forum*, Aug. 1951; reprinted in Frank Underhill, *In Search of Canadian Liberalism* (Toronto 1960), 209–10
14 Ibid.
15 Neatby Papers, Saskatchewan Archives Board, University of Saskatchewan, Saskatoon, A139 I 12 1, Massey to Neatby, 25 July 1951
16 Montreal *La Presse*, 2 June 1951; Ayre, 29
17 See Suzanne Myette, 'La Nation, l'état, et la culture: Quelques réactions québécoises à la Commission Massey, 1949' (MA thesis, Université de Montréal, 1979), 90–114. This was also the conclusion of the Ottawa *Evening Citizen* in an article of 13 June 1951 reviewing French-Canadian press reaction to the report entitled 'Quebec Applauds Massey Report.' See also Georges-Henri Lévesque, *Souvenances II* (Ottawa 1988), 273.
18 Ottawa *Evening Citizen*, 13 June 1951
19 Ayre, 'The Press Debates the Massey Report,' 29–30
20 *Le Devoir*, 5 June 1951, as cited in Frank Peers, *The Politics of Canadian Broadcasting* (Toronto 1969), 430
21 Michel Brunet, 'Le Rapport Massey: Réflexions et observations,' *L'Action universitaire*, 18 (Jan. 1952); reprinted as 'Une autre manifestation de nationalisme *Canadian*: Le Rapport Massey,' in Michel Brunet, *Canadians et Canadiens* (Montreal 1954).
22 St John's *Telegraph*, 7 June 1951
23 Ayre, The Press Debates the Massey Report,' 38. Historian Donald Creighton commented approvingly that the commission's 'conception of Canadian cultural development was a Laurentian one' ('Report of the Royal Commission on National Development in the Arts, Letters, and Sciences,' *Canadian Historical Review* 32, no. 4 [Dec. 1951], 378). Another prominent Canadian historian, Arthur Lower, made a similar observation and added that cultural development was the natural next step in the progress of the Canadian nation from adolescence to maturity ('The Massey Report,' *Canadian Banker* 59, no. 1 [1952], 22–32).

See also Wilfrid Eggleston, 'Canadian Geography and National Culture,' *Canadian Geographic Journal* 43 (Dec. 1951), 254–73.

24 Calgary *Herald*, 2 June 1951
25 Neatby Papers, A139 202 3, 'Notes on John L. McDougall'
26 *Le Devoir*, 7 June 1951
27 *Le Soleil*, 21 June 1951
28 Lévesque, *Souvenances II*, 276–82
29 *Standard* [Hodgeville, Sask.], 20 June 1951
30 MacKenzie Papers, 194 2–1, Massey to MacKenzie, 7 June 1951
31 Underhill, 'Notes on the Massey Report'
32 Allan Sangster, 'On the Air – the Massey Report (1),' *Canadian Forum*, July 1951
33 MacKenzie Papers, 194 1–4, Neatby to MacKenzie, 17 June 1951
34 Hilda Neatby, 'The Massey Report: A Retrospect,' *Tamarack Review* 1, no. 1 (Autumn 1956), 44–5
35 He came up with one argument that particularly impressed the prime minister. Noting that about half of the lawyers in the Justice Department were from the University of Saskatchewan law school – one of the best in the country – he asked St Laurent why Prairie wheat farmers should have to pay for the training of professionals destined for the Ottawa bureaucracy. This was a point that St Laurent, a former justice minister, could appreciate, and it pertained to other areas of the civil service as well (J.W. Pickersgill, interview, Ottawa 27 Mar. 1987).
36 Canada, *Official Report of Debates*, Fourth Session, Twenty-first Parliament, vol. 5 (19 June 1951), 4277–8
37 Conrad Black, *Duplessis* (Toronto 1977), 481
38 David Kwavnick, ed., 'Introduction,' *The Tremblay Report: Report of the Royal Commission of Inquiry on Constitutional Problems* (Toronto 1973), vii–ix. As a clerical counterbalance to Lévesque, Richard Arès, a Jesuit and editor of *Relations* (which had been quite critical of the Massey Report), was named a member.
39 Louis St Laurent Papers, National Archives of Canada, MG 26, L, vol. 146, R 35–1–R
40 W.L. Whittaker, 'The Canada Council for the Encouragement of the Arts, Humanities and Social Sciences: Its Origins, Formation, Operation and Influence upon Theatre in Canada, 1957–63' (PHD diss., University of Michigan, 1965), 137
41 'The Massey Report,' *Canadian Forum*, July 1951
42 'Cultural Time-Table,' *Food for Thought* 12, no. 3 (Dec. 1951)
43 Neatby Papers, A139 I 12 1, Neatby to Massey, 15 Sept. 1951
44 MacKenzie Papers, 194 2–1, Massey to MacKenzie, 7 Sept. 1951
45 The government provided $4,750,000 for the CBC for the remainder of the fiscal year and $6,250,000 a year for the next four years, bringing its income up to one dollar for every Canadian as the Massey Re-

port had suggested (*Debates*, Fifth Session, Twenty-first Parliament, vol. 1 [6 Nov. 1951], 739). The CBC was also given added responsibilities to ensure the use of Canadian talent on private stations and to monitor private programming in general. In reply to the private stations' complaints about arbitrary control by the CBC, rules about its procedures for enforcing its regulations were made more specific, and the Exchequer Court was made the court of appeal for questions of law regarding CBC rulings.

46 MacKenzie Papers, 194 2–1, MacKenzie to Day, 28 Mar. 1952
47 Ibid., Day to MacKenzie, 2 April 1952
48 'The Massey Report: Second Anniversary,' *Canadian Forum*, June 1953
49 Neatby, 'The Massey Report'
50 Whittaker, 'The Canada Council,' 138–40
51 MacKenzie Papers, 194 2–1, Day to MacKenzie, 17 Oct. 1951. Day added that 'I can tell you, but it is highly confidential, that the Government was to bring up in Parliament the Canada Council at this autumn session but later abandoned the notion until the regular meetings next year.'
52 MacKenzie Papers, 133 1–1, Pickersgill to MacKenzie, 1 April 1952. J.A. Corry, a political science professor at Queen's, informed MacKenzie that Pickersgill expected that the Canada Council might be introduced at the next session of Parliament, but scholarships would have to wait until the Council was underway (ibid., Corry to MacKenzie, 30 Sept. 1952). But J.R. Kidd wrote in late October that he doubted anything would be done that year (ibid., Kidd to MacKenzie, 28 Oct. 1952).
53 St Laurent in the House of Commons, as quoted in 'The Massey Report: Second Anniversary,' *Canadian Forum*, June 1953
54 MacKenzie tried flattery, appealing to Pickersgill's pride as a cultural nationalist: 'My own feeling is that you and your colleagues have a unique opportunity to organize the Canada Council and to get it successfully launched. I conclude this because of your victory, despite the kind of campaign the private broadcasters and others of their ilk carried on prior to the election. I realize your critics didn't attack the Canada Council directly, but it was, it seemed to me, implicit in what they wrote and said' (MacKenzie Papers, 133 1–1, MacKenzie, 22 Sept. 1953).
55 MacKenzie Papers, 133 1–1, Pickersgill to MacKenzie, 8 Oct. 1953
56 Whittaker, 'The Canada Council,' 142
57 MacKenzie Papers, 133 1–1, Pickersgill to MacKenzie, 30 Oct. 1954
58 *Globe and Mail*, 1 Nov. 1954
59 J.R. Kidd to H.H. Hannam, 2 Feb. 1955, as quoted in Ron Faris, *The Passionate Educators* (Toronto 1975), 125
60 Lévesque, *Souvenances II*, 288
61 Ibid., 289

62 Ibid., 289–90
63 Remarks by J.W. Pickersgill, Canada Council Twenty-fifth Anniversary Dinner, 12 June 1982, as quoted in J.L. Granatstein, 'Culture and Scholarship: The First Ten Years of the Canada Council,' *Canadian Historical Review* 65, no. 4 (Dec. 1984), 441. See also J.W. Pickersgill, *My Years with Louis St Laurent* (Toronto 1969), 318–19.
64 Granatstein, 'Culture and Scholarship,' 442. The quotations come from Lamontagne's remarks at the anniversary dinner cited above.
65 Bernard Ostry, *The Cultural Connection* (Toronto 1978), 67
66 John Robbins, 'The Massey Commission Recommendations: What Has Been Implemented, 1951–1960,' *Canadian Library* 17, no. 4 (Jan. 1961), 185

Conclusion

1 Claude Bissell, *The Imperial Canadian: Vincent Massey in Office* (Toronto 1986), 233. In Blair Fraser, *The Search for Identity: Canada, 1945–1967* (Toronto 1967), 104, the commission is presented as part of a 'great Canadian cultural revolution,' its report as 'a cultural bombshell in the upper megaton range.' See also Robert Fulford, Foreword, *An Introduction to the Arts in Canada* (Ottawa 1977). Maria Tippett challenges 'the popular view that government patronage of the arts began only with the founding of the Canada Council in 1957' (Maria Tippett, *Making Culture* [Toronto 1990], 91).
2 Georges-Henri Lévesque, *Souvenances* II (Ottawa 1988), 273. Measures such as the National Arts Centre (1966), the Canadian Film Development Corporation (1967), and the Art Bank (1972) were not even envisioned by the Massey Commission, although the creation of the Social Sciences and Humanities Research Council in 1978 fulfilled its hopes that, once established, an omnibus granting agency could later split into different specialized parts.
3 Bernard Ostry, *The Cultural Connection* (Toronto 1978), 63–4. In this same passage, however, Ostry makes the standard claim that 'almost all its recommendations were eventually implemented in some fashion or other.'
4 Hilda Neatby, 'The Massey Report: A Retrospect,' *Tamarack Review* 1, no. 1 (Autumn 1956), 44
5 'With the creation of the Canada Council, Canadian intellectuals finally achieved that state support for which many had pleaded ever since the late nineteenth century. They had attained, in fact, the intellectual parallel to the system of bounties that other social groups and classes had received since the inauguration of the National Policy' (Carl Berger, *The Writing of Canadian History* [Toronto 1986], 179). If 'intellectuals' is understood to exclude the scientists already supported by the NRC and other government funding, this comment is quite apt.

6 In her study of the ideology of the Massey Commission and other expressions of cultural nationalism during the 1950s, Erna Buffie traced similar premises through the thought of Arthur Lower, Harold Innis, Frank Underhill, Robertson Davies, Northrop Frye, B.K. Sandwell, and, of course, George Grant. See E.V. Buffie, 'The Massey Report and the Intellectuals: Tory Cultural Nationalism in Ontario in the 1950s' (MA thesis, University of Manitoba, 1979).

Primary Sources

The primary sources consulted in the process of writing this book can be roughly categorized into four groups:

1. sources relating to the political background of the commission
2. official records of the commission
3. private papers of commissioners
4. contemporary journalism

In the first category, critical information relating to the origins of the commission was found in the Brooke Claxton Papers in the National Archives of Canada (NAC, MG 32, B 5). These were supplemented by scraps of information found in the Lester Pearson Papers (NAC, MG 26, N) and the Louis St Laurent Papers (NAC, MG 26, L) in the same depository. An interview with Jack Pickersgill (Ottawa, 27 March 1987) provided additional information and the invaluable perspective of someone involved behind the scenes. Pickersgill also allowed the author access to his papers (NAC, MG 32, B 34). However, they proved less useful on this topic than the interview.

The briefs submitted to the commission and the transcripts of its hearings are deposited in the National Archives and are available on microfilm (NAC, RG 33 28, mfm C–1998 to C–2021). Research on the commission's hearings was based largely on this microfilm, while a group of papers relating to the commission donated to the University of Toronto Library by the commission's counsel, Peter Wright, provided originals for the study of the briefs (Government Publications Section, Robarts Library, University of Toronto, CA1 Z1 49A22). Both these sources were checked and supplemented by consulting the originals in the National Archives (NAC, RG

33/28). The NAC originals include a set of the minutes of the private meetings of the commission, but copies of these minutes found in the Norman MacKenzie Papers were the primary source used in this study.

These sources were supplemented by the study of private papers of the commissioners that were open to research. The Hilda Neatby Papers (Saskatchewan Archives Board, University of Saskatchewan, Saskatoon, A139) provided much useful information, but perhaps not as much as might be expected. Neatby apparently did not start saving her papers systematically until after the Massey Commission. Moreover, since much of her work on the commission was done in the commission's offices in Ottawa, where she would most often consult with the staff and other commissioners personally, there was relatively little correspondence relating to the commission in her papers. They do provide, however, a wealth of material on Neatby's and Massey's collaborative speech-writing in the years following the commission, material which provides many insights into their common beliefs. The papers of Norman MacKenzie (University of British Columbia Library, Special Collections) provided a much more comprehensive view of the behind-the-scenes life of the commission. Since MacKenzie stayed in close touch with Ottawa while attending to university business in Vancouver, he had more correspondence and memoranda in his papers, especially relating to the writing of the report, than those whose work in Ottawa allowed daily personal contact. These papers were unquestionably the single most valuable private collection employed in the writing of this study.

The Vincent Massey Papers, which were deposited in Massey College, University of Toronto, under the supervision of Massey's biographer, Claude Bissell, and the college librarian, Desmond Neil, were not opened to this researcher. This came as a surprise since many established historians had been allowed access to them before. Subsequently the papers were transferred to the University of Toronto Archives, where the stipulations of Massey's will, denying access for twenty-five years, are now being rigorously enforced. As consolation, Claude Bissell assured the author that there was not a lot of interesting documentation relating to the Massey Commission in the collection. P.B. Waite, who had access to the papers in the course of researching his biography of Norman MacKenzie, agreed with this assessment when asked by the author about the collection. This makes a certain amount of sense since the same geographical factors which limited Neatby's correspondence would have applied to Massey as well. It also proved impossible to obtain access to Arthur Surveyer's papers. They are neither in any public archives nor in the possession of his former company. His family was unhelpful in providing information on their existence or whereabouts.

The remaining member of the commission, Georges-Henri Lévesque, lives in Montreal, where he provided an informative interview (26 March 1987) and access to a manuscript of his memoirs relating to the commission (which has since been published). This study also benefited from the recollections and insight of Guy Roberge, the French-language associate counsel of the commission (Ottawa, 7 June 1988). An interview with Douglas LePan provided the perspective of someone who, while not directly involved, was an interested and well-connected observer of the commission's work (Toronto, 15 December 1987).

These sources were supplemented by references to numerous contemporary newspapers and periodicals, which contained an endless amount of fact and opinion on a subject that was something of a media sensation in its day. In consulting these sources, too numerous to list here, care was taken to obtain a geographical and partisan balance of viewpoints. The press was more than usually valuable in this study because Canadians who were interested and involved in the work of the commission were unusually articulate and quite often expressed their views in print.

Select Bibliography

This select bibliography is composed only of major works considered essential to an understanding of the Massey Commission. A more extensive bibliography can be consulted in Paul Litt, 'The Donnish Inquisition: The Massey Commission and the Campaign for State-Sponsored Cultural Nationalism, 1949–1951' (PHD diss., University of Toronto, 1990).

Ayre, Robert. 'The Press Debates the Massey Report.' *Canadian Art* 9 (Oct. 1951), 25–30, 36, 38

Berger, Carl. *The Sense of Power: Studies in the Ideas of Canadian Imperialism, 1968–1914.* Toronto 1971

– *The Writing of Canadian History: Aspects of English-Canadian Historical Writing since 1900.* 2d ed. Toronto 1986

Biggs, Karen L. Holland. 'Public Inquiries on Broadcasting and Cultural Policy in Canada, 1928–1982: Perspectives towards a Communicational Theory of Public Life.' MA thesis, McGill University, 1985

Bissell, Claude. *The Imperial Canadian: Vincent Massey in Office.* Toronto 1986

Brebner, J.B. *Scholarships for Canada: The Function of Graduate Studies.* Ottawa 1945

Buffie, E.V. 'The Massey Report and the Intellectuals: Tory Cultural Nationalism in Ontario in the 1950s.' MA thesis, University of Manitoba, 1979

Canada, Royal Commission on National Development in the Arts, Letters and Sciences. *Report.* Ottawa 1951

Canada. *Royal Commission Studies: A Selection of Essays Prepared for the Royal Commission on National Development in the Arts, Letters and Sciences.* Ottawa 1951

Creighton, Donald. *Dominion of the North*. Toronto 1957
– 'Report of the Royal Commission on National Development in the Arts, Letters, and Sciences' [book review]. *Canadian Historical Review* 32, no. 4 (Dec. 1951), 377–81
Culler, Dwight A., ed. *Poetry and Criticism of Matthew Arnold*. Boston 1961
Eggleston, Wilfrid. 'Canadian Geography and Canadian Culture.' *Canadian Geographic Journal* 43 (Dec. 1951), 254–73
Eliot, T.S. *Notes towards a Definition of Culture*. London 1948
Evans, Gary. *John Grierson and the National Film Board: The Politics of Wartime Propaganda*. Toronto 1984
Faris, Ron. *The Passionate Educators: Voluntary Organizations and the Struggle for Control of Adult Educational Broadcasting in Canada, 1919–1952*. Toronto 1975
Fee, Margery. 'English-Canadian Literary Criticism, 1890–1950: Defining and Establishing a National Literature.' PHD diss., University of Toronto, 1981
Fortier, André. *The Development and Growth of Federal Arts Policies, 1944–1985*. Ottawa 1985
Granatstein, J.L. 'Culture and Scholarship: The First Ten Years of the Canada Council.' *Canadian Historical Review* 65, no. 4 (Dec. 1984), 441–74
Hayden, Michael. *So Much to Do, So Little Time: The Writings of Hilda Neatby*. Vancouver 1983
Horkheiner, Max. 'Art and Mass Culture.' *Studies in Philosophy and Social Science* 9 (1941), 290–304
Jasen, Patricia. 'The English-Canadian Liberal Arts Curriculum: An Intellectual History.' PHD diss., University of Manitoba, 1987
Jones, D.B. *Movies and Memoranda: An Interpretive History of the National Film Board of Canada*. Ottawa 1982
Kirkconnell, Watson, and A.S.P. Woodhouse. *The Humanities in Canada*. Ottawa 1947
Kneller, George P. *Higher Learning in Britain*. Berkeley 1955
Kroker, Arthur. *Technology and the Canadian Mind: Innis / McLuhan / Grant*. Montreal 1984
Lévesque, Georges-Henri. *Souvenances II: Remous et éclatements*. Ottawa 1988
Lower, Arthur. 'The Massey Report.' *Canadian Banker*, 59, no. 1 (Winter 1952), 22–32
– *This Most Famous Stream: The Liberal Democratic Way of Life*. New York 1954
Macdonald, Dwight. 'A Theory of Popular Culture.' *Politics* 1, no. 1 (Feb. 1944), 20–3
– *Against the American Grain*. 1952, reprint, New York 1962
McKillop, A.B. *Contours of Canadian Thought*. Toronto 1987

– *A Disciplined Intelligence: Critical Inquiry and Canadian Thought in the Victorian Era.* Montreal 1979

McLeish, John A.B. *A Canadian for All Seasons: The John E. Robbins Story.* Toronto 1978

Massey, Vincent. *On Being Canadian.* Toronto 1948

Myette, Suzanne. 'La Nation, l'état, et la culture: Quelques réactions québécoises à la Commission Massey, 1949.' MA thesis, Université de Montréal, 1979

Neatby, Hilda. *So Little for the Mind.* Toronto 1953

Ortega y Gasset, José. *The Revolt of the Masses.* Trans. Arthur Kerigan. 1932; reprint, Notre Dame 1985

Ostry, Bernard. *The Cultural Connection: An Essay on Culture and Government Policy in Canada.* Toronto 1978

Owram, Douglas. *The Government Generation: Canadian Intellectuals and the State, 1900–1945.* Toronto 1987

Peers, Frank. *The Politics of Canadian Broadcasting.* Toronto 1969

Pickersgill, Jack. *My Years with Louis St Laurent: A Political Memoir.* Toronto 1969

Rickwood, R.R. 'Canadian Broadcasting Policy and the Private Broadcasters, 1936–68.' PHD diss., University of Toronto, 1976

Rosenberg, Bernard, and David Manning, eds. *Mass Culture: The Popular Arts in America.* Glencoe, Ill., 1957

Schafer, D. Paul. *Review of Federal Policies for the Arts in Canada, 1944–1988.* Ottawa 1989

Seldes, Gilbert. *The Great Audience.* New York 1950

Shea, Albert. *Culture in Canada: A Study of the Findings of the Royal Commission on National Development in the Arts, Letters and Sciences, 1949–1951.* Toronto 1952

Shortt, S.E.D. *The Search for an Ideal: Six Canadian Intellectuals and Their Convictions in an Age of Transition.* Toronto 1976

Smith, Frances. *André Biéler: An Artist's Life and Times.* Toronto 1980

Stager, David A. 'Federal Government Grants to Canadian Universities, 1951–1966.' *Canadian Historical Review* 54, no. 3 (Sept. 1973), 287–97

Stanké, Alain. *Georges-Henri Lévesque: Père de la renaissance québécoise.* Montreal 1976

Tippett, Maria. *Making Culture: English-Canadian Institutions and the Arts before the Massey Commission.* Toronto 1990

Vipond, Mary. *The Mass Media in Canada.* Toronto 1989

– 'The Nationalist Network: English Canada's Intellectuals and artists in the 1920s.' *Canadian Review of Studies in Nationalism* 5, no. 1 (Spring 1980), 32–52

Waite, P.B. *Lord of Point Grey: Larry MacKenzie of UBC.* Vancouver 1987

Whittaker, Walter Leslie. 'The Canada Council for the Encouragement of the Arts, Humanities and Social Sciences: Its Origins, Formation, Operation and Influence upon Theatre in Canada, 1957–63.' PHD diss., University of Michigan, 1965

Wise, S.F. 'The Conservative Tradition in Upper Canada.' In *Profiles of a Province*. Toronto 1967, 20–33

– 'God's Peculiar Peoples.' In W.L. Morton, ed., *The Shield of Achilles*. Toronto 1968, 36–61

– 'The Origins of Anti-Americanism in Canada.' 4th Seminar on Canadian-American Relations, Assumption University of Windsor, 1982

– 'Sermon Literature and Canadian Intellectual History.' In J.M. Bumsted, ed., *Canadian History before Confederation*. Georgetown 1972, 253–69

Woodcock, George. *Strange Bedfellows: The State and the Arts in Canada*. Vancouver 1985

Young, William R. 'Making the Truth Graphic: The Canadian Government's Home Front Information Structure and Programmes during World War II.' PHD diss., University of British Columbia, 1978

Index

Acadia University 152
L'Action catholique 228
L'Action nationale 224, 230
Adorno, Theodor W. 95–6
advertising: on CBC 124, 139, 144, 215–16, 236; economic role of 137, 249; magazine, examples of 58–9; and private radio 125
Aird Commission 70; public broadcasting system, creation of 20, 36, 124
Alberta Federation of Home and School Associations 160
Alberta Teachers' Association 160
Alcock, Dr F.J. 192, 298n.5
Aldwinkle, Eric 221
All-Canadian Mutually Operated Radio 136
All-Canadian Radio Facilities Limited 136
Andrew, Geoffrey 182, 208; background of 43; and Canada Council legislation 239; on report, anticipation of 209; and report, influence on 213
Angers. François-Albert 230
Anti-Americanism: in commission's

attitudes 250; and cultural superiority 106–7, 171; in press reaction to report 226; in report 212, 227
Arnold, Matthew: on high culture, value of 100–2, 253, 287n.37; influence on commissioners 99–100; quoted by commissioners 18, 287n.32; and *Scrutiny* 287n.31
Art Gallery of Toronto 202
Arthur, Eric 61
artists 23–4, 35, 171, 173, 253
Arts Centre of Greater Victoria 139
arts council. *See* Canada Council
Arts Council of Great Britain 48; model for Canada Council 181–3, 246
arts subsidies 13, 16, 24, 32, 36, 37, 45, 170–1, 175, 178
Association canadienne des éducateurs de la langue française 159
Association of Canadian Clubs 59, 78; and cultural elite 19–20
Association of Canadian Radio Artists 130

Association of Motion Picture Producers and Laboratories of Canada 196
atomic power 58, 90–1, 95
Augustine, Saint 210

Batterwood 21; broadcasting deliberations at 145; Canada Council deliberations at 183; July 1950 meetings at 143, 209
Bell, Bernard Iddings 286n.10
Bennett, R.B. 31, 124
Berger, Carl 101, 285n.1
biculturalism 6, 73, 113, 117, 120, 178, 196
Biéler, André 22
Birney, Earle 110
Bissell, Claude: on Lévesque as a commissioner 63; presentation for Canadian Writers' Committee 110–11
Bissett, Florence 72
Boag Foundation 286n.7, 291n.17
Board of Broadcast Governors 246
Brebner, J.B. 147
Brett, Gerard 298n.5
British Broadcasting Corporation 48, 98
British Council 48, 182
British North America Act 28, 160, 211
broadcasting 3, 184, 194, 203, 231, 233, 236; commercialization of 123, 129, 131, 137, 139; public, financing of 127–8, 140, 141–2, 144, 215–16; regulation 124–5, 128–9, 143–4, 215–17, 231–2, 246. See also radio; television
Broadcasting Act (1956) 246
Brock, David 179
Brown, George: Neatby, recommendation of 33; scholarships scheme 153; sub-committee on scholarships 148–9
Brunet, Michel 228

Burns, E.L.M. 152

Calgary Allied Arts Centre 70, 178
Calgary Business and Professional Women's Club 130
Calgary *Herald* 225, 230
Callaghan, Morley 57
Canada, an International Power 109
Canada Council 4, 45, 185, 203, 237; Arts Council of Great Britain, modelled on 182–3, 246; composition of 149, 182–4; establishment of, problems in 238–43, 246–7; *fait accompli* 32, 41, 180–1; recommendation of 214; recommendation of, press reaction 229
Canada Foundation 78
Canadian Art 224
Canadian Arts Council 23, 78, 171, 235, 239
Canadian Association for Adult Education: brief 49; on education and culture 94; on mass media 90; promotion of commission, role in 50; promotion of report, role in 235, 239
Canadian Association of Broadcasters: communism, invokes threat of 105; detractors 129–30; and House of Commons Select Committee on Broadcasting 236; on independent regulatory body 25, 128; and public interest 137–8; submissions 46, 60, 78; supporters 25, 125, 136, 232; television, interest in 142
Canadian Authors Association 20, 106–7, 110, 171–3
Canadian Ballet Festival Association 174
Canadian Banker 224
Canadian Broadcasting Act (1936) 141

Canadian Broadcasting Corporation 4, 12, 35, 169, 178, 194, 199, 203, 223, 231–2, 247; and advertising 124, 139, 144, 215–16, 236; creation of 124; criticism of 77, 133, 135, 139–140; criticism of by CAB 125, 128, 133, 135; culture, promotion of 131, 138; funding of 24–5, 127, 139, 144, 233–4; national role of 27, 129; postwar problems of 24–5; radio set licence fee 139–40; recommendations regarding 215–16, 306n.45; regulatory powers 125, 128; role in television development 141–2; submissions 60, 78; support for 136
Canadian Chamber of Commerce 200, 226
Canadian Citizenship Council 193, 203
Canadian Clubs (Association of) 19, 59, 77
Canadian Conference of Artists 23
Canadian Congress of Labour 138
Canadian Council for the Arts and Letters. See Canada Council
Canadian Council of Churches 50
Canadian Daily Newspaper Association 136
Canadian Federation of Agriculture 49–50, 53, 109, 240
Canadian Forum 224, 232, 235
Canadian Geographical Journal 224
Canadian Group of Painters 110
Canadian Handicrafts Guild 289n.17
Canadian Historical Association 21, 49, 190, 191
Canadian Institute of International Affairs 19–20, 78
Canadian League 19, 50
Canadian Library Association 39, 49–50, 190, 191

Canadian Music Council 168
Canadian Political Science Association 21, 22, 190
Canadian Press 223, 225
Canadian Psychological Association 22
Canadian Radio Broadcasting Commission 124
Canadian Teachers' Federation 160, 174
Canadian University Liberal Federation 14
Canadian Welfare 224
Canadian Welfare Council 78, 170, 224
Canadian Writers' Committee 105, 110–11, 133
Canadian Writers' Foundation 48
Canadian Youth Commission 21, 59
Carnegie Corporation 22, 288n.5
Central Mortgage and Housing Corporation 72
CFAR Flin Flon 132
CFCY Charlottetown 135
CFQC Saskatoon 138
Chambre de commerce de Québec 158
Christianity 91, 92
Church of England 90
'Citizen's Forum' 50, 132
CJCA Edmonton 135
CJOC Lethbridge 128
CKCL Verdun 136
CKEY Toronto 71, 139
CKOC Hamilton 139, 293n.38
classicism 91, 92, 95, 220, 253
Claxton, Brooke 11; and Canada Council 238, 242, 247; choice of commission chairman 29; commission, creation of 16, 24, 27–9, 36; cultural elite, place in 21; on federal aid to public schools 160–1; federal cultural institutions, conslidation of 11,

23, 188; 1948 National Liberal
Convention 12–16, 278n.2; universities, federal funding for 36,
165; voluntary associations, early
involvement with 19–20; Wartime Information Board, involvement with 282n.19; woman
commissioner, need for 34
Cold War 57–8, 85, 87, 95, 102,
104–5, 125, 133–5, 198, 212, 229,
249–50
Coldwell, M.J. 47
Comité permanent de la survivance
française en Amérique 107, 113,
159
Commercial and Press Photographers Association of Canada 197
Community Arts Council of Vancouver 235
community centres 169–70, 180–1
Competitive Festival of Music 87
Conservative party 25, 30, 31, 125,
139, 233
consumerism 88–9, 95, 124, 249
Cooke, Jack Kent 71–2, 138
Co-operative Commonwealth Federation 16, 30, 46, 233
Co-ordinating Committee of Canadian Youth Groups 107
Corbett, E.A. 46, 239; support for
commission, organizes 50; Wartime Information Board, role in
282n.19
Corporation des agronomes de la
province de Québec 20
Corry, J.A. 307n.52
Creighton, Donald 17–18, 305n.23
cultural elite 4, 29, 35–7, 56, 83,
120, 147, 152, 155, 184–5, 215,
248–54; arts subsidies, concerns
regarding 175–82; broadcasting
as education, advocacy of 133–4;
cosmopolitanism 109–13; edification of masses, problems with
130–1; description of 38–40; on

federal cultural institutions, decentralization of 191, 201, 203;
hearings, representation at 48–9;
leadership role 54; origins of
19–22; press membership 42;
staffing of commission 45–6
culture lobby 4, 38, 104, 120, 145,
173, 184–5, 203, 244, 251–3; CBC,
criticism of 140; concerns of
85–91; cultural nationalism of
109–12; culture, views of 83–4;
on federal cultural institutions,
decentralization of 191, 200–1;
humanities, views on 150; mass
culture, fear of 102; motivations
of 248–51; and National Library, origins of 191; public
broadcasting, support for 129,
133, 138; report, implementation
of 237–8; support for commission 50–5

Dalhousie University 152
Davies, Robertson 57, 309n.6
Day, Archibald 219, 221; appointment as secretary 43–4; on the
Canada Council 182; honours
and awards 299n.11; parody of
Surveyer and consequences 67;
on response to report 223,
236–8; scholarships, surveys opinion regarding 147; on UNESCO
175; witnesses, role in briefing
61; on writing the report 208
Department of External Affairs
43, 148–9, 174, 175, 236, 237
Department of National Defence
189, 197
Department of Veterans' Affairs
152
Desrochers, F. 299n.6
Deutsch, John 241
Le Devoir (Montreal) 74–6; commission, attitude towards 72–3;

report, response to 228; university funding 230
Dexter, Grant 67
Direct Veterans Assistance program 27, 152, 155, 156–7, 164, 166
Discussion Group of Hamilton 88, 169
Dominion Bureau of Statistics 148
Dominion Drama Festival 48, 169
Drew, George 30, 31
Dunn, James Hamet 242
Dunton, Davidson 144, 282n.19; brief for CBC, presents 127, 129; television, plans for 142; relations with commission 46
Duplessis, Maurice 28, 75, 76, 117, 162, 164, 230, 233–4, 239; ignores commission in Quebec 72; and Lévesque, relations with 34–5; objections to commission 47, 175

Edelstein, H.N. 78–9
Edmonton *Journal* 136
Eggleston, Wilfrid 42, 220, 281n.15, 282n.18, 305n.23
Eliot, T.S. 99, 287n.31
Elliot, W. 134–5
Elliot-Haynes Ltd. 134
Ewing, D.M. 66

Federated Women's Institutes of Canada 130
Fédération des sociétés Saint-Jean-Baptiste du Québec 74
Federation of Canadian Artists 22, 51, 65
Ferguson, George 42, 281n.15, 301n.5
Fiddlehead Poetry Society 89–90
Film Act (1950) 199, 245
Financial Post 197–8
Financial Times 225
Food for Thought 50, 224, 235

Fowler Commission 246
Frankfurt School 95–6, 98
Fraser, Blair 57, 282n.18
Fraser, G.K. 198
Fredericton Art Club 168
Fromm, Eric 95
Frye, Northrop 94, 309n.6

Garneau, René: appointment to commission 44; on Archibald Day 67; report, French version of 221; scholarships committee, liaison with 148, 153; Wartime Information Board, role in 282n.19
Geological Survey of Canada 188, 243
Gillson, A.H.S. 67
Gordon, Walter 46, 197
Gourd, J.J. 136
Gouzenko, Igor 194
Graham, Elsie 112
Grant, George 287n.32, 309n.6; *Lament for a Nation* 101–2, 249; special study on philosophy 46, 93
Grierson, John 282n.19, 300n.24
Group of Seven 110
Guild, William 128, 138

Hall, Margaret K. 168
Halton, Matthew 58
Hannam, H.H. 109, 240
Hardy, F.A. 299n.6
Harris, Lawren 23, 32
Harris, Walter 238–9
Hazelgrove, A.J. 201
Heeney, Arnold 68
Henry, G.S. 136
Herbert, Walter 282n.18
high culture 208, 229, 249–54; defined 84–5; dissemination through broadcasting 131–2; need for 87, 95, 100, 102, 103; origins of 91–3; popularization,

problems in 131, 180, 192, 252–3; public suspicions of 53, 57, 60, 65, 70–1, 76–7, 80, 101, 225–6; relationship to national identity 106–8, 200–1, 248–51; and universities 147, 157–8, 214
Historic Sites and Monuments Board 13, 188, 237, 243, 298n.1, 299n.6
hockey 170, 171
Hodgeville *Standard* 231
Horkheimer, Max 95–6
honours and awards 193–4, 298n.1, 299n.11
House of Commons Joint Committee of Both Houses on the Library of Parliament 190
House of Commons Select Committee on Radio Broadcasting 236
How, Douglas 225
Howe, C.D. 240–2
humanism 101, 252, 254; bicultural bridge 117; and Christianity 92–4, 103; commissioners' attitudes towards 91, 120, 220; as counterbalance to capitalism and science 90, 95, 100, 248–50; cultural elite, defining element of 38–40; liberal 102, 105–8, 112, 118, 120, 185, 211, 253–4
humanities: council for 182–3, 214; status in universities 149–51
Humanities Research Council of Canada 150

idealsim 92–3, 103, 250
Innis, Harold 97–8, 227, 309n.6
Irwin, Arthur 198, 289n.9, 300n.21

Jackson, A.Y. 23
James, F. Cyril 161–2, 295n.45
Johnson, Everson, and Charlesworth 135

Jones, J. Walter 77

Keenleyside, H.L. 59
Kerr, A.E. 152
Key, A.F. 70
Keynes, John Maynard 181
Kidd, J.R 193, 239–40, 282n.18, 307n.52
Killam, Isaac Walton 242
King, W.L. Mackenzie 11, 13, 23, 30, 114, 124
Kingston Conference of Artists 22–3
Kirkconnell, W. 152, 293n.8
Klein, Alan 170

Lamb, Kaye: decentralization of archives 193; records management 189; subcommittees, membership of 45, 298n.5, 299n.6
Lamontagne, Maurice 164, 240, 242
Laurendeau, André 228
League of Nations Society 19–20
learned societies 21
Leavis, F.R. 98–9, 287n.31
Léger, Jules 44
LePan, Douglas 42–3
Lesage, Jean 239
Lethbridge *Herald* 226
Lett, Sherman 44
Lévesque, Georges-Henri 6, 210, 218–19, 246; commissioner, chosen as 34–5; criticism of in French Canada 230–1; cultural elite, membership in 20–1; discussions regarding Canada Council 183–4, 240–1; and Duplessis 47; French-Canadian nationalist 116–17; and Neatby, compatibility with 93, 117; 1949 trip to Europe 48; report, promotion of 234–5; report, work on 208, 210, 221; Special Committee on Museums 298n.5; on universities,

federal funding for 150, 158, 163–4
Liberal party 12–14, 16, 35, 37, 48, 126, 238, 243, 247
Library of Parliament 48
Ligue d'action nationale 112. *See also L'Action nationale*
Lismer, Arthur 110, 289n.15
Livesay, Dorothy 110
Livingston, Richard 98
Lloyd, Woodrow 159–60
Loon's Necklace, The 196
Lortie, Léon: on humanities 150–1; sub-committee on scholarships 148, 153; universities, federal funding for, and scholarships 155–6
Lowenthal, Leo 95
Lower, Arthur 285n.1, 305n.23, 309n.6

McCann, J.J. 236
McCurry, H.O. 192, 298n.5
MacDermot, T.W. 44
Macdonald, Dwight 95
McGee, D'Arcy 126
McGill University 148, 150
Mackenzie, C.J. 148, 151
MacKenzie, N.A.M.: on Canada Council 183, 238–40; commission, promotion of 51; commissioner, chosen as 32–3; common touch 61, 63, 118–19, 280n.45; feature film industry 200; report, promotion of 232; report, writing of 209–10, 209–20; scholarships 152–5; on Surveyer's dissent 303n.30; UNESCO 297n.15; universities, federal funding for 32, 295n.45, 296n.51; voluntary associations, involvement with 20
McKiel, Harold 150
McKillop, A.B. 93
MacKinnon, Frank 77

MacLaren, D.L. 118
McLean, Ross 195, 197–8
Maclean's 58, 198; broadcasting, calls for commission on 25; report, reaction to 224, 232; television development 57
MacLennan, Hugh 282n.18
McLuhan, Marshall 98
McMahon, J.S. 176
MacMillan, Ernest 23, 46
Maheux, A. 299n.6
Manitoba Drama League 175
Mannheim, Karl 98–9
Marcuse, Herbert 95
Marsh Report 17
mass culture 5, 102, 105–8, 171, 173, 201, 212–13; criticisms of 95–7, 100, 178, 217, 227, 249–53; defined 84–5; threat to democracy 85, 89, 249
mass media 88–91, 96–7, 123, 210, 214, 249, 254
Massey, Alice 43, 209
Massey, Vincent 3, 11; arts council, composition of 182–3; CBC, support for 117; chairman, chosen as 15, 29–31; on commission's purpose 108–9; commissioners, relations with 116–17; constitutional scruples 175; honours and awards, opinion regarding 194; leadership style 62–3; National Film Board, approach to 197; and Neatby, dependence on 210, 304n.40; *On Being Canadian* 18, 32, 66, 86, 106, 181; political activism, techniques of 39–40; press conference regarding commission 41; public image 113–14; report, influence on implementation 235–6, 238, 240; scholarships 153–7; Special Committee on Museums 298n.5; Surveyer, opinion of 219, 232; UNESCO 297n.15; universities,

federal funding for, acceptance of 160–5, 295n.45; voluntary associations, involvement with 20; wife's illness and death 209

Massey Commission 3; Canadian identity, protection of 108; characteristics of members and supporters 20–1, 38–9; commissioners, choice of 29–30, 32–5; commissioners' relations 114–20; conservative bias 5, 6, 101–2, 249–50; culture, definitions of 83–5; deliberations on arts council 184; deliberations on broadcasting 143–5; deliberations on federal cultural institutions 201–3; deliberations on National Film Board 197, 199–203; deliberations on universities, federal funding for 162–3; education, association of culture with 146–7; hearings 46–8, 77, 207; ideological influences upon 95–9; ideology of 91–5, 99–103; influence of 245–54; influence of WIB upon 40; in the Maritimes 76–7; in Newfoundland 79; in Ottawa 48–9, 60, 77, 126, 147; in Quebec 73–6, 158–9; in Toronto 71–2; in Western Canada 64–71; mandate 35–6; multiculturalism, appreciation of 113–14; nicknamed 'Culture Commission' 4, 40; origins 4–5, 16, 23, 27, 36–7; press, relations with 42; private investigations 68; public image 40, 44, 61–2, 65–6; social activities 67; social context 56–60; special committee on libraries and public records 190; special committee on museums 190; special committee on scholarships 148; special studies 46; staffing 44; submissions to 51–2; submissions to, concerns of 85–91; submissions to re arts subsidies 167–83; submissions to re broadcasting 125–40; submissions to re federal cultural institutions 187–92; submissions to re federal funding for public schools 159–61; submissions to re National Film Board 195–7; submissions to re scholarships 147–8, 152; submissions to re universities, federal funding for 156–9; voluntary associations, support for 50–1

Massey Foundation 29

Massey Report: on American cultural influence 5; form of 210–11, 213–14; French-Canadian reaction to 228–31; implementation of 233–44; introductory sections 211–13; minority recommendations of Surveyer 216–20; press reaction to 223–32; promotional role 208; recommendations on broadcasting 215–16; recommendations on Canada Council 214; recommendations on federal cultural institutions 214; tabled in Parliament 221; translation difficulties 221; unanimity of commissioners in 208; writing of 208–10

Mawdsley, J.D. 53

Mayrand, Léon 148

Mazzoleni, Ettore 168–9

Mill, John Stuart 157

ministry of culture 180–1, 188, 196

Mitchell, W.O. 110

Moberley, Walter 98

Montréal Matin 228

Mount Allison University 150

multiculturalism 113, 290n.24

National Conference of Canadian Universities 234; on Canadian superiority 107–8; MacKenzie's

relationship with 32, 165; 1956 conference 242; publicity efforts of 233; and St Laurent, meeting with 161–2; submissions of 60, 157–8, 160–1
National Council of Women 87
National Farm Radio Forum 50, 132
National Film Board 12, 16, 35, 169, 191, 203, 243, 246, 298n.1; accommodations 236–7, 243; commission's conclusions regarding 200–1, 216–17; decentralization 186; opposition to 26–7, 187, 194–8; support for 49; Woods-Gordon report on 199
National Film Society of Canada 49
National Gallery 12, 22, 26, 35, 48, 186, 203, 246, 298n.1; accommodations 26, 188, 237, 243; administrative reforms to 189; decentralization of 192, 201–2; Massey's involvement with 45
National Home Monthly 57–8, 140–1
National Liberal Convention (1948) 11–12, 14, 27
National Liberal Federation 12, 14
National Library 12–13, 27, 45, 191, 246, 298n.1; commission's effect on 243; created 237; initiated by Parliament 190; role defined 191
National Library Act 237
National Museum 26, 186, 187, 246, 298n.1, 298n.3; administrative reforms to 189; commission's effect on 237, 243; decentralization 192–3; hearings on 48, 186–9
National Research Council 3, 33, 35, 147, 151, 182, 239
National War Museum 48, 189, 298n.1
nationalism 66, 102, 109–14, 202,

229, 248; broadcasting debate, influence on 124; commissioners' brand of 115; cultural 5, 19, 24, 37, 71, 104, 105, 107–9, 113, 120, 138, 171, 173, 176, 178, 187, 227, 250, 254; high culture, relationship to 108–13; in postwar era 16–17, 120; in press reaction to report 229; romantic 112–14; state support for culture, motive for 173–4
native cultures 113, 290n.24
Neatby, Hilda: commission, initial reaction to 45; commission, promotion of 51; commission, role on 64, 72, 115; commissioner, chosen as 33–4; commissioners, relations with 117–19; cultural elite, membership in 20–1; on humanities 150; on masses, edification of 66, 291n.17; on Matthew Arnold 99; philosophical outlook 91, 93, 98; public broadcasting, support for 144; publicity efforts 65; report, comments on reactions to 232, 237–8; report, promotion of 235; report, writing of 208, 213–14, 220; on scholarships 152–5; *So Little for the Mind* 94–5; Surveyer, criticism of 218–19; UNESCO, dislike of 183, 297n.15; universities, federal funding for 162, 295n.45; voluntary associations, defence of 54
New Westminster *British Columbian* 224, 226–7
Newman, John Henry 99
Newman, Robert 130–1
Nichols, Edward M. 107
Northern Ontario Art Association 170
Norwood, Gilbert 43
Nova Scotia Teachers' Union 175

Ontario Federation of Labour 50
Orchestre symphonique de Québec 180
Ortega y Gasset, José 95
Overstreet, H.A. 217

Page, P.K. 110
Parker, Tom 175
Parkin, George 288n.40, 290n.26
Partisan Review 95
Pearson, Lester 44, 68; Canada Council, support for 238–9; Canada's international image, and culture 14, 17, 174; commission, origins of 14–15, 31; cultural elite, membership in 21–2; Wartime Information Board, involvement with 282n.19
Pegis, Anton C. 86–7
Phelps, Arthur 18–19, 134, 292n.24
Pickersgill, Jack: Canada Council, support of 238–42, 307n.52, 307n.54; commission, origins of 14–15; cultural elite, membership in 21–2; on report, presentation of 304n.49; universities, federal funding for, support of 28, 36, 159, 164–5, 233, 296n.51, 306n.35
Plaunt, Alan 20
Pollock, John 53
Pontifical Institute for Mediaeval Studies 86
popular culture 84–5, 118, 184, 253
Poulin, Raoul 75
Prentice, Howard 53
La Presse (Montreal) 228
Prince Edward Island Adult Education Council 130
Prince of Wales College 77
private radio 124; arguments in support of 127, 133–4; and commission, agitation for 14; opposition to CBC 25. *See also* Canadian Association of Broadcasters
Progressivism 94
Public Affairs Institute 131
Public Archives 26–7, 35, 45, 48, 189, 298n.1; decentralization 193; effect of commission on 237, 243; historical collection 189; national role 186; records management 189, 237; sub-committee on 190

Quebec Co-operative Council 20
Queen's University 22, 148, 153

radio 4, 24–5, 35, 123–40. *See also* broadcasting
Radio League 20, 37, 124, 126, 190, 248
Robb, Wallace Havelock 78
Robbins, John 43; commission's impact, assessment of 243; scholarships plan 153, 155; scholarships sub-committee, appointment to 148–9
Roberge, Guy 44, 278n.8; hearings, role in 126; and Surveyer's reservations, help with 216–17
Rockefeller Foundation 288n.5
Rowell-Sirois Commission 226, 294n.27, 296n.51, 301n.9
Royal Architectural Institute of Canada 201
Royal Canadian Geographical Association 22
Royal Canadian Mounted Police 198
Royal Commission of Inquiry on Constitutional Problems. *See* Tremblay Commission
Royal Commission on Dominion-Provincial Relations. *See* Rowell-Sirois Commission
Royal Commission on National Development in the Arts, Letters

and Sciences. *See* Massey Commission
Royal Commission on Radio Broadcasting. *See* Aird Commission
Royal Ontario Museum 29
Royal Society of Canada 21, 48, 190
Rural Film Projection Service 195
Ruskin, John 99

Saint Dunstan's College 147
St John's *Telegraph* 229
St Laurent, Louis 14, 47, 235; Canada Council, founding of 238–43; commission, announces 30–1; commission, origins of 24; commission's mandate, supplements 193–4; constitutional controversy, fears of 28, 146, 158–9, 233, 306n.35; report, presentation of 209, 221–2; report, response to 233–4; universities, support for federal funding of 162–5
Saint Mary's College 105
Sandwell, B.K. 42, 46, 281n.15, 309n.6
Sangster, Alan 232
Saskatchewan Arts Board 177
Saskatchewan Council of Home and School Associations 90–1, 110
Saskatoon Archaeological Society 191
Saturday Night 57–8; commission on broadcasting, calls for 25; report, response to 224, 232
scholarships 3, 12–13, 28, 33, 35–6, 166, 237, 239, 243, 246; recommendations regarding 214; sub-committee on 148–55; submissions regarding 147, 152
Scott, Frank 110
Scrutiny 98–9

Seeley, R.S.K. 291n.17
Seldes, Gilbert 98, 217
Shea, Albert 304n.42
Siegfried, André 108–9
Siepmann, Charles 98, 143
Smallwood, Joey 79
Smith, David 177
Smith, Norman 61–2
Social Credit 233
Social Science Research Council of Canada 147, 190
social sciences 34, 39–40, 98, 149–51, 182–3, 214
Société d'éducation des adultes de Québec 20
Société des écrivains canadiens 20, 286n.7
Le Soleil (Quebec City) 228
Somerset, Dorothy 170–1
Special Committee on Historic Sites and Monuments 299n.6
Special Committee on Libraries and Public Records 190
Special Committee on Museums 190
Special Committee on Scholarships 148–9, 153–5
Special House of Commons Committee on Reconstruction and Re-establishment. *See* Turgeon Committee
Sports College Association 72
Spry, Graham 20
Stacey, C.P. 298n.5, 299n.6
state intervention 20, 22, 39, 248; Canadian tradition 5, 229; cultural development, requirement for 104–6; culture lobby, appeals for 170; and education 165–6; nationalist justification for 173; opposition to 177; press reaction to 229–30
Steeves, Dorothy 291n.17
Stratford Shakespearian Festival 18

Surveyer, Arthur: commissioner, chosen as 33; independent regulatory body, advocacy of 143–4; minority recommendations 216–20, 300n.22; philosophical outlook 151, 217–18; role on commission 63–4, 119–20, 208, 289n.15; universities, federal funding for 295n.45

television 4, 35, 124, 127–8, 140–2, 237, 245, 246; advent of 25; public anticipation of 57, 140–1; recommendations regarding 215, 302n.26; study of by Lévesque 48; study of by Neatby 48, 282n.25. *See also* broadcasting
Theatre Under the Stars 172
Theriault, Paul 196
Thomas Aquinas, Saint 93
Thompson, W.P. 152
Thomson, David 148–9
Thomson, J.S. 295n.40
Tocqueville, Alexis de 95
Toronto Board of Trade 171
Toronto *Globe and Mail* 41, 158
Tremblay, Paul 148
Tremblay Commission 234
Trilling, Lionel 99
Trotter, R.G. 148, 153
Trudeau, Pierre Elliott 230
Trueman, A.W. 295n.40
Turgeon Committee 13, 17, 23

Underhill, Frank 33, 99, 227, 232, 309n.6
UNESCO 30, 35, 41, 48, 49, 174–5, 182–3, 214, 297n.15, 297n.26
Union Nationale 230
United Church 94
Université de Montréal 73, 148, 163
Université Laval 34, 63, 74, 93, 112, 163–4

universities, federal funding for 36, 146, 184, 203, 214, 229–30, 233, 237, 245, 246–7; commission's consideration of 156–65; need for 27–8, 156
University of Alberta 130
University of British Columbia 21, 32–3, 118, 119, 170, 235
University of Manitoba 18
University of New Brunswick 32
University of Saskatchewan 33, 53
University of Toronto 15, 29, 33, 50, 148, 163
University of Toronto Press 111–12
University Women's Club of Regina 66

Vancouver Board of Trade 68–9
Vancouver Little Theatre 167
Vancouver *News-Herald* 69
Vancouver *Sun* 41, 59, 140
Vandry, Ferdinand 112, 164
Voaden, Herman 23
Voice of Radio 135–6
voluntary associations 3, 11, 24, 27, 38, 210; and adult education 94; CBC, criticisms of 139; and commission, support for 48–55; on feature film industry 200; in mandate of commission 35–6; and nationalism, post–World War I 21–2; public broadcasting, support for 129; report, support for implementation 240. *See also* culture lobby

Walker, Harold 202
Wallace, R.C. 295n.40
Wansborough, V.C. 72
Wartime Information Board 40, 282n.19, 282n.26, 304n.42
'Wednesday Night' 131

Western Stage Society 110–11
White, Thomas H. 76–7
Whitmore, Joseph 174
Windsor *Daily Star* 224
Winnipeg *Free Press* 41, 67
Winnipeg *Tribune* 226
Winters, Robert 198
Wood, E.C. 200
Woodhouse, A.S.P. 293n.8
Woods-Gordon Report 197–9, 245

Works Progress Administration 22, 279n.26
Wright, Peter: commission counsel, chosen as 44; hearings, questioning in regarding broadcasting 60, 69–70, 126, 136; hearings, questioning in regarding film 197
Writers and Players Club of Ottawa 78